# Mastering the Job Search Process in Recreation and Leisure Services

# Mastering the Job Search Process in Recreation and Leisure Services

## Second Edition

**Dr. Craig M. Ross**
Department of Recreation, Park, and Tourism Studies
Indiana University

**Dr. Brent A. Beggs**
School of Kinesiology and Recreation
Illinois State University

**Dr. Sarah J. Young**
Department of Recreation, Park, and Tourism Studies
Indiana University

**JONES AND BARTLETT PUBLISHERS**

*Sudbury, Massachusetts*

BOSTON    TORONTO    LONDON    SINGAPORE

*World Headquarters*

Jones and Bartlett Publishers
40 Tall Pine Drive
Sudbury, MA 01776
978-443-5000
info@jbpub.com
www.jbpub.com

Jones and Bartlett Publishers
Canada
6339 Ormindale Way
Mississauga, Ontario L5V 1J2
Canada

Jones and Bartlett Publishers
International
Barb House, Barb Mews
London W6 7PA
United Kingdom

Jones and Bartlett's books and products are available through most bookstores and online booksellers. To contact Jones and Bartlett Publishers directly, call 800-832-0034, fax 978-443-8000, or visit our website, www.jbpub.com.

Substantial discounts on bulk quantities of Jones and Bartlett's publications are available to corporations, professional associations, and other qualified organizations. For details and specific discount information, contact the special sales department at Jones and Bartlett via the above contact information or send an email to specialsales@jbpub.com.

**Production Credits**
Publisher, Higher Education: Cathleen Sether
Acquisitions Editor: Shoshanna Goldberg
Senior Associate Editor: Amy L. Bloom
Senior Editorial Assistant: Kyle Hoover
Production Manager: Julie Champagne Bolduc
Associate Production Editor: Jessica Steele Newfell
Associate Marketing Manager: Jody Sullivan
V.P., Manufacturing and Inventory Control: Therese Connell
Composition: Toppan Best-set Premedia Limited
Cover Design: Kristin E. Parker
Cover Images: (boat) © Ahmad Faizal Yahya/Dreamstime.com; (sky) © Cornelis Opstal/
    Dreamstime.com
Printing and Binding: Courier Kendallville
Cover Printing: Courier Kendallville

**Library of Congress Cataloging-in-Publication Data**
Ross, Craig M., 1952–
    Mastering the job search process in recreation and leisure services / Craig M. Ross, Brent A.
Beggs, Sarah J. Young. — 2nd ed.
        p. cm.
    Includes bibliographical references and index.
    ISBN 978-0-7637-7761-6 (pbk. : alk. paper)
    1. Leisure industry—Vocational guidance—United States.   2. Recreation industry—
Vocational guidance—United States.   3. Job hunting—United States.   I. Beggs, Brent
A.   II. Young, Sarah J., 1959–   III. Title.
    GV188.3.U6R67 2011
    790.07—dc22
                                        2009045821

6048
Printed in the United States of America
14  13  12  11     10 9 8 7 6 5 4 3 2

# Contents

# Preface

*How we Americans spend leisure time might seem to have little bearing on the strength of our nation or the worth and prestige of our free society. Yet we certainly cannot continue to thrive as a strong and vigorous free people unless we understand and use creatively one of our greatest resources—our leisure.*

—President John F. Kennedy

The fact that you are reading this text means that you are probably near completion of your academic study in recreation and leisure services. With an increased awareness by the American public of available recreation and leisure opportunities, we have seen a tremendous growth in participation in this field, which has responded with new and expanded programs to meet these needs. This growth has created a tremendous market as well as a new era with challenges that we, as recreation professionals, must meet. It also has created significant career choices and employment opportunities in a variety of recreation and leisure services settings.

Career development and planning by definition is a never-ending process—it continues throughout one's lifetime. Effective career planning in recreation and leisure services requires the acquisition of specific skills, a conceptual knowledge base, and accurate information. Common sense tells us that people make better decisions when they have as much information as possible. More specifically, effective career planning depends upon the identification and understanding of your current abilities, interests, skills, values, aptitudes, and priorities followed by the communication of these items to potential employers during the job search process.

Today the job search process has become far more sophisticated, complex, and complicated than ever before for new college graduates. Over the years, scores of how-to books have been published about the job search process in general, including networking, constructing and designing resumes, writing cover letters, and interviewing. Most of this information is subjective, opinionated, and written for individuals pursuing jobs in business-related positions. Furthermore, these opinions transform over time because of changes in the industry, new laws affecting the job search process, and employer demographic variations. The fact that there are no ground rules or standards results in a significant amount of contradictions and confusion for job applicants. Everyone seems to be an expert, but few agree. Many of the trade book publications on the job search process advocate a wide range of advice. To date, few publications have focused on the specifics of the job search process for those pursuing careers in recreation and leisure services.

*Mastering the Job Search Process in Recreation and Leisure Services, Second Edition*, is a guide full of practical tools and advice for future recreation and leisure service professionals. This text aims to simplify the process of securing a job in recreation and leisure services by explaining every step from both employers' and applicants' points-of-view. The information presented here is based on our years of practical experiences in the hiring process; reflects on research that we have conducted with over 1000 recreation and leisure services practitioners involved in the job search process; and includes our personal advice and secrets to success. This practitioner-research–based information, which is the cornerstone of this text, sets *Mastering the Job Search Process in*

*Recreation and Leisure Services, Second Edition*, apart from other general trade books on the same subject.

Chapter 1 begins with an overview of the job search process and focuses on the importance of conducting a personal self-assessment by identifying personal goals and career expectations. Chapter 2 describes the various career settings in recreation and leisure services, such as the emerging sports tourism setting. Chapter 3 illustrates various resources for locating job opportunities in the field and specifics on how to research a prospective agency as well as—new to the *Second Edition*—a section on how to use social networks to research different organizations. Chapter 4 explains how to organize and create a personal portfolio that highlights your strengths and abilities and includes information on the latest developments in electronic portfolios. Chapter 5 contains information on how to use the Internet to search for jobs specifically in the field of recreation and leisure services. Additionally, the impact of technology on the job search process is discussed with the latest information on the use of electronic resumes, blogs, and professional networks.

Chapters 6, 7, and 8 focus on cover letters, resumes, and interviews, respectively. Each chapter offers an in-depth look at how to successfully complete the step as well as information from practitioners in the field about current content preferences. New to Chapter 7 is a section on the use of video resumes. Chapter 9 explains the role and value of the internship process in recreation and leisure services. Chapter 10 guides you through the process of deciding which job offer to accept while Chapter 11 gives new ideas on how to realistically navigate the transition from college to professional life. Lastly, the appendices include lists of recreation and leisure organizations, online resources for newspapers and journals, questions most frequently asked by interviewers, and questions most frequently asked by candidates.

Each chapter in this text provides practical techniques for handling the various phases of the job search process as well as worksheets, checklists, and case studies to make this information more personal and specific. *Mastering the Job Search Process in Recreation and Leisure Services, Second Edition*, also incorporates the following graphical features in each chapter to help identify and illustrate important information:

- *Did You Know:* Spotlights interesting facts about careers and organizations in the field of recreation and leisure services.

- *Job Search Tip:* Coaches you through the job search with quick highlights on the process.

- *Time Out:* Features time-saving advice.

- *Be Alert:* Assists you in avoiding potential problems and pitfalls in the job search process.

- *Case Studies and Assignments:* Presents practical case studies and exercises where you can share your ideas and opinions.

- *Keys to Job Search Success:* Highlights, in liberal doses, short tips relating to success in the job search process.

Additional resources for students and instructors are available at **http://health. jbpub.com/recreationjobs/2e**, including Web links to field-specific career resources, a guide to identifying suitable careers, and a checklist for starting a new job in recreation and leisure services.

We live in an age where we are responsible for the development of our own careers. Bursting with valuable and pertinent information and interactive worksheet exercises, we have done our best to make *Mastering the Job Search Process in Recreation and Leisure Services, Second Edition*, a practical, up-to-date, and accurate tool for college graduates wanting to enter the field of recreation and leisure services. The rest is up to you!

## Acknowledgments

The authors would like to acknowledge Mr. Bill Ramos, a faculty member at Indiana University, for his creative ideas on teaching a careers course as well as his students' suggestions for additional content in this *Second Edition*. The authors also would like to thank Susan Hastings-Bishop, PhD, Ferris State University, and Douglas J. DeMichele, EdD, University of Florida, for their reviews of the *First Edition*.

# About the Authors

**Dr. Craig M. Ross** received his Bachelor of Science degree in Physical Education (1973) as well as his Master of Science degree in Recreation (1975) from Memphis State University. In 1980 he earned his Doctorate in Recreation from Indiana University (IU). He has been involved in recreation and sports programming and administration in a variety of work settings. Dr. Ross has worked with the Memphis Park Commission as playground director, community center director, and zone supervisor. He was the girls' high school athletic director/coach in a small, rural school community in Missouri and, for 14 years until 1993, he worked in collegiate recreational sports with the IU Division of Recreational Sports. At IU, he served as associate director with primary responsibilities in the campus intramural sports program. In July 1993, Dr. Ross was appointed as a full-time associate professor in the recreational sports management curriculum through the Department of Recreation, Park, and Tourism Studies at IU.

Dr. Ross has served on numerous university committees as well as National Intramural-Recreational Sports Association (NIRSA) committees, including the NIRSA Journal Editorial Board, Career Placement Center, Professional Development Committee–Recreational Sports Curriculum Subcommittee, Computer Utilization Committee, and Research Committee. He was past-chair of the Board of Regents for the NRPA/Oglebay Computer Use Institute for Parks and Recreation. Dr. Ross has made over 65 presentations at the NIRSA and Big Ten Recreational Sports conferences, published numerous articles, and is co-author of *Recreational Sports Management, Third Edition*.

**Dr. Brent A. Beggs** earned his Bachelor of Science degree in Recreation (1991) and his Master of Science degree in Recreation (1995) from Southern Illinois University. He completed his Doctorate in Leisure Behavior (2002) at Indiana University. Dr. Beggs is currently an associate professor at Illinois State University, teaching undergraduate and graduate courses in the management of sport and recreation, research methods, leisure theory, commercial recreation, and facility design. Prior to teaching at Illinois State, he served as a lecturer and internship coordinator for the Department of Recreation, Park, and Tourism Studies at IU. Dr. Beggs began his career in leisure services with the Collinsville Area Recreation District in Illinois and moved on to the Maryland Heights Parks and Recreation Department in Missouri.

Dr. Beggs has served on the Illinois Association of Park Districts Research Advisory Council, as a board member for the Indiana University Executive Development Program, and on the American Park and Recreation Society Student Task Force. He also is an active member of NRPA and NIRSA and is a Certified Parks and Recreation Professional. In addition, he serves on the editorial board for the *Recreational Sports Journal*, *Schole*, and *LARNet* and has been a reviewer for multiple journals and textbooks. He is co-author of *Recreation Facility Management* and has published scholarly papers and presented research findings at international, national, and regional conferences.

**Dr. Sarah J. Young** earned her Bachelor of Science degree in Recreation and Park Administration from Illinois State University and earned both her Master of Science degree in Recreational Sport Administration and her Doctorate in Leisure Behavior with a minor in Law from Indiana University. She currently is an associate professor with the Department of Recreation, Park, and Tourism Studies at IU–Bloomington. Dr. Young also worked as an assistant director of Intramural Sports for 9 years with the Division of Recreational Sports at IU. In between her IU experiences, Dr. Young was an assistant professor with the Leisure Studies program in the College of Hotel Administration at the University of Nevada–Las Vegas for 4 years. She is an active member of NIRSA, the National Recreation and Park Association, and Sport and Recreation Law Association, and she has conducted over 60 presentations on national, state, and local levels. She is a Certified Park and Recreation Professional. Dr. Young teaches courses in recreation management and legal aspects of recreation. Her research focuses on recreational sport settings, legal liability and risk management, scholarship of teaching, and health/wellness issues.

# The Job Search Process: Where to Begin?

For most college students, their primary purpose in selecting a school, taking courses, choosing a major, attending class, writing papers, and studying for exams is so that they can obtain an education and subsequently land a job. Some students assume that because they have labored hard in gaining an education, finding a job should be relatively easy. However, because employers are constantly looking for ways to stretch their budgets while obtaining the most for their money, competition for positions has increased. As a result, it is not enough for job seekers to be ready and willing to work. A successful job search requires a calculated effort of organization and preparation.

# Chapter 1

Visit the Web site for this book to learn more about the organizations and topics covered in this chapter. http://health.jbpub.com/recreationjobs/2e

**Job Coach Tip**

The more organized and prepared you are in your job search, the more successful you will be.

To complete the job search process successfully, candidates not only need marketable skills, they also need the skills to market themselves. The Minnesota Workforce Center (2003) stated that although job candidates may be motivated toward employment, and they may be very good at what they do, if candidates are not able to convince a potential employer they are the most qualified, they will not be the one who wins the job. So, another key to being successful in the job search involves communicating one's qualifications.

The field of recreation and leisure services is no different from any other in that employers seek the best qualified candidates for open positions. Whether candidates for recreation positions are just graduating from college or have been working in the field a few years, they must use a variety of skills and strategies to land their coveted job successfully. The information contained in this book is designed to assist job seekers interested in recreation and leisure services in planning and organizing each step of their job search process. Furthermore, this text provides qualified candidates the strategies to communicate effectively with potential employers in the recreation and leisure service setting so that both candidates and employers can find the best match for the job.

The job search process is a linear process involving different phases, each of equal importance. To progress successfully through the job search process, candidates must be able to master each phase. Not fully understanding or appreciating just one phase could result in candidates not achieving the job offer. So, candidates must know what steps to take and the expectations of employers in recreation and leisure services for each phase of the job search. The purpose of this book is to help candidates successfully progress through each phase of the job search process on their way to a career in recreation and leisure services. Ready for the challenge? Let's get started by reviewing the steps of the job search process:

1. *Self-assessment:* This involves candidates understanding their values, skills, personality traits, and job priorities along with how to utilize these attributes throughout the job search process. The assessment process is covered in this chapter.

2. *Identifying career opportunities:* Understanding and utilizing the multitude of resources available in locating job opportunities in recreation and leisure services is crucial to the job search process. A review of career opportunities in recreation and leisure service settings is addressed in Chapter 2.

3. *Researching an agency:* Candidates must learn as much as possible about any recreation agency they are considering for a job opportunity. The more candidates know about an agency, the more complete their application for the position will be, thereby, enhancing their opportunity to obtain an interview. Chapter 3 addresses the steps to take in researching an organization.

4. *Job search tools:* These tools are key elements in the application process and consist of preparing a portfolio, understanding how to use technology effectively, and developing both the cover letter and resume. Details on each of these tools can be found in Chapters 4, 5, 6, and 7, respectively.

5. *Interviewing:* In addition to answering questions and being aware of interview behavior, candidates must spend a considerable amount of effort preparing for the interview. Chapter 8 provides candidates insight into preparing for this very important dimension of the job search process.

6. *Internship:* The role and value of the internship process in recreation and leisure service are discussed in Chapter 9.

**Be Alert!**

The job search process is linear. Failure to master any phase will most likely prevent you from getting to the next phase.

7. *Evaluating the offer:* Should candidates be offered a position, they must have a strategy prepared for responding to that offer. Their preferred strategy is often influenced by individual needs and priorities, and is explained in detail in Chapter 10.

8. *Navigating the transition:* Even after candidates accept their position, there are still tasks to be accomplished. Newly hired employees should be aware of the expectations and realities their new position will demand. Chapter 11 addresses issues candidates will want to know and consider regarding this transition.

## The Assessment Process

The first step in the job search process is for candidates to conduct a self-assessment. The self-assessment starts by candidates reflecting upon values, strengths, limitations, and preferences for a career area in recreation and leisure services, and perhaps even a specific job. From this reflection, candidates then develop a personal philosophy, establish career and personal goals, and establish job-related priorities.

The personal philosophy is a reflective narrative of what is important to candidates. When writing a personal philosophy, candidates should describe themselves, their values, and the personal meaning of their lives. Many people have a personal philosophy, yet have never taken the time to write it down. By capturing one's personal philosophy on paper, candidates are more easily able to recognize what is important to them. This reflection can then be extrapolated to the candidate's short- and long-term goals. Although there are a variety of ways to write a personal philosophy, the most common method for getting started is to reflect on values, people, and experiences that have had the greatest impact on the candidate's life. It is important to remember that a personal philosophy is personal for candidates, with the ultimate purpose being to identify candidates' values.

Once a personal philosophy has been developed, the next step is for candidates to establish goals, both personal and career. The primary difference between the personal philosophy and individual goals is that the personal philosophy is a reflection of the past representing current values, whereas goals are an indication of the future. These goals should be grounded in the candidate's personal philosophy and focus on short- and long-range expectations. In other words, the desired future of candidates should be a reflection of their values. The process of establishing goals is different from the personal philosophy in that career and personal goals consist of a listing of the candidate's specific desired outcomes and expectations.

Career goals help candidates focus on professional aspirations for a career, rather than just drifting from job to job. The focal point of a career goal can be a specific job or a particular sector of recreation and leisure services in which a candidate wants to work. Once candidates have established career goals, they should think strategically about the

**Time Out**

Take time to do a self-assessment prior to identifying potential jobs.

**Job Coach Tip**

Establishing career goals and using them to guide career choices will result in meaningful jobs that meet individual career objectives.

**Keys to Job Search Success**

Writing a personal philosophy allows an individual to reflect on his or her value system. Personal values play an important role throughout the job search process. Take some time to think about what really matters to you. You'll be surprised how important this is in establishing career goals and prioritizing factors related to the job.

steps to accomplish their goals. Understanding and accomplishing career goals will be easier if the candidate outlines specific steps to achieve each goal. These steps are called objectives and become measurement points for goals (Rossman & Schlatter, 2008). By this definition, objectives should be written in a way that can be measured. For example, stating that a job search task should be accomplished by a specific time or date allows for that objective to be measurable.

**Job Coach Tip**

Preparation-based planning is the way you acquire, enhance, and organize the skills and resources needed to enact your plan.

Rosenberg

Personal goals help candidates to focus on issues outside their careers, such as family, health, and living location. Candidates' personal goals are generally influenced by their personal philosophy. Specific objectives for personal goals should also be listed. Career goals and personal goals will undoubtedly overlap for many candidates. As a result, the values in the personal philosophy also play an important role in prioritizing career and personal goals. A final consideration is that career goals and personal goals will change throughout life, so it is important for candidates to revisit this process each time they consider a particular job.

The next step in the assessment process is for candidates to evaluate their personal attributes, such as skills and personality traits. This helps candidates become more aware of their strengths while helping them understand areas needing improvement. The best method of carrying out this evaluation is, once again, to put it in writing by completing the Self-Assessment of Skills Worksheet and the Personality Traits Inventory Worksheet.

The Self-Assessment of Skills Worksheet (Figure 1.1) is completed by candidates using a plus ( + ), check ( √ ), or minus ( − ) to indicate their assessment of a specific item. A plus ( + ) indicates candidates have experience or are very skilled; a check ( √ ) indicates candidates have some experience or adequate skill; and a minus ( − ) suggests an area in which candidates have little to no experience or are not skilled. Skills include the basic competencies that recreation and leisure service professionals should possess, such as leadership, programming, and communication skills. If the self-assessment reveals areas where candidates need to improve, then they should focus upon the Action column corresponding to that skill. In the Action column, candidates identify the action needed to improve the skill. For example, if candidates have a minus for budgeting, they can write down actions that will help them bump budgeting from a minus to a plus, such as attending a professional development session on budgeting or taking a class on finance and budgeting. For those candidates already in the workforce, improving a skill may be a decision to take on a greater role in their current position that will provide them with this experience. Once all of the minus areas have been addressed, then candidates should address those items receiving a check. Although the check indicates skills in a specific area are adequate, candidates may wish to strengthen that area. The goal of such an exercise is to identify areas needing improvement to maximize the number of attributes a candidate can promote to potential employers.

Although understanding strengths and weaknesses is crucial to the self-assessment process, candidates should also understand their personality traits. Personality traits address a wide variety of characteristics applicable to most jobs in leisure services and other disciplines. The Personality Traits Inventory Worksheet (Figure 1.2) allows candidates the opportunity to address the strengths and weaknesses of their personality traits using the same plus ( + ), check ( √ ), or minus ( − ) system. A plus indicates candidates possess and have refined a specific personality trait; a check indicates candidates possess a specific personality trait, but need to refine it; and a minus suggests candidates are very weak or do not have a specific personality trait.

Figure 1.1

Self-Assessment of Skills     Date _____

**Skills**                         **Action**

Mark each item with: +, √, –

_____ Budgeting               _____

_____ Communication (oral)    _____

_____ Communication (written) _____

_____ Computer skills         _____

_____ Creativity              _____

_____ Delegating              _____

_____ Employee supervision    _____

_____ Evaluation              _____

_____ Facility supervision    _____

_____ Initiative              _____

_____ Leadership              _____

_____ Marketing               _____

_____ Negotiating             _____

_____ Organizing              _____

_____ Planning                _____

_____ Problem solving         _____

_____ Programming             _____

_____ Scheduling              _____

_____ Team building           _____

_____ Time management         _____

_____ _____         _____

_____ _____         _____

Self-Assessment of Skills Worksheet

**Job Coach Tip**

When conducting a self-assessment, try to be objective. This will be of greater benefit to you in understanding your strengths and weaknesses.

Once candidates have assessed their skills and personal traits, it is much easier for them to understand their strengths and weaknesses.

The last step in the self-assessment is determining job-related priorities. Candidates can do this by completing the Job Preferences Worksheet (Figure 1.3). Establishing priorities will help candidates determine the types of jobs for which they want to consider applying. There are many different job-related priorities that candidates may want to consider, such as the following:

■ *Career setting:* Candidates may be interested in a position because of the way it fits with their career goals and objectives. If candidates are moving from one position to another, or are seeking to meet career objectives, they may seek a position with a specific title. Additionally, the job title, level of the position within the organization, the supervisor for the position, and the supervisory role

Figure 1.2

Personality Traits Inventory    Date _____

| **Personality Traits** | **Action** |
| --- | --- |
| Mark each item with: +, √, − | |
| _____ Ability to say no | _____ |
| _____ Accepting criticism | _____ |
| _____ Confident | _____ |
| _____ Considerate of others | _____ |
| _____ Determined | _____ |
| _____ Empathetic | _____ |
| _____ Enthusiastic | _____ |
| _____ Ethical | _____ |
| _____ Flexible | _____ |
| _____ Friendly | _____ |
| _____ Good listener | _____ |
| _____ Hard worker | _____ |
| _____ Honest | _____ |
| _____ Open minded | _____ |
| _____ Patient | _____ |
| _____ Punctual | _____ |
| _____ Reliable | _____ |
| _____ Resourceful | _____ |
| _____ _____ | _____ |
| _____ _____ | _____ |

Personality Traits Inventory Worksheet

**Job Coach Tip**
Establishing job priorities will help you determine the type of jobs that you should apply for.

of the position may be important to candidates seeking specific professional experiences.

- *Organizational climate:* The working conditions of an organization are quite often important to candidates considering a position with that organization. Many factors affect working conditions, such as:

 **Keys to Job Search Success**

A self-assessment is used to identify strengths and weaknesses and serves as an action plan for self-improvement. Make an effort to follow up on the action plans outlined in your self-assessment. It will make you a stronger candidate in the job search process.

Figure 1.3

| Job Preferences | | Date_____ |
|---|---|---|
| **Issue** | **Specific Preference** | **Rank** |
| Career setting | _____ | _____ |
| Organizational climate | _____ | _____ |
| Agency philosophy | _____ | _____ |
| Types of services | _____ | _____ |
| Job scope | _____ | _____ |
| Salary | _____ | _____ |
| Geographic location | _____ | _____ |
| Travel | _____ | _____ |
| Agency reputation | _____ | _____ |
| Other | _____ | _____ |
| _____ | _____ | _____ |
| _____ | _____ | _____ |
| _____ | _____ | _____ |
| _____ | _____ | _____ |

Job Preferences Worksheet

- ◆ How well employees get along
- ◆ Policies of the organization
- ◆ Facilities
- ◆ Independence provided employees in doing their jobs
- ◆ Empowerment
- ◆ Opportunities for professional development
- ◆ Opportunities for advancement

■ *Agency philosophy:* Being able to match a personal philosophy with the philosophy of an organization can be an important factor for candidates. This factor is more common in candidates already employed but who are dissatisfied with the philosophy of their current agency. Therefore, it becomes an important job preference as they seek different employment.

■ *Types of services:* Because some recreation and leisure service agencies provide a wide variety of programs or services for their clients and others specialize in certain areas, candidates may be interested in a position with an organization based on the types of services offered.

■ *Job scope:* Responsibilities that accompany the position can be motivating factors for candidates seeking a specific job. Although candidates frequently seek jobs where their skills or interests match the skills required for the job, some candidates seek positions of greater challenge that will require them to use skills that they currently are not utilizing.

- *Salary:* Candidates need to determine their basic salary needs. In other words, what salary must they make to maintain a certain level of living? If candidates are considering the job search in an effort to find a higher paying job, they should outline their salary requirements. Although many entry-level positions in recreation and leisure services meet basic salary needs, salary requirements become more important to candidates moving from an entry-level position to mid- and upper-level positions.

- *Geographic location:* In many instances, the geographic location of a job is the most important factor for candidates. For example, if a candidate desires to work in a specific region because of family or issues related to climate, then that becomes a significant factor in deciding which jobs to apply for. If candidates establish geographic location as an important factor, then their pool of job opportunities may be significantly narrowed.

- *Travel:* Those working in commercial recreation or tourist destination settings may have opportunities to travel that are not provided in other sectors of leisure services. Travel may be an appealing factor to some candidates, while others may not be interested in a position requiring travel.

- *Agency reputation:* There are some instances where candidates are interested in working for a specific agency because of its reputation as a leader in the field. Additionally, candidates may prefer to work with certain people who have established reputations as excellent professionals.

**Job Coach Tip**

A job scope that matches individual interests is important to many people. Unfortunately, they don't realize this until they've accepted a job where this isn't the case. Make sure to set job scope a priority for you.

When candidates establish their priorities in finding a job, the process of deciding what jobs to apply for becomes more focused and much easier. The self-assessment not only helps candidates establish what is important to their career and personal goals, but also helps candidates understand what they do well and areas in which they should improve. Candidates may feel that once they have completed the self-assessment they are ready to move onto the next step. However, the reason the self-assessment is the starting point for the job search process is because of its integral role throughout the process. Candidates will likely find themselves coming back to their self-assessments throughout the job search process. It serves as a reference point for decisions on pursuing specific jobs, writing the cover letter, preparing for the interview, evaluating the job offer, and even negotiating the final deal. The assessment is the cornerstone of the job search process and the first step in matching candidates with their most desired position.

## Building a Network Through Professional Associations

Wherever there are communities, organizations, or institutions, there is networking. People network every day, some without realizing it and most without giving it much thought. Formal networking is systematically pursuing new contacts and gathering new information, and it is another key starting point in the job search process. In the past, networking was largely informal and random, yet to be successful in the job search process today, networking must be calculated and structured. Candidates must organize and plan to build their network, and becoming a member of a professional association is an excellent way to start.

There are a variety of professional associations in recreation and leisure services with each serving a similar purpose to advance the effective delivery of leisure services through research, training, and certification (Kraus, Barber, & Shapiro, 2001). These associations provide a multitude of benefits for their members including publications, training seminars, workshops, and conferences. Publication offerings range from feature articles and current research information in leisure services to job postings and contact information of other members in the organization. Professional association publications are generally available in both print and electronic formats.

Professional organizations also offer conferences, workshops, and training seminars. These professional development meetings provide candidates with opportunities to participate actively in the association by facilitating and attending sessions, earning continuing education units (CEUs), participating in social events, and viewing exhibits. Attending and participating in the conferences, workshops, and seminars of a professional association are excellent ways to build one's network. For some candidates who join an organization, the only benefit received from their membership is listing it on their resume. Being a member of a professional organization should be much more than a bullet point on a resume. Candidates should feel a professional obligation to learn and grow within their chosen area of recreation and leisure services, and participating in conferences is the best way to maximize the benefits of membership in professional organizations. There are several keys for candidates to consider in making the most of attending professional conferences:

- *Get to know the leaders:* It is very easy for a member of a professional organization (especially a new member!) to attend a professional conference and wait to get noticed. Leaders of professional organizations are often busy and in demand at these events, but most do like to take time to get to know their members. Candidates attending conferences for the first time should consider introducing themselves to officers, speakers, and conference exhibitors when presented with these opportunities. Taking the initiative to meet others is a good way for candidates not only to become known in a professional organization, but to build their network.

- *Be prepared to learn:* Conferences provide numerous educational and research sessions assisting candidates in gaining more knowledge and introducing them to new ideas. In recreation and leisure services, many new programs and services come from adopting and applying the ideas of other agencies and professionals. Conferences provide an excellent arena for this exchange. Additionally, many conferences and training sessions provide opportunities for specialized certifications or CEUs that can be applied to certification requirements.

- *Come with a purpose:* Many times members of professional organizations will attend conferences without thinking of their purpose in attending. Candidates using professional conferences as a way to build their network can ill afford to make that mistake. Most professional organizations provide a schedule of activities prior to their conference and distribute this to their members. Examining this schedule and establishing an individual agenda for the conference will help candidates enhance their conference experience and make the most of this opportunity.

**Job Coach Tip**

Get the most out of professional conferences. The relationships you establish in this environment can help you for years to come.

**Be Alert!**

If you apply for a job that you are not qualified for, you are just wasting your time. Know your strengths and weaknesses!

- *Help others:* As a professional in recreation and leisure services, contributing to the field might mean looking for ways to provide information, resources, or referrals to other members at the conference. By helping others, candidates can establish good relationships, broaden their professional network, and build a good reputation in the field.

- *Keep it professional:* Conferences provide a variety of organized and casual social opportunities that are excellent occasions to network and meet others in the field. Candidates should be mindful that while these opportunities are social events, they still take place within the context of a professional environment. As a result, candidates should maintain their professional demeanor.

- *Follow-up:* While at a conference, candidates should collect business cards and contact information from the people they meet. Once the conference is over, candidates should follow up via e-mail, telephone, or written correspondence with those individuals they would like to maintain a longer-term relationship. The content of the follow-up may include something related to a conversation at the conference or just simply be a message that they were pleased to make acquaintance and look forward to keeping in touch.

Becoming a member of a professional association is particularly advantageous to students currently enrolled in recreation and leisure studies curricula. Not only does becoming a member help to build students' professional networks, but it displays commitment to the field. It is important to employers in recreation and leisure services that students seeking internships and full-time positions have established memberships in appropriate professional organizations (Ross & Zabriskie, 2001; Young & Ross, 2003). Furthermore, many professional organizations offer reduced membership dues for student members, encouraging their participation and professional development. Specifically, benefits students can gain from membership in professional organizations are as follows:

- *Knowledge:* A student can advance classroom learning by attending educational and research sessions at professional conferences. In addition, students can further their knowledge about their chosen field of interest and learn about jobs and other recreation and leisure careers.

- *Getting to know alumni:* Using many of the same strategies professional candidates would use, students can develop their own network of professional contacts. One very important tool for students in networking is meeting alumni from their university who already work in the field. Having a common educational background provides a link for students to meet professionals, possibly paving the way for internships or even future full-time employment. Many universities have organized socials at recreation and leisure service conferences, making this a wonderful opportunity to meet alumni. Furthermore, faculty members attending these conferences can introduce current students to alumni

**Time Out**

Take time to follow up with people you meet at a conference.

---

**Keys to Job Search Success**

Professional conferences should be viewed as more than just an opportunity to attend sessions, socials, and exhibit halls. The professional conference is an excellent place to network and learn about jobs. When attending a conference, go with a plan and act professional at all times.

in conference settings. Finally, some professional organizations incorporate networking opportunities through mentor development programs or organized activities such as take-a-student-to-lunch programs.

- *Internships and jobs:* Whereas networking at a conference can create contacts to professionals with internships, many professional organizations post internships and jobs at the conference career center. Additionally, some professional organizations sponsor internship fairs, internship postings, and educational sessions about pursuing internships and jobs. These career centers may consist of job boards, listings of job announcements, and rooms for group and individual interviews.

- *Resume and portfolio review:* Some conferences provide opportunities for students to meet with professionals to review their resumes and portfolios. This feedback can be very helpful when a student is preparing to apply for an internship or job.

- *Interviewing:* Some professional conferences provide opportunities for students to interview for internships and jobs during the conference. In some instances, students apply for positions prior to the conference and a representative from the agency conducts interviews during the conference. These interviews can be scheduled outside the regular conference schedule, may take place over lunch, or may occur in a room reserved for interviews by the hiring organization. Another method used by agencies is to collect and review resumes on the first day of the conference and then interview candidates on subsequent days. In these situations, students often end up interviewing with multiple agencies. This is a great way for students to learn about different opportunities with agencies as well as a cost-effective way for an agency to conduct interviews.

A wide variety of professional associations in recreation and leisure services is available for students and professional candidates to join, thereby enhancing their professional networks. In deciding which associations are most appropriate, students and professional candidates should consider those associations matching their current position, desired job, or career goals. To learn more about professional associations in recreation and leisure services, refer to Appendix A in this book.

## Conclusion

A successful job search involves a number of steps the job candidate must take to land the most desired position. This chapter provides insight into those steps while emphasizing the importance of job candidates being organized, being well prepared, and developing good communication skills. Two starting points in the job search process require candidates to look both within (reflection through assessment) and outside themselves (developing a professional network). The assessment process is the starting point from which a successful job search emerges, helping candidates to recognize that which is important to them both personally and professionally. Additionally, investigating a variety of professional organizations related to specific careers and jobs within recreation and leisure services is a good place to begin developing a professional network. Membership in professional organizations is relatively easy, inexpensive, and provides candidates with a link to practitioners, agencies, and jobs! This chapter provides the details of how to begin the job search process in recreation and leisure

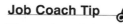

**Job Coach Tip**

The preferred choice of hard-copy portfolios is three-ring binders.

**Job Coach Tip**

Don't just join any professional association. Find one that matches your interests, job, or career goals.

services. As a result of reading this chapter, candidates should know not only the steps to take, but the expectations of employers in recreation and leisure services for each phase of the job search.

# References

Kraus, R., Barber, E., & Shapiro, I. (2001). *Introduction to leisure services: Career perspectives.* Champaign, IL: Sagamore.

Minnesota Workforce Center. (2003). *Creative job search.* St. Paul: Minnesota Department of Economic Security.

National Park Service. (n.d.). Retrieved May 1, 2009, from http://www.nps.gov

National Sporting Goods Association. (2008). Retrieved May 1, 2009, from http://www.nsga.org

Rosenberg, A. D. (2009). *101 ways to stand out at work.* Avon, MA: Adams Media.

Ross, C. M., & Zabriskie, R. B. (2001). An examination of resume preferences among therapeutic recreation professionals. *Annual in Therapeutic Recreation, 10,* 33–44.

Rossman, J. R., & Schlatter, B. E. (2008). *Recreation programming: Designing leisure experiences* (5th ed.). Champaign, IL: Sagamore.

Young, S. J., & Ross, C. M. (2003). Teaching resume effectiveness: Results from a recreation administrators' study. LARNet: The Cyber Journal of Applied Leisure and Recreation Research [Online]. Retrieved from http://www.larnet.org/2003-3.html

# Assignment: Self-Assessment

It's time to learn more about yourself by conducting a self-assessment. Follow the steps below:

**1. Write your personal philosophy:**

a.   Reflect on the values, people, and experiences that have affected your life.

_____

_____

_____

_____

b.   Use this information to describe yourself, what is important to you, and what gives your life meaning.

_____

_____

_____

_____

**2. Record your career goals and objectives:**

a.   Establish your career goals first.

_____

_____

_____

_____

b.   Beneath each goal, write specific objectives that will help you achieve that goal.

_____

_____

_____

_____

**3. Complete the Self-Assessment of Skills Worksheet (Figure 1.1)**

**4. Complete the Personality Traits Inventory Worksheet (Figure 1.2)**

**5. Complete the Job Preferences Worksheet (Figure 1.3)**

By completing a self-assessment, you can learn something about yourself. That is the purpose of the exercise. Write a brief summary reflecting on what you learned about yourself during this process.

_____

_____

_____

_____

_____

Assignments

## Assignment: Professional Association Investigation

Professional associations play an important role in career development. In leisure services, students and leisure service professionals can join a multitude of potential organizations. Your assignment is to identify three professional associations that would be a good match for your career interests. For each professional association, you should provide the following information:

- Name of the professional association
- Address and phone number of the professional association
- Web site address of the professional association
- Mission of organization
- Cost of student membership or cost of professional membership
- Why this organization is a good fit for you

Use resources available in this textbook, on the Internet, from faculty, or any other resources you have to start your research.

_____

_____

_____

_____

_____

_____

_____

_____

_____

_____

_____

_____

_____

_____

_____

_____

_____

_____

_____

_____

_____

_____

# Chapter 2

# Careers

Careers—what an all-encompassing term. The word *career* comes from the Latin word *carrus,* referring to a race track where horses competed in an effort to win a race. Ever had this feeling? Today, the word *career* is used interchangeably with job, job title, occupation, and vocation.

Now, more than ever, the field of recreation and leisure services offers a wide variety of rewarding and fulfilling careers to candidates who possess a strong academic background, practical experience, and a passion, commitment, and dedication to the profession. From event planners to park rangers to recreational sport programmers, there are numerous career opportunities and literally thousands of jobs worldwide.

Because recreation and leisure is approximately a $400 billion per year industry, the field offers more variety and career choices on a global basis than do many other professional fields. Employment of recreation and leisure service personnel is expected to continue to grow in years to come. This is primarily because of an increasing number of people with an abundance of leisure time and the resources to purchase associated services; changing work patterns; increased interest in fitness and health; and the rising demand for recreational opportunities for older adults in retirement communities and senior centers.

## Career Exploration

In regard to careers in recreation and leisure services, it is important to discuss two important aspects associated with employment in this field. Potential candidates must consider both the expectations of working in recreation and leisure services along with the career settings.

## Expectation 1: What Is Expected of an Entry-Level Professional

The following are basic career expectations or assumptions that apply to individuals entering the field of recreation and leisure services in any position:

1. Day-to-day programming requiring a great deal of effort and hard work.

2. Because leisure service agencies provide recreation opportunities for the general public, most activities are conducted during the *public's* leisure time hours, which means leisure professionals lunch time, evenings, and weekends are spent working.

3. Many participants take recreation programming for granted, perceiving it as frivolous or requiring no formal training. Subsequently, professionals in this field sometimes receive little respect. Seldom will participants express thanks for a great program. Most do not appreciate the many leadership and programming skills that are incorporated into activities and events, such as planning, organizing, promotion, safety precautions, equipment needs, facility maintenance and preparation, legal liability, eligibility policies, rules and regulations, budgeting, staff training, scheduling, and evaluation to name just a few! Frequently, recreation professionals will receive very little recognition or attention *until* something goes wrong!

4. A recreation professional *must* be a people-oriented person. If an individual does not like working with people, this is the wrong career choice. A friendly, outgoing personality is a must.

5. Individuals must be willing to work long hours. It is not unusual for a professional to work 50–65 hours per week during peak times of the year. This is not a "Monday through Friday, 9 a.m.–5 p.m." profession as some would think.

6. Entry-level salaries for recreation programmers vary depending on the setting, specific agency, and population size of the community. Salaries, in general, will not be comparable to similar management positions in the business or corporate setting.

# Expectation 2: What a Candidate Can Expect

1. As noted earlier, recreation and leisure services is a people-centered profession. Professionals in this field have an opportunity to work with diverse groups of participants. In the course of a typical day, a professional may work with preschool kids in a day camp program, young adults playing in an after-school basketball league, and adults and senior citizens in an "Over 50" special event at night. On the other hand, professionals have the flexibility to choose the age group and setting they are most interested in, whether it is youth sports, armed forces recreation, tourism, or any of the many other groups and settings available.

2. There are many opportunities to work hand in hand with a variety of great people and volunteers who assist on boards, councils, special interest groups, and so on.

3. Professionals have a number of opportunities to be involved with participant development, that is, using recreation and leisure services as a medium to influence lives positively. What a great feeling it is to be able to take a negative situation that has occurred in an event and use it to turn a person's life around. Contributions to society like this are hard to measure in quantitative terms or put a price tag on.

4. The field provides a great deal of flexibility. Many agencies are experimenting with flextime schedules in which employees may work late one evening but will not report to work the next day until midmorning.

5. Generally, an entry-level recreation professional does not work behind a desk all day in a suit or dress. A typical day would include performing a number of different assignments from working the front office counter and presenting at a participant's meeting to supervising events at night.

6. The most exciting part of a job is conducting an event from start to finish and looking back upon its completion and seeing the participants' satisfaction and enjoyment. For some, it is strictly an intrinsic feeling of knowing that they "beat" all of the obstacles presented to them and that the participants had a really great time.

# Career Settings

The second aspect associated with employment in the recreation and leisure services field is the various career settings in which one may work. Because of the increase in the scope and demand of recreation and leisure service programs and facilities, there is a great deal of diversity in the types of entry-level career opportunities in both the public and private sectors. Because recreation professionals can choose from such a broad range of careers, opportunities are generally grouped into the following 10 categories of leisure service organizations and providers:

- Public or governmental agencies at the federal, state, and local levels
- Nonprofit organizations, both religious and nonreligious agencies
- Commercial recreation

**Job Coach Tip**

Flextime allows an employee to work a nontraditional workweek, such as four 10-hour days, to meet personal needs.

**Did You Know...**

There are approximately 7500 employees of the U.S. Fish and Wildlife Service.

U.S. Fish and Wildlife Service

**Job Coach Tip**

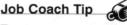

To manage your career path effectively, develop and use a personal career network.

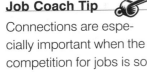
- Armed forces recreation
- Employee services and recreation
- Campus recreation
- Private membership organizations
- Therapeutic recreation services
- Sports management
- Tourism and hospitality (Kraus, Barber, & Shapiro, 2001)

The remainder of this chapter provides a brief overview of these 10 categories of career opportunities.

## Public or Governmental Agencies at the Federal, State, and Local Levels

Public parks and recreation, the traditional source for many job opportunities in this field, offers careers with federal, state, county, and city governments focusing on recreation and leisure services. At the federal level, most public recreation and leisure service agencies are primarily involved with outdoor recreation and natural resources such as national parks and forests, and are responsible for the management of these resources. In addition, several federal agencies also have responsibilities associated with tourism, military recreation, and education to name a few. Careers include interpretation of the many national parks and cultural resource centers, outdoor recreation planning and management, forestry and wildlife management, park maintenance, and law enforcement at these resources.

Similar to responsibilities found at federal agencies, each state is responsible for the provision and maintenance of wilderness areas, state reserves or natural preserves, historical monuments and cultural preserves, and recreational areas and facilities such as campgrounds, cross-country skiing areas, backpacking trails, and water sites for boating, swimming, fishing, and other recreational outlets.

At the local municipal and county levels, recreation professionals are responsible for the planning, management, and supervision of public parks and playgrounds, community recreation centers, camps, sports facilities, and recreation activities and programs that meet the leisure needs and interests of the tax-paying public.

With federal, state, or local agencies, a number of exciting and challenging jobs are available in recreation and leisure services in the public and governmental sectors.

## Nonprofit Organizations

In 2008, there were more than 1,500,000 nonprofit organizations in the United States alone (National Center for Charitable Statistics, 2008). Many of these organizations are religious-based organizations such as the YMCA/YWCA, the YMHA/YWHA/ Jewish Community Center, and the Catholic Youth Organization. However, others are nondenominational and include such organizations as Boy Scouts, Girl Scouts, Big Brothers/Big Sisters, and Boys and Girls Clubs of America. Many of these community service agencies are youth-serving agencies providing recreation programs, facilities, and professional staff to promote the constructive use of leisure time, along with developing enriched lifestyles for the youth membership of their organizations.

## Commercial Recreation

Private recreation and leisure service businesses provide needed leisure services, products, and programs to the public for a fee and have a long-term goal of making a profit. The *for-profit* motive and primary purpose of commercial recreation distinguish these recreation businesses from the other types of leisure service providers found in the field. This is not to say that recreation business owners and managers care only about making a financial profit. Many of these businesses have overall missions, goals, and actual products that meet the needs and wants of the paying public. But the bottom line, as with any agency or organization in the business world, is that they must make a profit to stay in business. Examples of commercial recreation include the following:

- Health and fitness centers
- Clubs and health spas
- Tennis and racquet clubs
- Ski areas
- Private country clubs
- Athletic clubs
- Golf courses
- Condominiums
- Bowling lanes
- Billiard parlors
- Sporting goods stores
- Campgrounds
- Skating rinks
- Aquatic centers
- Splash or water theme parks

- Marinas
- Squash and racquet centers
- Cruise ships
- Yachts
- Golf courses
- Theme parks
- Auditoriums
- Arenas and stadiums
- Movie theaters
- Dance studios
- Amusement parks
- Craft stores
- Casinos
- Resorts

The gaming or gambling industry is a prime example of commercial recreation and has increased in popularity throughout the United States. More than a decade ago, if a person desired to take a chance at the blackjack table, keno lounge, or slot machine, he or she had to travel to Atlantic City, New Jersey, or Nevada. Today, gambling casinos and gaming operations are more prevalent in a number of states (e.g., California, Illinois, Indiana, Iowa, Louisiana, Mississippi, Missouri) as state governments have welcomed gambling as a major source of revenue. The industry consists of approximately 500 commercial casinos and 160 Native American casinos located on reservations with combined annual revenue of nearly $85 billion (Hoover's, Inc., 2008). One of the largest growth areas within the casino industry is racetrack casino facilities, or racinos, which include horse or dog tracks with on-site gaming machines. Positions in management, entertainment, security, marketing, food and beverage, and hotel operations illustrate the variety of employment opportunities in the gaming industry.

## Armed Forces Recreation

Each branch of the armed forces provides morale, welfare, and recreation (MWR) programs that contribute to the readiness and combat capability, retention, and the mental, physical, and emotional well-being of its service members, their families, and other members of the Department of Defense. These programs and facilities provide sport and physical fitness activities, child development and youth programs, and a variety of food and beverage services. They are generally self-supporting using only nonappropriated revenues generated internally from their base operations. The military also operates a number of Armed Forces Recreation Centers and resort locations around the world for the enjoyment of the men and women serving in the military.

## Employee Services and Recreation

Numerous industries, businesses, and corporations provide recreation and leisure service programs and facilities for benefits of their employees and families. Opportunities for employment in this setting are becoming more plentiful because Stoltzfus (2009) reports employees in the public and private sectors have greater access to wellness programs and employee assistance programs than they did a decade ago. Once referred to as industrial or corporate recreation, these programs provide services such as nutrition education, physical fitness, and stress management—proactive measures aimed at reducing the employer's medical care costs and improving the employees' quality of life. Employee services and recreation programs improve relations between employees and management, increase overall employee productivity, enhance employee morale, reduce absenteeism and turnover, and contribute to reduced health insurance costs and expenses. In other words, a happy, healthy employee is a more productive employee!

## Campus Recreation

Campus recreation programs and facilities provide participatory recreation, sport, and fitness opportunities for college and university students, faculty, staff, and in some cases, the local public. Campus recreation promotes active, healthy lifestyles and fosters a sense of community through programs, facilities, and services. This is accomplished by providing a diverse array of recreation and *nonvarsity* sports opportunities, state-of-the-art sport facilities and equipment, student development opportunities, and professional staff leadership. Individuals working in this career setting focus on the management of people and resources in recreational sports rather than professional or varsity athletic sports. Positions in campus recreation are involved in programming and managing intramural sports, informal sports, club sports, instructional sports, aquatics, fitness and wellness, and various special event programs, activities, and facilities throughout the year.

## Private-Membership Organizations

Private-membership recreation and leisure service organizations provide programs and services specifically for their members, families, and guests. Private-membership organizations customarily include country clubs, residential-based organizations and associations, and fraternal or service organizations. The country club setting generally consists of golf clubs, tennis clubs, hunt and polo clubs, yacht clubs, athletic clubs, swim clubs, and many other leisure-oriented clubs. Residential-based agencies and

 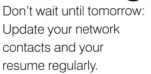
**Time Out**

Don't wait until tomorrow: Update your network contacts and your resume regularly.

associations, such as Leisure Living Resales and Leisure World, are retirement communities offering a "life of leisure" to retired homeowners. Other residential-based associations provide recreation programs and facilities at apartments, condominiums, and other housing developments for those who have not yet reached retirement age. Groups such as the Knights of Columbus, Shriners, and Kiwanis International are examples of private-membership organizations.

## Therapeutic Recreation Services

Therapeutic recreation programs and services involve the use of recreational programs and activities as therapeutic interventions to improve health, functional ability, and the quality of life. These programs are designed to provide rehabilitative services in clinical and nonclinical settings such as hospitals, hospices, mental health agencies, halfway houses, children's homes, senior centers, and nursing homes. Therapeutic recreation services can also help special populations such as burn victims, the terminally ill, drug users, or at-risk youth. A therapeutic recreation specialist works with youth and adults who may have physical, mental, emotional, psychiatric, or learning disabilities.

## Sport Management

With an increased awareness of available leisure opportunities by the American public, there is a tremendous growth in participation in recreational sports. The field has responded with new and expanded programs and opportunities to meet these needs. This growth has created an expanded market for sports along with a new era and challenge that must be met. It has also brought about significant career choices as well as employment opportunities in a variety of settings. There are entry-level sport management positions in literally thousands of public, nonprofit, commercial, and private agencies. Sports programs, conducted on a recreational basis, are intended for the enjoyment of all age groups regardless of race, gender, or athletic skill level.

Of the 10 recreation and leisure service categories, sport management represents one of the largest participation-based categories in the group. With the increasing interest in recreational sports participation and fitness activity for all age groups, there has arisen a need for broad-based recreational sports programming that reflects these needs and interests. In turn, this requires professionals who possess programming and management skills in sport management.

## Tourism and Hospitality

As the third largest industry in the world, and one of the fastest growing, a career in the tourism and hospitality industry offers numerous career opportunities at a variety of levels of service, production, and management. Just in the past 30 years, tourism industries have grown by more than 500%. According to the World Travel and Tourism Council (WTTC) (2009), the travel and tourism industry employs more than 225 million people worldwide and is expected to continue to grow by as much as 4% annually over the next decade. Further, the WTTC speculates "the contribution of the travel and tourism economy to total employment is expected to rise from 219,810,000 jobs in 2009 (1 in every 13.1 jobs) to 275,688,000 jobs (1 in every 11.8 jobs) by 2019." In addition, the nature of tourism has developed and been reshaped in scope and direction. Once considered as going to the beach for sunshine and sand during one's

**Time Out**

Put your dreams into action. Take the necessary steps now that will ensure success as a candidate for your dream job!

**Did You Know...**

Nearly 11 million college students use recreational facilities operated by National Intramural-Recreational Sports Association's (NIRSA's) members with more than 1.1 million intramural contests scheduled each year.

NIRSA

vacation, tourism now includes a wide range of new activities such as cultural tourism, adventure tourism, and ecotourism.

Employment opportunities, such as for event planners, tour directors, festival directors, and program coordinators, exist in resort management, convention center management, visitors bureau management, meeting and event planning, cruise hospitality, hotel and restaurant hospitality management, transportation and travel, theme parks, fairs and festivals/expositions, tourism planning, and commercial recreation settings to name just a few.

A hybrid of sport management and tourism is the emerging area of sport tourism. Identified by Biddiscombe (2006) as one of the hottest new businesses, sport tourism involves people traveling to actively participate in or to passively observe sports. Although sporting events have long influenced travel, the term *sport tourism* to describe this type of travel has become more ubiquitous within the past decade (Gibson, 2006). Furthermore, sport and tourism professionals have begun to realize the significant potential of travelers seeking to participate in or spectate at sporting events creating a demand for sport experiences (Neirotti, 2003). Ritchie and Adair (2004) claim, "Sport and tourism are among the 'developed' world's most sought after leisure experiences" (p. 2). Whether a golf vacation to the Grand Strand of Myrtle Beach or a bicycle tour through California wine country, the implications for professionals with experience and expertise in the event planning and the leisure service industry are plentiful.

This chapter provides a brief overview of the 10 major career categories in recreation and leisure services. A major challenge now is for candidates to narrow these possibilities down to a few select career settings based on their particular career interests and desires. Visit this book's website, http://health.jbpub.com/recreationjobs/2e, for information that can be used as a tool or guide in helping to identify suitable careers by listing possible job titles for each career category as well as skills and typical leisure activities associated with each career setting. In reviewing the chart, job seekers should circle all of the job titles that are of interest to them as well as skills and experiences they might have. In the last column, job seekers can circle the leisure activities they enjoy participating in currently or in the past. In some cases, favorite hobbies or activities can lead to full-time job opportunities. In the recreation and leisure services field, professionals really can earn a living working in a job that they enjoy doing!

Please keep in mind that information provided about career opportunities in the chart is only representative of the possible job opportunities in the field. Many more related occupational titles, skills, and leisure activities are not listed that certainly could be a match for some job seekers. The main purpose of the chart is to serve as a beginning tool that assists further career exploration and information gathering on possible career settings.

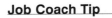

**Job Coach Tip**

Ask, listen, and learn! You can learn a lot by being a good listener, especially in the job search process.

**Keys to Job Search Success**

Before you start planning and getting serious about a future career in recreation and leisure services, identify your dream job as well as short-term and long-term goals that will be necessary to get this job. Reach for the stars!

# Conclusion

Starting a new career is an exciting and important phase in one's life. Individuals seeking positions in recreation and leisure services should realize that a number of paths lead to a variety of rewarding and exciting careers. However, one of the most important steps that job seekers can take to ensure success in a career is to be well prepared during the job search process. The following chapters in this book help prepare candidates for the many steps in this process.

# References

Biddiscombe, R. (2006). *The business of sport tourism report.* Retrieved May 24, 2009, from http://www.sportbusiness.com/files/tourism_sum.pdf

Bureau of Labor Statistics, U.S. Department of Labor. (2008). *Occupational outlook handbook, 2008–09 edition, recreation workers.* Retrieved May 24, 2009, from http://stats.bls.gov/oco/ocos058.htm#nature

Gibson, H. (2006). Sport tourism: Concepts and theories. An introduction. In H. Gibson (Ed.), *Sport tourism concepts and theories* (pp. 1–9). New York: Routledge.

Hoover's Inc. (2008). *Gambling resorts & casino industry trends.* Retrieved May 25, 2009, from http://industries.hoovers.com/leisure/gambling/gambling-resorts-and-casinos/industry_trends

Kraus, R., Barber, E., & Shapiro, I. (2001). *Introduction to leisure services: Career perspectives.* Champaign, IL: Sagamore.

LeisureTRAK (2008, December). *The unemployed still play.* Retrieved May 17, 2009, from http://www.leisuretrends.com/ShowArticle.aspx?ID=372&EID=151&sid=BH186JCLEJRGLBRGINNHHEE

National Center for Charitable Statistics. (2008). *Nonprofit almanac 2008: Public charities, giving, and volunteering.* Retrieved May 24, 2009, from http://nccs.urban.org/statistics/profiles.cfm

National Intramural-Recreational Sports Association. (2007). *NIRSA's rich history.* Retrieved May 24, 2009, from http://www.nirsa.org/Content/NavigationMenu/AboutUs/History/History.htm

National Park Service. (n.d.). *Work with us.* Retrieved September 23, 2009, from http://www.nps.gov/aboutus/workwithus.htm

Neirotti, L. D. (2003). An introduction to sport and adventure tourism. In S. Hudson (Ed.), *Sport and adventure tourism* (pp. 1–25). New York: Haworth Hospitality Press.

Ritchie, B. W., & Adair, D. (2004). Sport tourism: An introduction and overview. In B. W. Ritchie & D. Adair (Eds.), *Sport tourism interrelationships, impacts and issues* (pp. 1–29). Tonawanda, NY: Channel View Publications.

Stoltzfus, E. R. (2009, April 22). Access to wellness and employee assistance programs in the United States. *Compensation and Working Conditions Online*, U.S. Bureau of Labor Statistics. Retrieved May 25, 2009, from http://www.bls.gov/opub/cwc/print/cm20090416ar01p1.htm

USDA Forest Service. (2009). *General careers overview.* Retrieved May 17, 2009, from http://www.fs.fed.us/fsjobs/jobs_overview.shtml

U.S. Fish and Wildlife Service. (2007). *About the U.S. Fish and Wildlife Service.* Retrieved September 23, 2009, from http://www.fws.gov/help/about_us .html

World Travel and Tourism Council. (2009). *Travel and tourism economic impact 2009 executive summary.* Retrieved May 17, 2009, from http://www.wttc.org/bin /pdf/original_pdf_file/exec_summary_2009.pdf

YMCA of the USA. (2009). *About the YMCA.* Retrieved May 17, 2009, from http://www.ymca.net/about_the_ymca

## Assignment: Reflecting on a Career in Recreation and Leisure Services

As you prepare to enter the recreation and leisure services field as a career, now is the time to take stock of yourself seriously. In order to do this, you should have a solid foundation in what the field has to offer in terms of career opportunities, expectations, job placement, salary levels, and so on.

Specifically, in your opinion, what are the advantages and disadvantages of a career in recreation and leisure services? Recommend a course of action that you will follow as you pursue your first job, with a complete justification of your recommendations.

_____

_____

_____

_____

_____

_____

_____

_____

_____

_____

_____

_____

_____

_____

_____

_____

_____

_____

_____

_____

_____

_____

_____

Assignments

Assignments

## Assignment: Investigating Recreation and Leisure Service Settings

As you contemplate your career in the recreation and leisure services field, it is crucial to determine your strengths and weaknesses as you think about the setting that most interests you. For this assignment, select the top three recreation and leisure services settings that most interest you, and list the advantages and disadvantages of each setting as in the first assignment. Then, take your strengths and areas that need improvement from your assessment in Chapter 1. Review both lists together and write a paragraph for each of your selected settings, reflecting upon the best fit for you. Be sure to justify your best fit based on how your strengths and weaknesses match up with the advantages and disadvantages of each setting.

# Researching an Organization

Researching an organization is one of the most critical steps in the job search process and can either encourage or discourage the candidate from pursuing a career or job in this field. To be successful in the job search process and as a way to set him- or herself apart from the rest of the applicant pool, the candidate must do the homework and learn as much as possible about the leisure services industry in general, and specifically more about the different types of organizations in this field. The key to success is having accurate, timely, and sufficient information to make educated decisions and choices. Candidates can think of this as a research project for a class, but instead of conducting research on, let's say, the constraints to leisure participation, the candidate's research focus is effectiveness of career exploration in the job search process. Research should strengthen and help clarify the candidate's career aspirations and job objective (Krannich & Krannich, 2003).

Visit the Web site for this book to learn more about the organizations and topics covered in this chapter. **http://health** **.jbpub.com/recreationjobs/2e**

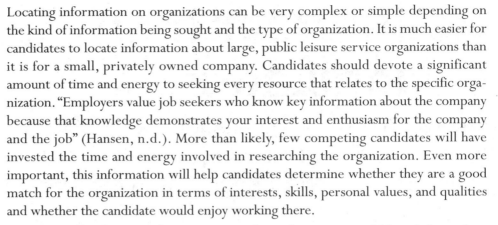
Locating information on organizations can be very complex or simple depending on the kind of information being sought and the type of organization. It is much easier for candidates to locate information about large, public leisure service organizations than it is for a small, privately owned company. Candidates should devote a significant amount of time and energy to seeking every resource that relates to the specific organization. "Employers value job seekers who know key information about the company because that knowledge demonstrates your interest and enthusiasm for the company and the job" (Hansen, n.d.). More than likely, few competing candidates will have invested the time and energy involved in researching the organization. Even more important, this information will help candidates determine whether they are a good match for the organization in terms of interests, skills, personal values, and qualities and whether the candidate would enjoy working there.

A number of books, journals, magazines, and newsletters are available to help explore career options and specific organizations. With the growth, popularity, and ease of use of the Internet, more and more organizational information is becoming available. The World Wide Web provides a vast source of information. At an unprecedented rate, organizations of all types and sizes are hosting their own Web sites and are being included in Web-based directories and virtual lists.

Although there is an abundance of information available, there is no one way to research a particular organization. The approach taken and the resources used will depend upon the type of organization and the amount of information candidates would like to receive.

At the very least, employers generally do expect candidates to know:

1. The exact organization name
2. Their programs, facilities, and services
3. The location of the main office and whether or not they have satellite facilities. If so, where are they located?
4. Their target audience
5. The organization's size (both in terms of professional staff and program participants/clients)
6. The specific interests of candidates about their organization
7. The candidate's familiarity with the position job announcement
8. The supervisor of the department or division with which the candidate would potentially be working
9. The potential career paths of the candidate within the organization. In other words, is the candidate familiar with the organizational flowchart?

**Job Coach Tip**

For information on jobs in recreation and leisure services, contact employers such as local departments of parks and recreation, YMCAs, Boys and Girls Clubs, local social or religious organizations, resorts, sport organizations, military recreation programs, or other settings that employ recreational specialists.

### Keys to Job Search Success

Recruiters report that the students who most impress them at career fairs, job interviews, professional conferences, and so on are those who demonstrate they have conducted job search research and have gained a familiarity and basic knowledge about an organization, have intelligent questions to ask based on this research, and have given previous thought to the way they might fit into the organization.

Employers have indicated that exceptional candidates who have done their research well:

- Are aware of noteworthy news items related to the employer
- Are aware of organization or industry trends
- Know the reputation of the employer
- Talk with current employees, participant/clients, and competitors for more detailed information about the organization (these groups can provide insight to the rewards and demands of a particular occupation)
- Attend local, state, or national presentations presented by the organization's professional staff
- Have a good idea of the working conditions, required education and training, salaries, qualifications, and other personal and professional characteristics associated with their particular organization
- Talk with alumni who are employed with their organization

## Steps in Researching an Organization

There are many places job candidates can discover information about an organization in recreation and leisure services. One simple premise job seekers can follow in researching a career or organization is to start generally and move toward specifics. In other words, they should browse information before searching for specific jobs at targeted organizations. The following section provides tips on the most effective ways to conduct this research. These tips include talking with friends, colleagues, faculty members, and alumni who might know about the organization; using the Internet; and obtaining information directly from the organization. Reference materials are available in print format at local public or university libraries. However, many are now available as online versions via the Internet.

### Researching Careers

In the first step of researching an organization, it is assumed the candidate has already decided upon a career in recreation and leisure services. Although a decision may have already been made to focus upon a specific organization, it is a good idea to gain an overview of the field of recreation and leisure services for a better research context. The *Occupational Outlook Handbook* Web site is the place to begin researching particular industries and occupations. It is the U.S. Department of Labor, Bureau of Labor Statistics, official handbook and is a nationally recognized source of career information. The handbook, revised every 2 years and published in print and on the Internet, contains the nature of the work, working conditions, training and other qualifications needed, job outlook, earnings, and sources of additional information for each occupation listed.

### Information Interviews

Although the Internet can provide excellent information about an organization, it cannot answer all questions candidates might have. One of the best ways to fill this gap and to research an organization is to speak with professionals who are currently working in the field. This technique of providing a personal perspective of an industry or organization is referred to as *information interviews*. It is an excellent way to explore and

**Job Coach Tip**

Prepare for the information interview exactly as you would for a job interview.

expand network contacts as well as to obtain firsthand information about day-to-day operations in the field.

After conducting several information interviews, candidates will not only be more informed, but better able to make good decisions based on accurate, current information. More specifically, information interviews can aid in the decision-making process regarding the following:

- Career setting in recreation and leisure services: The information interview can help candidates be more familiar with various career paths. Additionally, they may learn numerous ways to prepare for a particular career, such as academic majors, work experiences to gain, and college activities.

- Specific occupation in recreation and leisure services: Following the information interviews, candidates should be more aware of position titles, job descriptions, qualifications, types of employers, skills required, as well as the interests and values expressed in several occupations.

- Specific positions in recreation and leisure services: The information interview assists candidates in familiarizing themselves with potential employer contacts and the hiring process. As a result of participating in the information interviews, candidates have developed interviewing skills and received feedback on resume and job-hunting strategies. Finally, candidates have demonstrated assertive job-hunting behaviors by selecting, scheduling, participating in, and following through interview appointments.

## Obtain Information Directly from the Organization

In many instances, it is sometimes easier to obtain information about the organization directly from them. Ask the Human Resources Department or other appropriate offices or staff members for departmental annual reports, job descriptions, organizational flowcharts, recreation program policies or guidelines, vision/mission/goal statements, strategic plans, brochures, publicity and promotional materials, press releases, and other pertinent information that can provide a better picture of the agency or organization.

## Talk with Friends, Colleagues, Career Advisors, Faculty Members, and Alumni

At the research stage in the job search process, talk to everyone who might be familiar with the organization. Ask friends or contacts if they know of anyone who is or has worked at the organization. Speak with academic and career advisors or faculty members who might know about the organization or know of colleagues who might have valuable information. Last, try to locate any alumni from your university who might be working in the organization or in the geographical area of the organization.

## The Better Business Bureau

According to the Better Business Bureau (BBB), their organization does not endorse, recommend, or disapprove of any company on which it reports. It simply states the facts about a company's customer service record, as the bureau knows it. If the BBB has a report on a company, it will indicate: (1) whether the company is a member of the BBB; (2) if the company has a satisfactory or unsatisfactory customer service record

**Time Out**

Always take the time to follow up with a thank-you note to those who participated in your information interview.

**Be Alert!**

The information interview is not a job interview; it is used to gain information about an occupation and to obtain valuable networking contacts.

with the BBB; and (3) details on how the company handles customer disputes. From a job research standpoint, this information can be important because it illustrates how many complaints an organization might have against it as well as how the organization handled these complaints.

## Annual Reports

An organization's annual report can provide a great deal of general industry information as well as a good overview of specific organization information. Annual reports are available from various sources:

- Several companies now list their annual reports on their Web sites or use a third party to post them online. About 3000 annual reports are available at AnnualReports.com.
- Public Register's Annual Report Service (PRARS) is America's largest annual report service; it provides free annual reports on more than 3600 public companies.

## Professional Associations

Professional associations are powerful resources providing many research and networking opportunities. Associations are excellent sources for career research purposes because one of their major functions is to promote and provide professional development for their profession. Students in virtually every major in recreation and leisure services can benefit in a variety of ways through membership and participation in professional associations. There is no better way to demonstrate enthusiasm and commitment to the field than by joining and becoming an active member. Memberships offer excellent opportunities to build network contacts, learn up-to-date information about trends emerging in the field, and earn and maintain professional certifications. Once a member, candidates should plan to attend and get involved in local, state, and national association conferences, workshops, and seminars.

Key professional associations in the parks, recreation, sports, and tourism fields include the following:

- *National Recreation and Park Association (NRPA):* NRPA has been the voice promoting parks, open green space, recreational opportunities, facilities, and programs that are available to all Americans.
- *American Alliance of Health, Physical Education, Recreation and Dance (AAHPERD):* AAHPERD is one of the largest associations of professionals

**Time Out**

Don't skip employer Web sites even if you found they have listed jobs in other locations. Many employers post even more job listings on their own sites, plus you can probably find a way to contact their HR department to find out about additional opportunities not posted.

Riley Guide

**Job Coach Tip**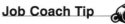

Joining a student branch or chapter of a professional association is an excellent and inexpensive way to further your career exploration.

---

**Keys to Job Search Success**

The Internet cannot be the only resource you use for your job search! You must continue to utilize all contacts, information resources, and services available to you for the most effective and efficient search for employment. Continue to attend meetings, pick up the phone and call people, and use the reference books in your library. Limit your time online to 25% of the total time you can dedicate to your job search.

Riley Guide

**Job Coach Tip**

Because approximately 65–75% of job opportunities are never posted, it is critical that you know how to network properly to find this hidden job market!

promoting healthy lifestyles through various educational programs involved in health, physical education, and recreation/leisure services.

- ***International Association of Amusement Parks and Attractions (IAAPA):*** IAAPA is a nonprofit organization dedicated to the preservation and prosperity of the amusement industry worldwide.

- ***International Festivals and Events Association (IFEA):*** IFEA is a voluntary association involving event-related professionals who provide various festivals and community events and celebrations.

- ***Meeting Professionals International (MPI):*** For meeting and event planning professionals, this global professional organization is the connection for more than 24,000 members in more than 80 countries.

- ***National Intramural-Recreational Sports Association (NIRSA):*** NIRSA is the leading resource for professionals programming collegiate or campus recreational sports programs and activities.

- ***Resort and Commercial Recreation Association (RCRA):*** RCRA is a non-profit organization established to further the resort and commercial recreation industries and to increase the profitability of commercial recreation business and entities.

- ***Cruise Lines International Association (CLIA):*** CLIA is the world's largest cruise association dedicated to the promotion and growth of the cruise industry. CLIA is composed of 24 of the major cruise lines representing 97% of the cruise capacity marketed from North America. CLIA exists to promote a safe, secure, and healthy cruise ship environment; educate and train its travel agent members; and promote and explain the value, desirability, and affordability of the cruise vacation experience.

- ***Student Conservation Association, Inc. (SCA):*** The SCA provides a variety of educational programs for students interested in pursuing careers in natural resource conservation.

Many associations provide career opportunity resource centers offering up-to-date information on career paths and actual job listings of position openings. For example, the National Recreation and Park Association (NRPA) sponsors a career page. See Appendix A for a listing of associations.

Job seekers may find other printed sources of information in the *Encyclopedia of Associations and the National Trades* and *Professional Associations of the United States*. These publications can be viewed at most public libraries and university career resources libraries.

Job seekers can also use online databases of associations to identify various associations in leisure services. These databases can produce membership directories, journals, and newsletters that provide valuable information. Some online resources are as follows:

- Directory of Associations
- AssociationCentral.com

## Industry Publications, Magazines, and Newsletters

Several organizations print internal publications for employees and the public that are placed in local libraries or available by contacting the organization itself. Reading

**Did You Know...**

At least 60% of all jobs are found through networking.

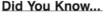
Doyle

relevant articles about the organization enables the candidate to gain a better perspective of the organization. Tools are available for finding publication titles in a field of interest:

- The best way to begin searching is through a university library Web site. Most of these sites include links to Lexis/Nexis, Academic Search Elite, and others.
- Magazines can be identified online in the National Directory of Magazines.
- Hoovers Business Library provides free "organization capsules" and for a fee, "organization profiles." They also have links to major corporate Web sites.
- PR NEWSWIRE has recent organization press releases.
- ABI/Inform Global has abstracts from more than 1000 business periodicals.

## Newspaper Articles, Press Releases, and Periodical Articles

The next step in the research process is to review local newspaper articles, press releases, and periodical articles about the organization. According to Messmer (1995), job search candidates should be reading three types of periodicals on a regular basis: (1) general business publications or publications that are being read by top managers in a professional field; (2) trade publications specifically geared toward the candidate's particular field; and (3) local newspapers and other related publications. These resources can provide extensive information on organizations such as advertising, marketing, special events, new recreation programs, facilities, and so on. These local sources can be accessed through the Web, and even newspapers in the smallest communities have Web sites these days.

The local or city newspaper serves as a great starting point to obtain organizational information. Newspaper resources generally have articles and features on programs provided by the organization. A number of Web sites provide links to online newspapers throughout the world; for example, NewsLink connects you to more than 3600 newspapers and magazines from around the world—even college newspapers—and it is searchable by state. Others include the following:

- NewsCentral
- E&P MediaInfo
- NewsPaperLinks
- News Alert
- Northern Light Group, LLC
- Excite News
- U.S. Newspapers

**Job Coach Tip**

Knowledge is power. Gathering, processing, and using information is the lifeblood of any job search.

Krannich & Krannich

**Did You Know...**

Newspapers only produce 7 percent of hiring results while the Internet accounts for 33 percent with company Web sites producing about 53 percent of those jobs!

Beatty

## Keys to Job Search Success

Networking is the art of building alliances, not contacting everyone you know when you are looking for a new job and asking if they know of any job openings. Networking starts long before a job search, and you probably don't even realize you are doing it!

Riley Guide

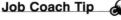
Don't forget about local and campus newspapers, many of which can be found in most local public or university libraries.

For periodicals, try the following:

- American City Business Journals (owned by Advance Publications, Inc.)
- Forbes' People Tracker
- TIME.com
- NewsDirectory.com
- Newslink

## Nonprofit Organizations

For nonprofit organizations, valuable information can be found at a number of key Web sites:

- Guidestar provides a searchable directory of nonprofit organizations.
- Idealist is another site with lists of nonprofit organizations categorized by field, state, and country. This directory covers more than 120 countries worldwide.
- The Foundation Center offers a searchable database of philanthropic literature and links to nonprofits with Web sites.

## Use the Internet

Thanks to the Web, job seekers can learn more about an organization quickly at little or no cost. Most companies use their home pages as a marketing or communication tool for generating and retaining business. As such, corporate sites may provide annual reports, news articles, business ventures, and information about programs, services, and staff. A good portion of the candidate's research time should be spent reviewing the information available at the organization's home page.

### Searching for the Organization's Web Page

If candidates have not yet located the organization's home page, they should try guessing the address. Many businesses have a Web site address that looks like this: http://www.organizationname.com. The standard beginning of most Internet sites is www and the standard ending for sites is one of the following:

- .com: Commercial
- .org: Nonprofit organization
- .gov: Government
- .mil: Military
- .edu: Education

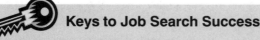 **Keys to Job Search Success**

The amount of knowledge (research) you have about a potential employer and the recreation and leisure services industry can give you a significant edge in the job search process.

For an organization such as Disney, try typing the address as described above in the browser's address box. If that does not lead to immediate results, Whois.net allows candidates to search a database of registered domain names. Lycos is a search engine that is particularly effective for locating organization home pages. Dogpile is a meta-search engine that searches the major search engines providing top results from each. These resources allow candidates to determine quickly if any of the search engines have indexed a home page for the organization.

Another organization research tool is the business metasite. These Web sites link to a very large number of online business resources from around the world. Some of the more popular metasites are these:

- A Business Researcher's Interests provides access to thousands of business resources.
- Business.com provides an extensive list of industries, products, and services. This is one of the few free industry sources with access (Riley Guide, 2009e).
- CEO Express is a great place to start the research process.
- CompaniesOnline from Lycos provides a business directory featuring detailed information on 60,000 public and private U.S. companies, all with sites on the World Wide Web.
- Corporate Information.com offers an extensive list of links to public, private, domestic, and international resources and company profiles.
- Hoover's Online database of 12 million companies, with in-depth coverage of 40,000 of the world's top business enterprises, provides excellent background research information.
- Gary Price's List of Lists is a comprehensive clearinghouse of links to journal articles listing industry outlooks, overviews, surveys, and product/industry information to the top ranked industries, organizations, schools, products, and people.

Once candidates have located the Web site of the organization, they can browse a number of pages because of the valuable information they might contain. These include the following pages (or their equivalents):

- *What's New:* This page provides the most current information about the organization and staff and may mention new programs that might be of interest.
- *Annual Reports or Strategic Plans:* If the Web site has links to annual reports, strategic plans, mission/goals/objective statements, organizational charts, and so on, read them very carefully to gain a better understanding of the overall direction of the organization.
- *Staff:* This page provides professional staff contact information such as names, titles, addresses, phone numbers, and so forth. This information will become very valuable later in the job search process.

**Time Out**

Be patient! Researching an organization takes time and energy, but it will pay off in the long run!

**Did You Know...**

Casino hotels, which account for the majority of gaming industry revenue, have become larger, generating average annual revenue of more than $100 million.

Hoover's, Inc.

**Keys to Job Search Success**

Don't wait for potential employers to post jobs or find your resume! Your go out and find them! Targeting employers puts you in full control of your search.

Riley Guide

**Job Coach Tip**

Use the research information you have gathered to make a great first impression in the interview!

- *Employment / Career Opportunities:* Many larger organizations provide links to current job listings in their organization as well as employment application procedures.

### Obtaining Organization Addresses and Phone Numbers

Candidates can use the following sites to obtain company contact information:

- *Yahoo! Business and Economy: Companies: Directories:* Here the candidate can find links to business directories and yellow pages that include company and industry profiles, news, financials, statistics, and more.

- *Big Book Nationwide Yellow Pages* provides phone and map information for businesses and is updated monthly.

- *FEDSTATS* provides access to statistics of many government agencies.

- *The Better Business Bureau's Philanthropic Advisory Service* reports on major charitable organizations.

- *The National Center for Charitable Statistics* collects statistics on nonprofit organizations and is the national clearinghouse of data on the nonprofit sector in the United States.

**Did You Know...**

Americans are spending so much of their time on the job that, in a quest to improve their quality of life, they are looking for more leisure-type activities and comforts at work.

LeisureTrak

### Using Social Networks

Social networking is a phenomenon that has become wildly popular within the last 10 years with the under-40-years-of-age group. The primary use of social networks is to interact with others online by creating a virtual network that potentially stretches around the world. Social networkers create profiles that share personal and / or professional information and that result in reconnecting with old friends as well as linking up with new acquaintances. Because of the global nature of online networking, someone in Gnawbone, Indiana, could be "friends" with someone in Beijing, China. Although the idea of networking is not new, "how people are networking and connecting to great opportunities is changing with next-generation job sites that combine job search and networking" (Goldberg, n.d.).

**Be Alert!**

Keep in mind that just about anything that is online can be read by someone—or everyone! If you don't want the world to read what you've posted, make sure they can't!

Doyle

With a plethora of social networks available, the job seeker might wonder which social media are most beneficial in researching organizations or allowing potential employers to notice the candidate's strengths for a posted job. The general consensus of the literature identified LinkedIn as the best site for networking because it is designed for professional networking (Doyle, 2009b). LinkedIn also allows employers to post jobs on their site, and most positions listed are for professional, high-quality jobs (Levy, 2009). Schawbel (2009) also recommends Twitter, Jobster, Facebook, and Craigslist as social networking sites for job searching and discovering information about organizations that may be of interest to the job seeker.

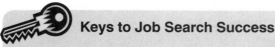

### Keys to Job Search Success

"The employer's Web site told me what they wanted me to know, but I found what I wanted to know by doing more searching online."

Riley Guide

Because first impressions are hard to overcome, it is essential that job seekers using social networking sites understand that anything posted on the Internet can be viewed by anyone, including potential employers. Some organizations regularly search social networks for additional information on candidates for their jobs. The implication of this for job seekers is to be cautious and thoughtful about the information they post online about themselves.

## Conclusion

The more time spent in the researching stage, the better prepared candidates will be during the interviewing phase of the job search process. The old adage "Fish where the fish are" is very appropriate in job searching. To be successful in this process, job seekers should do their best to get caught by acquainting themselves with the recreation and leisure services field in general and the specific organization of interest. Candidates must read, explore, and expand their knowledge of the field, as well as talk to professionals. The quality of the candidate's research will be only as good as the questions asked. There are plenty of resources available that can help in conducting the necessary research; yet, the bottom line is candidates must be willing to devote the time and energy it will require!

**Be Alert!**

Don't include a link on your resume to any site that includes inappropriate content that is not appropriate for a business audience.

Doyle

## References

Beatty, R. H. (2006). *The ultimate job search.* Indianapolis, IN: Jist Publishers.

Better Business Bureau. (2009). *Vision, mission, and values.* Retrieved May 27, 2009, from http://www.bbb.org/us/bbb_mission

Bureau of Labor Statistics, U.S. Department of Labor. *Occupational Outlook Handbook, 2008–09 Edition.* Recreation and Fitness Workers. Retrieved May 27, 2009, from http://www.bls.gov/oco/ocos058.htm

Doyle, A. (2009a). Successful job search networking: How to use job search networking to find a job. Retrieved May 27, 2009, from http://jobsearch.about.com/cs/networking/a/networking.htm

Doyle, A. (2009b). To blog or not to blog? How blogging and social networking can impact your job search. Retrieved May 30, 2009, from http://jobsearch.about.com/od/jobsearchblogs/a/jobsearchblog.htm

Florida State University Center. (2009). *Conducting an information interview.* Retrieved September 17, 2009, from http://www.career.fsu.edu/experience/information_interviews_guide.html

Goldberg, J. (n.d.). The power of networking: How networking can help with your job search. Retrieved May 30, 2009, from http://jobsearch.about.com/od/networking/a/jobster.htm

Hansen, R. S. (n.d.). *Step-by-step guide to researching companies.* Retrieved May 27, 2009, from http://www.quintcareers.com/researching_companies_guide.html

Hoover's, Inc. (2008). Gambling resorts & casino industry trends. Retrieved May 25, 2009, from http://industries.hoovers.com/leisure/gambling/gambling-resorts-and-casinos/industry_trends

**Be Alert!**

When considering employment within the cruise line industry, bear in mind that your choice of positions may vary depending on a ship's size, where it's registered, its itinerary, and to some extent, the type of passenger the cruise line attracts.

Krannich, R. L., & Krannich, C. R. (2003). *The job hunting guide: Transitioning from college to career*. Manassas Park, VA: Impact Publications.

Levy, R. (2009). How to use social media in your job search: Using LinkedIn, Facebook, and Twitter to job search. Retrieved May 27, 2009, from http://jobsearch.about.com/od/networking/a/socialmedia.htm

Messmer, M. (1995). *Job hunting for dummies*. Foster City, CA: Robert Half International, Inc.

Riley Guide. (2009a, February). How to use the Internet in your job search. Retrieved May 27, 2009, from http://www.rileyguide.com/jobsrch.html

Riley Guide. (2009b, February). Netiquette: The fine art of correct behavior on the Internet. Retrieved May 27, 2009, from http://www.rileyguide.com/network.html

Riley Guide. (2009c, February). Use the Internet to find job leads. Retrieved May 27, 2009, from http://www.rileyguide.com/jobleads.html

Riley Guide. (2009d, February). Do the research that supports your job search. Retrieved May 27, 2009, from http://www.rileyguide.com/jsresearch.html

Riley Guide. (2009e, February). How to research employers. Retrieved May 27, 2009, from http://www.rileyguide.com/employer.html

Schawbel, M. (2009, February 24). Top 10 social sites for finding a job. *Mashable The Social Media Guide*. Retrieved May 28, 2009, from http://mashable.com/2009/02/24/top-10-social-sites-for-finding-a-job

U.S. Travel Association. (2009, March 16). Americans' leisure travel intentions trend slightly upward. Retrieved May 27, 2009, from http://www.tia.org/pressmedia/pressrec.asp?Item=952

U.S. Travel Association. (2008, February 13). Travel and Tourism Works for America tell the impact of the nation's fifth-largest private industry sector. Retrieved May 27, 2009, from http://www.tia.org/pressmedia/pressrec.asp?Item=873

# Assignment: Information Interview

Each student should conduct two information interviews with professionals in their field. For each interview, they can write a 3- to 4-page summary report of the meeting. The interview summary report should be written in a question and answer format. Students should comment on what they learned, particularly if they were surprised or interested in the answers received. Each report should be typed and organized in a professional format. Students should start with an introduction that indicates the overall impression of the organization and a list of the areas they will discuss. The body of the report should provide information on those areas (e.g., background, work environment) to make it easier to find specific information at a later time. The conclusion should summarize the student's overall evaluation of the organization. The report will be graded on content, organization, professional appearance, documentation of sources, and mechanics (e.g., grammar, spelling, punctuation).

## Possible Questions for the Information Interview

1.  (Background) Tell me how you got started in this field. What was your education? What educational background or related experience might be helpful in entering this field?

2.  (Work environment) What are the daily duties of the job? What are the working conditions? What skills and abilities are utilized in this work?

3.  (Problems) What are the toughest problems you deal with? What problems does the organization as a whole have? What is being done to solve these problems?

4.  (Lifestyle) What obligation does your work put on you outside the workweek? How much flexibility do you have in terms of dress, work hours, and vacations?

5.  (Rewards) What do you find most rewarding about this work, besides the money?

6.  (Salary) What salary level would a new person start with? What are the fringe benefits? What are other forms of compensation?

7.  (Potential) Where do you see yourself going in a few years? What are your long-term goals?

8.  (Promotional) Is turnover high? How does one move from position to position? Do people normally move to another company/division/agency? What is your policy about promotions from within? What happened to the person(s) who last held this position? How many have held this job in the last 5 years? How are employees evaluated?

9.  (The industry) What trends do you see for this industry in the next 3 to 5 years? What kind of future do you see for this organization?

10. (Advice) How well-suited is my background for this field? When the time comes, how would I go about finding a job in this field? What experience, paid or volunteer, would you recommend? What suggestions do you have to help make my resume more effective?

11. (Demand) What types of employers hire people in this line of work? Where are they located? What other career areas do you feel are related to your work?

Assignments

12. (Hiring decision) What are the most important factors used to hire people in this work (education, past experience, personality, special skills)? Who makes the hiring decisions for your department? Who supervises the boss? When I am ready to apply for a job, who should I contact?

13. (Job market) How do people find out about your jobs? Are they advertised in the newspaper? If so, which ones? By word of mouth? If so, who spreads the word? By the personnel office?

14. (Referral to other information opportunities) Can you name a relevant trade journal or magazine you would recommend I review? What professional organizations might have information about this career area?

15. (Referral to others) Based on our conversation today, what other types of people do you believe I should talk to? Can you name a few of these people? May I have permission to use your name when I contact them?

16. Do you have any other advice for me?

*Source:* Adapted from Florida State University Career Center. http://www.career.fsu.edu/experience/information-interviews-guide.html

_____

_____

_____

_____

_____

_____

_____

_____

_____

_____

_____

_____

_____

_____

_____

_____

_____

_____

_____

_____

_____

_____

# Assignment: Career Research Presentation

By this time, you should have explored and researched various careers in recreation and leisure services. Now, it is time to find the one career or occupation of the most interest to you and continue with the research in this area. For this assignment, you will develop a PowerPoint presentation to deliver to your classmates. This will serve as an assessment of your research skills and knowledge of this career or occupation.

## This assignment includes the following:

A three (3) minute informational presentation that includes the following aspects of your research:

- A brief description of the nature of the work that is performed by entry-level employees
- Working conditions
- Starting salary for entry-level employees
- The characteristics needed for a person to be most successful in this career
- Education and training background required
- Advantages and disadvantages of the job
- Career advancement opportunities
- Employment outlook
- Related occupations

A double-spaced, typed report should be submitted at the time of your presentation with all the preceding information included.

_____

_____

_____

_____

_____

_____

_____

_____

_____

_____

_____

_____

_____

_____

_____

_____

Assignments

# Portfolios

Although portfolios are not new, using a portfolio in the job search process is a growing trend and becoming a standard requirement in many professional fields and occupations. Teachers, artists, musicians, and writers—both students and professionals—have traditionally used portfolios to record or document their skills and accomplishments. Now, portfolios have gained importance and are more widely used as a job search tool in business, arts and sciences, and, most recently, recreation and leisure services.

Visit the Web site for this book to learn more about the organizations and topics covered in this chapter. **http://health .jbpub.com/recreationjobs/2e**

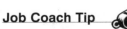
# What Is a Portfolio?

There are various terms associated with portfolios, such as *career portfolio*, *job portfolio*, *professional portfolio*, *presentation portfolio*, and *interview portfolio*. Regardless of the terminology used, the portfolio is a very practical job search tool used in career exploration that captures and showcases a complete picture of a candidate and provides a glimpse of the person's career accomplishments—both from a student and professional perspective. Often, it is referred to as a pictorial resume (Bolles & Bolles, 2008). "A portfolio is a portable collection of materials that showcase your skills, achievement, experience, academic excellence, and anything else that is relevant for the interviewer to see. While the resume is a great tool for summarizing your background, the portfolio actually *proves* the existence and the depth of your skills, education, and other experiences" (Turner, 2009). In this case, a picture truly is worth a thousand words! A portfolio goes well beyond a cover letter and the traditional resume. It is a portable means of storing, tracking, and presenting samples (known as *artifacts*) illustrating candidates' skills and achievements.

Unique to the portfolio, it allows (and requires!) candidates to be reflective about what they have accomplished while in college. In many instances, this reflection process needed for developing the portfolio can be just as important and beneficial as the final product! The candidates' reflection focuses on demonstrating, documenting, and displaying evidence of how much they have learned, grown, and developed over time (Klenowski, Askew, & Carnell, 2006). "It is a reflection of the student as a person undergoing continuous personal development, not just a store of evidence" (Rebbeck, 2008). The value of the portfolio is its objectivity and illustration of the candidates' best work. As a result, the job interviewer will be more likely to remember the candidates who actually *show* and *demonstrate* actual skills, rather than merely list these skills in their resume.

# Why Use a Portfolio?

Developing a portfolio can be a time-consuming and daunting task. However, if crafted in a professional manner so that it contains an abundance of supportive material, the portfolio can be an excellent tool for self-learning as well as a means of marketing one's capabilities in a job interview. "Although the ultimate goal of a portfolio is a product, the *process of* creating that product is where much of the learning takes place. Learning to become conscious of one's skill development impacts career planning, goal setting, and personal confidence for a lifetime" (Alberta Learning, 2002). Employers today want more than a resume, which is only a summary of what candidates say they have done. Being able to look at the student's work ahead of the interview can give the potential employer a deeper insight into the candidate's skills and abilities. Employers want documentation showing proof of the knowledge, skills, and abilities not depicted in the resume. At the same time, many candidates are often hesitant and do a poor job

 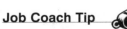
## Keys to Job Search Success

Although the cover letter and resume are critical tools in the job search process, a portfolio can give you the edge over other candidates by visually and graphically demonstrating to an interviewer your knowledge, skills, and abilities.

of communicating this information to employers. Oftentimes, candidates may not know just what skills they have, how those skills are relevant to the job position, and what employers are really looking for in a candidate. A portfolio not only helps candidates collect pertinent information about their knowledge, skills, and abilities, but it requires the student to reflect and analyze each item in the portfolio and determine how relevant this item is in terms of the employers' needs and wants.

## Types of Portfolios

Because the portfolio is really a collage of important documents and artifacts, one of the first decisions candidates have to make is to determine the best method of storing and presenting this material. Several choices are available, ranging from the traditional, three-ring notebook or zippered binder with plastic sheet covers to the electronic or Web version, which includes multimedia such as floppy disks, VHS or digitized video clips, CDs, and Web sites on the Internet.

## Developing and Preparing the Portfolio

There are five basic steps to compiling any kind of portfolio: assessing one's skills, experiences, and achievements; selecting a timeline and strategies for portfolio development; content to include in the portfolio; design, arrangement, and assembly of the portfolio; and final review of the portfolio.

### Step 1. Assessing Skills, Experiences, and Achievements

Self-assessment is the first step in developing and preparing the portfolio. During this self-assessment step, reflection and subsequent identification of candidates' knowledge, skills, and abilities are absolutely essential. It is important to document and specifically describe all of the candidates' experiences that have contributed to the development of professional recreation skills or to the development of life skills such as teamwork, leadership, creativity, communication, and so forth.

### Step 2. Selecting a Timeline and Strategy for Portfolio Development

Ideally, undergraduate students should document their skills and experiences from their freshman through senior years, and graduate students will merely add artifacts to their undergraduate portfolio (assuming they have developed a portfolio while an undergraduate student). The following is a suggested timeline and strategy that has been adapted from the Evergreen University Career Development Center (2009) for tracking and managing the development of the portfolio:

- *First Year:* Focus on developing academic competencies and integrating the college experience. Initiate the portfolio planning process. If nothing else, establish a place to store all the materials that may make up the portfolio (kitchen drawer approach). Gain practical experience, paid or volunteer, relating specifically to the field of recreation and leisure services.

**Did You Know...**

When designing your portfolio, allow for continuous growth and improvement of your material.

Eckerd College

**Job Coach Tip**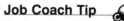

Keep your portfolio simple. Avoid repetitive pages, text, or photos, and make sure that your notebook is neither too large nor too small for the number of artifacts you have.

**Keys to Job Search Success**

Portfolios, like the resume, are "works in progress." Your portfolio should always be kept up-to-date, accurate, and well organized.

- *Second Year:* Focus on individual assessment. Document any relevant work completed that relates specifically to academic direction, personal growth, relationships, skills, career development, and competencies. Remember, it is essential to gain practical experiences in the recreation field.

- *Third Year:* Focus on values and exploring options. Students should keep track of professional affiliations, research, informational interviewing, travel experiences, and any record of their efforts to seek out new experiences or "adventures." Now is the time for students to start developing a network system by attending professional conferences and workshops.

- *Fourth Year:* Focus on transition. Knowing that this may be their busiest and most stressful year, students' attention should be given to reviewing the journey (job search process), acknowledging endings, summarizing learning experiences, and preparing for new beginnings. Toward the end of this year or prior to the beginning of the actual job interviews, students are encouraged to review their completed portfolio and make sure they have documented all pertinent artifacts.

### Step 3. Determining the Content of the Portfolio

The portfolio is more than a hodgepodge of documents and artifacts hastily and randomly placed in a notebook. It is a well-planned collection of information and artifacts deliberately included and strategically placed in some type of storage system (see Figure 4.1).

When determining how much to include in the portfolio, the decision is certainly affected by the format. For the traditional, three-ring notebook portfolio, many experts suggest including 5 to 10 artifacts but avoiding more than 15 artifacts because the

Figure 4.1

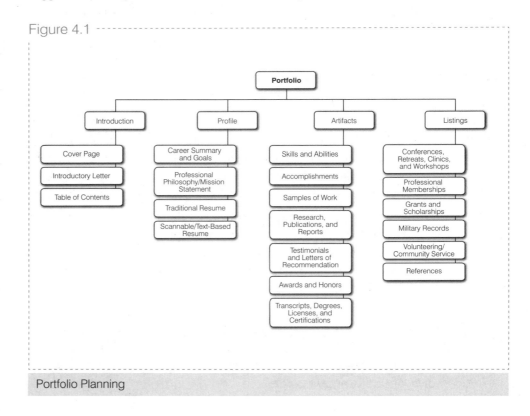

Portfolio Planning

portfolio becomes too clumsy and difficult to carry. Remember, the portfolio is a *portable* storage system. It is also important to consider that employers are extremely busy and limited in time and will not devote more than a few minutes to review the material during the interview.

Although portfolios can vary in form, length, and purpose, the following list of what to include was adapted from Randall Hansen's (2009) original listing. These sections are typically found in the paper portfolio separated by tab dividers. It is important to note that all of these sections do not have to be included in one's portfolio. Rather, candidates should choose only those that apply and portray them in the most positive manner.

**Time Out**

Keep a journal or some type of record-keeping system as you proceed in college to document any possible activity, event, or artifact that could possibly be included in your portfolio.

## Introduction

1. *Cover page:* One page that includes the candidate's name, address, phone number, and so on.

2. *Introductory letter:* A short letter that introduces the reader to highlights found in the portfolio (especially candidate's strengths!) and explains how the portfolio is arranged.

3. *Table of contents:* The table of contents, similar to that found in a book, clearly outlines sections of the portfolio that can help the reader locate material and artifacts quickly and easily.

## Profile

4. *Career summary and goals:* A brief description of a candidate's core values (such as work habits and style, organizational interests, personal attitudes that influence decisions, management philosophy, intellectual challenge) and where the candidate sees him- or herself in 2 to 5 years. Avoid broad statements and limit goals to three to five specific career-focused goals.

5. *Professional philosophy or mission statement:* A short description of the guiding principles driving candidates and giving them purpose. This professional philosophy section can include candidates' philosophy of work and beliefs about the future and a description of their ideal working conditions, geographical locations, and so on.

6. *Traditional resume:* A summary of candidates' education, personal achievements including work and academic accomplishments, and work experience, using a chronological, functional, or hybrid format. For ideas on how to write a traditional resume, refer to Chapter 7.

7. *Scannable/text-based resume:* A text-only version of the candidate's resume should also be included. See Chapter 5 for more information about how to develop this type of resume.

## Artifacts

8. *Skills, abilities, and marketable qualities:* This section is a detailed examination of candidates' related skills and work experiences they may have acquired. Include the name of the skill area; the performance or behavior, knowledge, or personal traits that contribute to success in that skill area; and their background and specific experiences demonstrating their application of the skill. Work

experiences can include internships, practicum, fieldwork experience, and so on, related to recreation and leisure services. If needed for the position, document computer skills and knowledge of various software applications in this section. Additionally, if candidates are fluent in other languages, this is a good section for documentation of that skill.

9. *Accomplishments:* Accomplishments are one of the most important elements of any good job search and highlight strengths in recreation event planning and programming.

**Job Coach Tip**

To hold materials in the portfolio, use nonglare top-loading sheet protectors.

10. *Samples of previous work:* A cross-section or sampling of the candidate's best student and/or professional work providing examples of problem solving, creativity, or leadership abilities. Include reports, term or research papers, studies, brochures, projects, presentations, photographs, flyers, sport tournament brackets developed, facility or department master plans, special event programs, risk management plans, public service announcements about a specific recreation program, research surveys conducted in a course, annual reports, and so on. Besides print samples, include photographs of the candidate publicly speaking or bulletin boards or posters created for a specific course, program, or event. Use CD-ROMs, videos, and other multimedia formats to show animated samples of work.

11. *Research, publications, and reports:* A good way to showcase multiple skills, including candidates' written communications abilities, is to include samples of written work. Include published papers and conference proceedings, PowerPoint presentations, survey instruments developed, pictures of research poster presentations, or articles written as a result of independent studies.

12. *Testimonials and letters of recommendation:* Another consideration for inclusion in the portfolio is a collection of letters of recommendation, commendation, or appreciation for outstanding performance received from coworkers, past and current employers and supervisors, program participants, and professors.

13. *Awards and honors:* A collection of documents related to education or past experience such as certificates or awards, honors, and scholarships should be included. This is a good section to include letters of recommendation to honorary and/or academic organizations and societies.

14. *College transcripts and degrees, professional licenses, and certifications:* A description of relevant courses and proof of degrees, licenses, and certifications are valuable to include. College graduates can include official undergraduate or graduate college transcripts.

### Listings

15. *Conference, retreats, clinics, and workshops:* Include a listing of recreation and leisure services conferences, retreats, clinics, professional development

**Keys to Job Search Success**

If you decide not to create an electronic portfolio, you can use inexpensive screen capture software to take screen shots of Web sites that you have created and include these graphics in your portfolio.

seminars, and workshops candidates have participated in and/or attended with a short description of each event. This is also a good section to include all certificates for attending or completing a seminar or workshop as well as selected copies of brochures and programs from professional development events.

16. *Professional memberships:* Include a listing (and confirmations) of professional memberships and associations.

17. *Grants and scholarships:* Mention all grants or scholarships secured for candidates' education.

18. *Military records, awards, and badges:* List military service, if applicable.

19. *Volunteering/community service:* Include a description or certificate of any community service activities, volunteering, or pro bono work candidates have completed, especially as it relates to their career in recreation, parks, sports, and tourism.

20. *References list:* List three to five individuals (including full names, agencies, titles, addresses, and phone/e-mail) with at least one former supervisor and faculty member who are willing to speak about the candidate's strengths, abilities, and work experience.

## Step 4. Design, Arrangement, and Assembly of the Portfolio

Most experts agree that the traditional paper portfolio should be stored in a professional-looking three-ring binder, the kind available at all office supply stores. When using binders, always include a table of contents with respective tabs or notebook dividers to separate the various sections and thus help the reader locate pertinent information quickly. The table of contents can be organized in one of two ways:

1. *Chronologically:* Sections are organized and arranged according to job description and dates the portfolio samples represent, for example, Recreation Supervision 2004–2006. This organizational scheme helps candidates who have been in a particular field over time to demonstrate a growing number of improvements and accomplishments.

2. *Functionally:* Sections are organized and assembled according to job description only, for example, Event Planning. This organizational scheme works when candidates have varied experiences that need to be pulled together to demonstrate ability in specified areas.

Once candidates decide on a format, a key element in producing a successful portfolio is organization. By spending extra time organizing the portfolio properly, it will come across as a very attractive and professional-looking documentation of the candidate's credentials. Remember, items should be logically placed into different sections by theme, category, or timing. Candidates should select one format and then consistently follow that format throughout the portfolio.

**Job Coach Tip**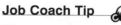

When necessary, tape or staple a typed explanation about artifacts or samples of your work including:
- Title
- Description
- Date it was produced
- Brief description

**Be Alert!**

Never place original documents (or documents that you cannot replace) in your portfolio if you plan to leave your portfolio with an employer.

 **Keys to Job Search Success**

Because portfolio development requires reflection and documentation of knowledge, skills and abilities, portfolios can provide the details and information needed for writing cover letters and preparing for job interviews.

Regardless of the scheme chosen, effective portfolios must create a descriptive caption for each artifact explaining the following:

- A description of each piece
- Why it was included in the portfolio
- Its main function and purpose
- The candidate's skills or abilities needed to produce the item

To protect the confidentiality of the candidate's work, Ryerson University Career Services (2009) suggests the following statement either at the end of the portfolio or selected artifacts:

> This portfolio is the work of _____. Please do not copy without permission. Some of the exhibits, work samples, and/or service samples are the property of the organization whose name appears on the document. Each has granted permission for this product to be used as a demonstration of my work.

### Step 5. Reviewing the Portfolio

Once assembly of the portfolio is complete, candidates must take time to review it, making sure the artifacts selected capture the best portrait of their knowledge, skills, abilities, and accomplishments. It is also a good idea to have others review the portfolio and provide feedback on how well key points are clearly communicated. By completing the review, candidates should be thoroughly knowledgeable of the content material and feel confident as they approach the interview.

## Using the Portfolio in an Interview

Portfolios are typically presented and displayed at the job interview. Depending on candidates' college and professional experiences, a portfolio can become quite extensive. If this is the case, candidates cannot realistically expect the interviewer to go through every item. A better strategy is to create and customize a smaller interview version of the portfolio with carefully selected and relevant key items most pertinent to that specific position.

**Time Out**

After you accept a job offer, keep your portfolio current. This will save you time if you ever want to apply for a job promotion.

## Electronic Portfolios

The concept of portfolios in an electronic format is gaining popularity as rapidly as the traditional paper copy portfolio. The electronic portfolio is a simple *technology-based* form of self-assessment and reflection, whereas the traditional portfolio is a *paper-based* form. "The electronic portfolio (also known as an ePortfolio, e-portfolio, efolio, digital portfolio, webfolio, and so on) is essentially an electronic version of a paper-based portfolio, created in a computer environment, and incorporating not just text, but graphic, audio, and video material as well" (Butler, 2006, p. 1). Sutherland and Powell

 **Keys to Job Search Success**

If one of your accomplishments happens to be confidential information and you cannot include an actual document for legal reasons, try to summarize your work and carefully share evidence, if possible, that it really occurred.

(2007) suggest that an "e-portfolio is a purposeful aggregation of digital items—ideas, evidence, reflections, feedback etc., which 'presents' a selected audience with evidence of a person's learning and/or ability."

With an electronic portfolio, information is stored digitally on a CD, floppy disk, Zip disk, digital or VHS video tape, or on the Internet rather than on paper in three-ring binders, folders, or boxes. Thus, it requires very little physical space, is easier to access, and can be more appealing to the interviewer. Once organized, electronic portfolios can also be enhanced with the addition of sound, graphics, photographs, music, and even digitized video clips. Other advantages of an electronic portfolio include the following:

- They reach a large audience in a relatively short period of time.
- They are inexpensive to develop (assuming candidates already own the technology equipment or have access to the equipment).
- Information can be updated very quickly.
- Various technology media can be used to more effectively demonstrate comprehension, learning, and growth.
- Various sections of the electronic portfolio can be connected via hyperlinks.
- Original artifacts are less likely to get lost, misplaced, or damaged.

The advantages of the electronic portfolio seem endless, yet a word of caution is in order. Because it is so easy to include many artifacts in an electronic portfolio, the tendency of candidates is to include too much, or even focus too heavily upon the sophistication of the technology rather than the content (Heath, 2005). In an interview with Education World, Helen Barrett, an expert in developing electronic portfolios, stated:

> *Many people emphasize the* electronic *side of electronic portfolios. People often approach electronic portfolios as a multimedia or Web development project and lose sight of the portfolio component. Reflection, however, plays a critical role in the development of a portfolio. An electronic portfolio is not a digital scrapbook (Brown, 2008).*

So, in developing an electronic portfolio, candidates must be selective in choosing and professionally displaying those artifacts that best reflect the three or four key attributes necessary for the position.

## Web Portfolio

The Web portfolio, a format of an electronic portfolio, is a professional-looking Web site that highlights a candidate's career. As was the case with the paper portfolio, a Web portfolio is a compilation of the candidate's career documents such as student college work, personal reflections, and accomplishments. However, rather than being stored and displayed in a three-ring notebook, it is stored and displayed on the World Wide Web. Web portfolios are skillfully crafted and showcase the education, career,

 **Keys to Job Search Success**

One way that the electronic portfolio is different from the paper portfolio is that prospective employers can review the portfolio before, during, and after an interview.

and personal achievements of a job candidate and allow prospective employers to view both an individual and educational perspective of these accomplishments. There is no specific way that a Web portfolio must be designed. Candidates should simply use their creativity and imagination!

Before creating a Web portfolio, it is strongly recommended candidates first create a paper version. Sections typically found in a paper portfolio are also applicable for the Web portfolio. For example, candidates wanting to illustrate their writing samples would include word processing files; candidates wanting to demonstrate specific achievements would include scans of appropriate photos and certificates; and candidates wanting to illustrate their flair for design might include Adobe Acrobat (PDF) files of graphics of their recreation program brochures. Other materials appropriate for a Web portfolio might include an expanded version of the candidate's resume with e-mail link, audio and streaming video clips of presentations, hyperlinks to Web sites created, and other pertinent links to material not possible to include with the paper portfolio. Other advantages of creating a Web portfolio are these:

- Universal compatibility
- Enhanced appearance using multimedia features
- Three-dimensional
- 24/7 accessibility
- Continual and reflective process (Whitcomb & Kendall, 2002)

For an excellent in-depth discussion on understanding and creating electronic portfolios, refer to Helen Barrett's Web sites; http://electronicportfolios.org/portfolios/howto/index.html and http://electronicportfolios.org/balance.

## Conclusion

**Job Coach Tip**

If possible, display and use your portfolio during the first few minutes of your interview.

By carefully examining, reflecting, and celebrating their knowledge, skills, abilities, and experiences, candidates provide interviewers with a wealth of positive information to judge their potential as employees. The portfolio, both paper and electronic, can be a tremendous tool and asset that can support candidates' comments and responses made during the interview. If done well, the portfolio can be an added advantage and one that can put candidates a step above the rest of the candidate pool applying for a given position.

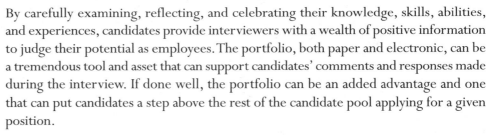

**Keys to Job Search Success**

Many universities now support the development and implementation of online career portfolio programs for current students enrolled in their university. Check with your campus career services department to see if such a program exists at your institution.

## References

Alberta Learning. (2002). *CALM guide to interpretation: Personal career portfolios.* Edmonton AB: Alberta Learning.

Barrett, H. (2000a). *Balancing the two faces of ePortfolios.* Retrieved June 5, 2009, from http://electronicportfolios.org/balance

Barrett, H. (2000b). *Electronic teaching portfolios: Multimedia skills + portfolio development = powerful professional development*. Retrieved June 5, 2009, from http://electronicportfolios.org/portfolios/site2000.html

Bolles, M. E., & Bolles, R. N. (2008). *Job-hunting online* (5th ed.). Berkeley, CA: Ten Speed Press.

Brown, M. D. (2008). *Electronic portfolios in the K–12 classroom*. Education World. Retrieved May 19, 2009, from http://www.educationworld.com/a_tech /tech/tech111.shtml

Bureau of Labor Statistics, U.S. Department of Labor. (2009a). Arts, entertainment, and recreation. *Career Guide to Industries, 2008–09 edition*. Retrieved May 18, 2009, from http://www.bls.gov/oco/cg/cgs031.htm

Bureau of Labor Statistics, U.S. Department of Labor. (2009b). Recreation workers. *Occupational outlook handbook, 2008–09 edition*. Retrieved May 18, 2009, from http://www.bls.gov/oco/ocos058.htm

Butler, P. (2006). *Review of the literature on portfolios and electronic portfolios*. Retrieved May 15, 2009, from https://eduforge.org/docman/view .php/176/1111

Evergreen University Career Development Center. (2009). *Portfolio construction*. Retrieved April 17, 2009, from http://www.evergreen.edu/career/job /portfolio.htm

Hansen, R. (2009). *Your job skills portfolio: Giving you an edge in the marketplace*. Retrieved January 14, 2009, from http://www.quintcareers.com/job_ search_portfolio.html

Heath, M. (2005). Are you ready to go digital? The pros and cons of electronic portfolio development. *Library Media Connection*, *23*(7), 66–70.

Klenowski, V., Askew, S., & Carnell, E. (2006). Portfolios for learning, assessment and professional development in higher education. *Assessment and Evaluation in Higher Education, 31*(3), 267–286.

Rebbeck, G. (2008). *Effective Practice with e-Portfolios*. Retrieved September 23, 2009, from http://www.jisc.ac.uk/media/documents/publications

Ryerson University Career Services. (2009). Portfolio writing. Retrieved May 14, 2009, from http://www.firefly.ryerson.ca/careercentre/students/tools/FT_ Portfolio_Writing.cfm

San Jose State Career Center. (2009). Portfolios: Build your portfolio. Retrieved May 15, 2009, from http://www.careercenter.sjsu.edu/students/launch /Resume_covLet/portfolio/portfolio.html

Sutherland, S., & Powell, A. (2007). Cetis SIG mailing list discussions—July 9, 2007. Retrieved May 21, 2009, from http://www.jiscmail.ac.uk/archives /cetis-portfolio.html

Turner, V. K. (2009). Portfolio: Add power to your job search with a portfolio. Retrieved May 22, 2009, from http://careercenter.missouristate.edu/assets /careercenter/Portfolio.pdf

Whitcomb, S. B., & Kendall, P. (2002). *e-Resumes*. New York: McGraw-Hill.

**Assignments** *(vertical side text)*

# Assignment: Reflecting on Your Knowledge, Skills, and Abilities

Before you can begin developing and preparing your portfolio, you need to reflect upon and document key knowledge, skills, and abilities that you have. Use the space below to list and document your accomplishments in each area.

## A. Goals

1. _____
2. _____

Give an example of how you could document one or all of the above:

1. _____
2. _____

## B. Professional Philosophy/Mission Statement

1. _____
2. _____

Give an example of how you could document one or all of the above:

1. _____
2. _____

## C. Skills, Abilities, and Marketable Qualities

1. _____
2. _____
3. _____
4. _____

Give an example of how you could document one or all of the above:

1. _____
2. _____
3. _____
4. _____

## D. Accomplishments

1. _____
2. _____
3. _____

Give an example of how you could document one or all of the above:

1. _____
2. _____
3. _____

## E. Samples of Your Work

1. _____
2. _____
3. _____
4. _____
5. _____

Give an example of how you could document one or all of the above:

1. _____
2. _____
3. _____
4. _____
5. _____

## F. Research, Publications, Reports

1. _____
2. _____

Give an example of how you could document one or all of the above:

1. _____
2. _____

## G. Testimonials and Letters of Recommendation

1. _____
2. _____
3. _____

Give an example of how you could document one or all of the above:

1. _____
2. _____
3. _____

## H. Awards and Honors

1. _____
2. _____

Give an example of how you could document one or all of the above:

1. _____
2. _____

## I. Transcripts, Degrees, Licenses, and Certifications

1. _____
2. _____

Assignments

Assignments

Give an example of how you could document one or all of the above:

1. _____
2. _____

### J. Conferences, Retreats, Clinics, and Workshops

1. _____
2. _____

Give an example of how you could document one or all of the above:

1. _____
2. _____

### K. Professional Memberships

1. _____
2. _____

Give an example of how you could document one or all of the above:

1. _____
2. _____

### L. Grants and Scholarships

1. _____
2. _____

Give an example of how you could document one or all of the above:

1. _____
2. _____

### M. Military Records, Awards, and Badges

1. _____
2. _____

Give an example of how you could document one or all of the above:

1. _____
2. _____
3. _____

### N. Volunteering/Community Service

1. _____
2. _____
3. _____

Give an example of how you could document one or all of the above:

1. _____
2. _____
3. _____

## O. References List

1. _____
2. _____
3. _____

Give an example of how you could document one or all of the above:

1. _____
2. _____
3. _____

_____
_____
_____
_____
_____
_____
_____
_____
_____
_____
_____
_____
_____
_____
_____
_____
_____
_____
_____
_____
_____
_____
_____
_____

Assignments

# Technology's Impact on the Job Search Process

Technology is changing not only the way people work, but has sparked new ways people look for and obtain jobs. "In our technology-driven era, job hunting online is a given, but navigating the enormous amount of information that is accessible with just a few clicks of the mouse can be overwhelming" (Bolles & Bolles, 2008).

Chapter 5

Visit the Web site for this book to learn more about the organizations and topics covered in this chapter. http://health .jbpub.com/recreationjobs/2e

The Internet is a very innovative and efficient way to find and apply for jobs, research organizations, conduct interviews, and communicate in a timely fashion. In yesterday's job search, applicants typically reviewed printed job listings, networked at national and regional conferences, created and mass mailed a 1-page resume to various agencies, waited for a call for an on-site interview, and then hoped they would be hired. It was a time-consuming and laborious "reactive" process. However, this is changing. The increase in technology and the popularity and growth of the Internet and the World Wide Web have created a whole new dimension in the job search process and are becoming essential resources in job searching. The Internet can be a helpful job search tool if you use it in "active" ways and combine it with other active methods (Farr, 2006).

Even if candidates do not plan to use the Internet and other technologies, they should become familiar with the various technologies that will undoubtedly save time and effort (Farr, 2004). How electronic resumes and other documentation are created and transmitted could affect whether candidates obtain an interview and positively influence a prospective employer.

An increasing number of for-profit and nonprofit organizations are conducting online employment searches for new employees and are finding it not only easy but also very inexpensive as compared to the traditional search process. But what about other recreation and leisure services? Is online job search really a wave of the future in leisure services or just a fad for corporate America? The key to being successful using technology in the job search process is being familiar with what prospective employers want and having the ability to implement strategies in developing these items.

This chapter helps job candidates better understand the dynamics and the role that technology plays in the job search process. Various technological innovations currently available to administrators and job candidates during the employment job search are explored.

## The Job Search Process

The current trends in technology are changing the way the job search process is conducted. The rapidly changing workplace will no longer solely support the traditional and sometimes outdated steps in the job search process. To be successful, job candidates should not follow a singular or linear job search path; instead they should keep the job search planning flexible by using a multidimensional approach involving traditional plus electronic methods. Technological advances in electronic recruiting tools such as blogging, online application, job postings, video and Web conferencing, and comprehensive Web sites, have changed how employers communicate with applicants.

The procedures that are generally followed during the traditional job search process can, and often do, prove to be tedious and exhausting for both the employer and the job candidate. For this reason, most individuals choose to break the process down into several distinct and workable phases. These phases, like those of any process, are constantly changing with the needs of both parties involved. Quite often, the phases are heavily influenced by technological developments that establish a faster, more convenient, and usually more economical way of improving the process. To understand technology's impact on the entire job search process, Figure 5.1 further outlines the individual phases of the job search process and how the process can be improved with the use of technology.

Figure 5.1

| Phases | Traditional Job Search | Electronic Job Search |
|---|---|---|
| **I. Getting Started** | ■ Campus career center<br>■ Library search<br>■ Personality and work style tests<br>■ Skill and interest assessment tests | ■ Job search Web sites<br>■ Personality and work style tests<br>■ Skill and interest assessment tests |
| **II. Researching an Organization** | ■ Local and campus newspapers<br>■ Departmental hard copy information | ■ Departmental Web pages<br>■ Electronic bulletin boards<br>■ Electronic classified ads<br>■ Electronic newspaper search<br>■ Job search agents<br>■ Online job posting<br>■ Resume database search<br>■ Web searches |
| **III. Networking** | ■ Contacts<br>■ Conferences, workshops, etc.<br>■ Social networking | ■ Blogs<br>■ CD business cards<br>■ Contacts<br>■ Electronic bulletin boards<br>■ E-mail<br>■ Listservs<br>■ Newsgroups<br>■ Social networking |
| **IV. Communication and Documentation** | ■ Job descriptions posted<br>■ Cover letters<br>■ Resumes<br>■ Portfolios<br>■ Follow-up and thank-you letters | ■ ASCII plain-text resumes<br>■ ASCII rich-text resumes<br>■ CD portfolios<br>■ Database of candidates<br>■ Electronic cover letter<br>■ Electronic resumes<br>■ E-mail<br>■ Follow-up and thank-you letters<br>■ Job descriptions on the Web<br>■ Posting resumes on Web<br>■ Scannable resumes<br>■ Video resumes<br>■ Web portfolios<br>■ Web resumes |

*(continues)*

*(continued)*

| Phases | Traditional Job Search | Electronic Job Search |
|---|---|---|
| *V. Interviewing* | ■ Face-to-face interviews<br>■ Telephone interviews<br>■ Conference group interviews | ■ Chat rooms<br>■ Conference calls<br>■ Interactive video technology<br>■ Videoconferencing<br>■ Videotaping responses |
| *VI. Job Offer* | ■ Reference checks<br>■ Letters of recommendation | ■ Letters of recommendation<br>■ Reference checks<br>■ Videoconferences with references |

Traditional vs. Electronic Job Search Phases

## Phase I: Getting Started

The key component traditionally conducted during the initial phase of the search process includes performing a self-assessment of skills, interests, and abilities (as discussed in Chapter 1) to identify what career path to pursue. If candidates have not yet identified a career path that best suits their skills and talents, they can use several tools and resources to find that career path. Most campus career centers offer a variety of self-assessment surveys that help students to distinguish where their skills lie and that point to the career path that best utilizes those skills. University and public libraries are valuable resources for finding these types of surveys or assessments. Also, a number of Web-based assessment surveys are available, and many are free of charge. Some of the more popular Web sites include the following:

■ Keirsey Temperament Sorter II

■ Motivational Appraisal of Personal Potential

■ Type Focus Personality Assessment

Once a career path has been identified, then the next phase of the job search process can begin.

## Phase II: Research an Organization

The second phase consists of several elements: (1) identifying what jobs are available, (2) studying prospective organizations, and (3) contacting key professionals who have information and/or making personal contact with individuals in these organizations. Chapter 3, "Researching an Organization," discusses various Internet resources that job applicants can use during this phase of the job search process.

For those job seekers who are more technologically inclined, the Internet provides several options in the form of newspaper employment ads, resume databases, department job postings, and bulletin board services. Candidates who feel more comfortable looking in the Help Wanted section of their local newspaper can take advantage of computer technology because the Web offers a whole new perspective on this simple type of job search. It is possible to access most major (and some minor) city newspapers online (help wanted or classified ad sections included). This allows the job candidate the advantage of browsing for a job in a Los Angeles newspaper while sitting in his/her living room or dorm room in Florida.

Employers look for qualified applicants in resume databases that offer the service of matching candidates with job openings electronically. There are several advantages to posting an electronic resume on one of the many databases currently found on the Web. The first is worldwide access. The opportunity exists for candidates to post their resume to an unlimited number of recreation departments in an unlimited number of cities, states, and countries. These numbers far exceed the amount of resumes one could send by postal mail economically. The second advantage is that this service is often free to the job candidate. In addition, resume databases providing prospective employers with information regarding job candidates' qualifications and background can be analyzed or dissected (when looking for individuals who meet specific requirements) in minutes using a variety of resume-scanning software programs available on the market today. Job search agents such as Jobsleuth.com and Careermosaic.com are automated programs that search job databases and notify users when a match occurs with their qualifications.

Jobs posted by specific recreation agencies can be found either on their own Web sites or on job listing Web sites used by many universities and recreation organizations.

There are also many online job posting Web sites that offer the job candidate access to a wide variety of work interests. The job openings listed on these servers can be searched by function, industry, location, or any combination of these. Because this service requires the candidate to have some knowledge of computers and the services offered on the Web, employers have noticed an increase of highly qualified candidates who are replying to these postings. However, a word of caution is needed. Research has shown that when using job listings alone for Internet job hunting, the success rate of obtaining a job is very low… approximately only 4% to 10%! In other words, the Internet is not the solution to job hunting, but rather it should be just one tool used in the job search process (Bolles & Bolles, 2008).

In today's world of high-tech communication, the utilization of Web sites is fast becoming the easiest, and most economical, way for agencies to present information about their recreation program. For this reason, department Web sites can communicate their standards, policies, and values as well as provide job candidates with information on job openings, qualifications/requirements, hiring procedures, and any number of specific items of interest.

## Phase III: Networking

One of the most important, and often overlooked, aspects of the job search process is that of networking or e-networking. From candidates' perspectives, this is when they make the first contact with the administrators in the departments they are applying to. These first contacts are not only an excellent opportunity to find out more information about the program, but this is a chance to lay the groundwork of the first impression. The use of electronic mailing lists generated and managed by computer programs called *listservs* are a way for both recreation administrators and candidates alike to stay abreast of the most current information regarding discussion topics, questions, and concerns that relate to a candidate's particular interest area.

**Be Alert!**
Because of the increase in identity theft, never publish your social security number in job search correspondence on the Internet.

**Did You Know…**
ENIAC, the first electronic computer, appeared 50 years ago. The original ENIAC was about 80 feet long, weighed 30 tons, and had 17,000 tubes. By comparison, a desktop computer today can store a million times more information than an ENIAC, and is 50,000 times faster.

Angelfire.com

A form of computerized e-networking is newsgroups. Newsgroups consist of group discussions that take place via the Internet. These groups discuss all types of topical categories ranging from entertainment to job listings. These are an often untouched resource for those seeking jobs; however, there are in fact hundreds of jobs to be found through newsgroup use. These postings are usually local; although there are national newsgroups that post jobs as well.

Another often used online resource for job information is bulletin board systems (BBSs). This method is utilized for the exchange of information, discussion of ideas, and the posting of jobs just like a traditional bulletin board found in a hallway.

Although the candidate may not initially see the benefits of the BBSs, it should be known that some may contain as many as 10,000 job openings, and they are an excellent way to network with others in the same area of interest.

Whereas most job candidates are familiar with the standard business card, technology now allows one to create electronic business cards or CD business cards. A CD business card, usually capable of storing approximately 50 MB of data, is simply a CD-ROM that has been cut into the shape of a business card and fits into the inner ring on a CD or DVD drive. A CD business card is more likely to help the candidate be noticed and is more effective than an average paper business card. These unique eye-catching discs can hold a resume text, portfolio, offline Web site, links to the candidate's Web site and e-mail, pictures, voice narration, and other documents regardless of the software that created it. With a CD business card the candidate will appear more professional as well as make a lasting first impression.

### Job Coach Tip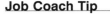

Include the URL of your Web resume in the text of your electronic cover letters.

An excellent way to demonstrate one's knowledge, authority, and networking skills is to create and maintain a blog (Burns, 2009). Blogs (short for "Web logs") are online, ongoing journal entries that are typically interactive between the writer and reader and are a great way to grab the attention of a potential employer. Unfortunately, sometimes job hunters will have to sort through a substantial number of entries to find meaningful information that can assist in the job search process. Rivera (2009) offers several suggestions and advice to those interested in blogging as part of the job search process:

1. Be prepared to spend a considerable amount of time being "engaged" in a conversation.

2. Be able to promote your knowledge, ideas, and passion (as well as writing skills—always check for grammatical and typographical errors!) on job-related topics.

3. Blogs are a good way to promote particular professional philosophies, beliefs, values, and goals about a topic.

4. Don't be afraid to disagree, but do be cautious not to offend anyone with written remarks.

5. Respond to reader comments and queries promptly.

E-mail (electronic mail), the sending and receiving of text messages by computer, has become an integral part of networking and communication during the job search process. It can be used not only for the initial contact with a potential employer or employee, but it can also be used as a means of transferring a resume or other pertinent materials about the job being discussed. E-mail allows candidates to send their resumes and additional correspondence quickly while avoiding regular postal mail delays.

## Computer-Supported Social Networking

As discussed in Chapter 1, wherever there are communities, organizations, or institutions, there are networking opportunities that are essential in the job search process. The traditional networking "tools" included the business card, the phone number, the home address, or the next professional meeting location. Although still effective, these networking tools are time consuming to use and are generally distributed at an event or location. Once the event is over, interactions with contacts sometimes are forgotten or lost.

With the introduction of Web 2.0 (the second generation of the World Wide Web, which emphasizes the movement away from static Web pages to dynamic, social networking platforms) in the past 2 years, social networking technologies and tools available today are completely unique and have expanded to include the Internet as well as mobile phone technology. "The tools of the networking trade changing and moving online, where e-mail, IM, and social-networking Web sites as LinkedIn, Facebook, and some specific to industry and career are the means to make new contacts and interact with current ones" (Fogarty, 2009, p. 1). This computer-supported social networking phenomenon is dramatically changing the way people interact in their everyday lives as well as when involved in the job search process. These sites encourage and enable people to exchange information about themselves, share pictures and videos, and use blogs and private messaging to communicate with friends, others who share interests, and even strangers in the global world.

Social networking is very popular with all age groups. "Two-thirds of the world's Internet population visit a social network or blogging site and the sector now accounts for almost 10% of all Internet time. These sites account for one in every 11 minutes online. 'Member Communities' has overtaken personal Email to become the world's fourth most popular online sector after search, portals, and PC software applications" (Nielsen Online, 2009, p. 1). In addition, recruiters and employers looking to learn more about candidates they're considering for employment are becoming active users of these various Web sites during the selection process.

Some of the more popular computer-supported social networking sites include the following:

- *LinkedIn:* This business networking site is generally considered the number 1 site for job seekers. It allows candidates to connect to people they already know as well as profiles of anyone else on LinkedIn. In addition, LinkedIn allows members to conduct company searches, look at job postings, link blogs, and look at discussions from Twitter.

- *Facebook:* Facebook has the highest average time per visitor than any of the major social networks. Facebook started out as a service for university students and now almost one third of its global audience is between 35 and 49 years of age and almost one quarter is older than 50 years! Facebook users can connect with friends or people they know or have known in the past such as high school classmates. The Facebook marketplace lists job openings and the opportunity to join various groups to find and network with people who have common interests.

- *Eacademy:* Eacademy allows users to connect and build relationships with people all over the world through its automated management of the user's profile, unlimited blogs, messages, club forums, marketplace listings, and more and to get found on most search engines by job head hunters.

■ *Twitter:* Twitter is a social networking and microblogging service that uses instant messaging to allow users to keep in touch with friends and strangers through the exchange of quick and frequent answers to simple questions.

■ *Jobster:* This is a networking platform with employers who have job opportunities. Users can search for open job positions, see the contact person responsible for the position, and then add that contact to their network and connect with him or her to learn more about the position.

■ *MySpace:* This free Web site is the most popular social networking site and is composed of personal profiles aimed mostly at a younger membership. A MySpace profile typically includes a digital photograph and in-depth information about personal interests.

**Be Alert!**

Never use ALL CAPS (shouting) or emoticons (☺—too casual) in your e-mail cover letter.

A word of caution: Although there are many advantages and rewards to using computer-supported social networking tools, this type of networking will not replace the "old-fashioned" handshake and also comes with some risks. Whenever personal information is placed on the Internet, there are inherent dangers. Some words of advice for using the Internet for networking are as follows:

■ Always proof online submissions using the lens of a potential employer.

■ Be very careful in what is written and posted online and never include any inappropriate content (personal or professional) on the Web site. This includes blogs, video, pictures, and so forth.

■ In regard to personal information, only a cell phone number and an e-mail address for the point of contact information is necessary. Including city and state is acceptable, but never post a home street address.

■ Nothing is private. Potential employers who visit the various social networking Web sites use them as a way to scope out potential candidates for employment. Even if information is not on a candidate's resume, if their blog, Web site, or profile contains information about them, prospective employers will also have access to this same information. Any inappropriate information can be viewed as a reflection of a candidate's character and can be damaging to a potential employer's impression of a job candidate.

■ Candidates should regularly review profiles and blogs to see what comments have been posted. Any unwanted comments that could be detrimental to the job search and career should be removed.

## Phase IV: Communication and Documentation

### Cover and Thank-You Letters

Although the advances of technology have clearly affected the way the job search is carried out by both employers and applicants, there are some constants that have remained the same. One of those constants is a cover letter. Job candidates should *always* submit a cover letter with their resume, regardless of whether the resume is sent in a hard copy or electronic format. In fact, the value and importance of the cover letter increases for candidates applying online or submitting their resumes electronically. Because many resumes must be sent using ASCII plain-text format, cover letters play a more significant role in marketing, selling, and providing excitement for candidates and their resumes. In accompanying an electronic resume, the cover letter should be short with only a few paragraphs briefly highlighting key points of the candidate. The cover letter sent via e-mail should be included in the body of the message and never sent as an attachment. (For more details on cover letters and other letters of correspondence, see Chapter 6.)

Thank-you letters, on the other hand, will always remain an effective way for the candidate to show appreciation and added interest in the job opening. Whether the thank-you letter is sent via e-mail or the postal service depends on the individuals within the particular department who were contacted. Some may still prefer a hard copy of the letter while others may feel that having it sent electronically is acceptable. The key point is for job seekers to remember that a thank-you should always be sent!

## Resumes

There are basically two broad categories or versions of resumes: the traditional paper resume and the electronic resume.

As illustrated in Figure 5.2, the paper resume category is further divided into two types: the traditional paper resume and the scannable resume, and electronic resumes have four types: Web resumes and Web portfolios, video resumes, ASCII plain-text (.txt), and ASCII rich-text (.rtf) resumes.

### *Paper Resumes*

Traditional paper resumes are typed using word-processing programs such as Microsoft Word and include various formatting enhancements such as bold, color, various font

Figure 5.2

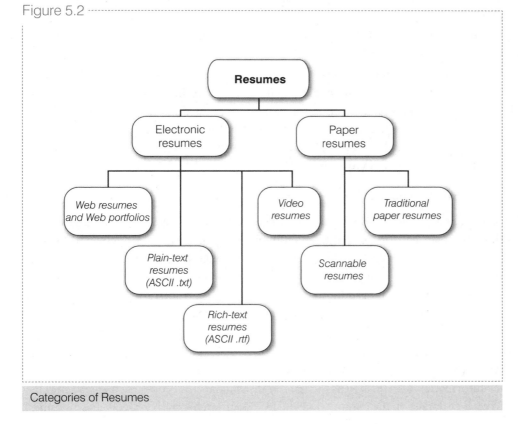

Categories of Resumes

types, font sizes, horizontal/vertical lines, graphics, boxes, and so on. Because the focus of this chapter is upon technology's impact on the job search process, and more specifically technology's impact on resumes, our discussion of the traditional paper resume is abbreviated. Creating traditional paper resumes is discussed in detail in Chapter 7.

The other type of paper resume is a scannable paper resume. Scannable resumes are basic resumes without any enhanced formatting characteristics. They are formatted in such a way that computerized applicant tracking systems (such as Webhire) can use an optical character reader (OCR) that scans or searches the resumes using criteria identified by the employer. These criteria include applicant's name, address, phone numbers, and predefined keywords along with optional information such as former employers, schools attended, and references. Applicant tracking systems can also be programmed to identify specific job skills, qualifications, and areas of expertise in a text resume. It is imperative that candidates do their homework and review their research information regarding the potential agency and job target when developing keywords because this is the key to a successful search by a tracking system.

The inclusion of keywords or industry buzzwords is the primary content difference between scannable resumes and traditional paper resumes. While the traditional paper resume incorporates action verbs (e.g., initiated, developed, assisted) and adjectives (e.g., increased participation, decreased forfeits, excellent), keywords in a scannable resume are typically nouns (e.g., tourism, event planner, team player, customer service, self-starter, achievement oriented, master's degree, personnel management). Once resumes have been scanned, they are scored in relation to keywords, terms, and topics, and then all job candidates are ranked based upon the results. The candidate with the greatest number of desired keywords rises to the top of the list. Note: it is acceptable to include one or two lines at the beginning or end of the scannable resume that include the term "keywords" and then a list of keywords that are separated by commas (Farr, 2007). (See Job-hunt.org for an excellent discussion on developing keywords for an Internet resume.)

The major *layout* difference between scannable resumes and the traditional paper resumes is that scannable resumes are saved in the ASCII file format resulting in a very simple, plain-text format with no formatting characteristics such as bold, underline, italics, and so on. Figure 5.3 describes various tips for creating a scannable resume. For a more detailed explanation of the ASCII file format, see the discussion later in this chapter pertaining to ASCII plain-text .txt files.

### Electronic Resumes

A term being used frequently in the last several years is *electronic resume*. Many may think this is just a resume sent to an employer via e-mail instead of delivered through traditional mail service. Although it is true that electronic resumes are submitted to employers via e-mail, there are unique and specific steps that candidates must take in preparing their resume to use this format. As a result, it is important that the electronic resume is written so that the employer's computer can easily recognize and understand it.

The electronic resume category consists of file formats all created and coded in ASCII. ASCII (pronounced ASK-ee), which is the acronym for the American Standard Code for Information Interchange, is the universally standardized code that assigns a number to each character on the computer keyboard. Computers simply process these numbers

## Job Coach Tip

Keywords often determine which resumes are selected in an optical scanning screening system. Make sure you use recreation and leisure services job-specific keywords throughout your resume so that it will be found in a resume database search.

Figure 5.3

Even though there is little standardization in optical scanning hardware and software, there are several steps that you can take to optimize the success of your scanned resume:

### *Do Not:*

- Use **bold**, *italics*, or other special formatting such as superscript, subscript, etc.
- Underline words or use horizontal/vertical lines because they might touch a letter.
- Insert borders, graphics, shades, or boxes.
- Use %, &, ( ), [ ], or foreign characters.
- Include page numbers or page headers/footers.
- Create tables or use two-column newspaper formats.
- Use association or agency acronyms; spell out the full name.
- Staple your resume. Paper clipping your resume is encouraged.
- Fax your resume because it will decrease the quality and sharpness of the print.
- Center text. . . . Don't use the Tab key!

### *Do:*

- Use scanner friendly, sans serif fonts such as Arial or Helvetica and font sizes between 10 and 14 points.
- Use solid bullets (such as • ) rather than hollow bullets (such as ○) because hollow bullets could be interpreted as the letter o. Symbols such as *, +, and – signs are acceptable.
- Limit line length to 60 characters maximum.
- Use ALL CAPITAL LETTERS for emphasis even though many scanners do not recognize the difference.
- Include as many keywords as possible. There is no need to put all keywords in one section of the resume because the scanner will locate words placed throughout the resume. However, do not misspell keywords; they will automatically be omitted in a keyword search.
- Use as many pages as necessary because the scanner is just looking for words, and include your name at the top of each page.
- Use left justification only; never center or right justify text.
- Divide large blocks of text into smaller sections. Use all capitals for section headings.
- Print (laser preferred) your resume on white, plain paper and use only black ink.
- Mail your resume in a 9 × 12" flat mailer/envelope to eliminate the crease created when folding your resume in a #10 business envelope.

Tips for Creating a Scannable Resume

**Be Alert!**

Because of the destruction caused by Internet viruses, many prospective employers refuse to open e-mail attachments.

by converting them into letters, punctuation marks, symbols, and, of course, numbers.

The three most popular file formats for the job search process are Web resumes (hypertext) and Web portfolios (discussed in Chapter 4, "Portfolios"), ASCII plain-text resumes, and ASCII rich-text resumes. Although all three formats have their advantages, it is important for candidates to prepare their resume material according to the appropriate file format requested by the prospective employer.

### Video Resumes

With the growth of broadband technology and the increased number of easy-to-use video-making software and hardware such as webcams and hand-held video cameras, more and more job seekers are posting video resumes on the Internet.

A video resume is a way for applicants to introduce themselves to potential employers by highlighting or showcasing skills, talents, or abilities that might not be possible with a traditional paper resume. It is a technique that allows candidates to "get acquainted" with the employer in a very controlled environment. Its purpose is not to replace the traditional paper resume but rather to complement the paper resume in an attempt to get a chance for a face-to-face interview. A word of caution: Some employers might be wary of video resumes because they put front and center information that it is illegal to use in hiring decisions—information such as the age, race, and gender of their candidates. With simple edits on a computer, an applicant can "direct" and customize a video message to a prospective employer or tailor a video resume for a specific job opening. This version of the resume can then be linked in an e-mail, placed on a personal Web site or blog, or used in social networking. The primary advantage of incorporating a video resume into a candidate's job search repertoire is that it "allows a potential employee to demonstrate his public speaking, inter-personal, creative or technical skills to a potential employer in a way that a text-only resume can not" (SearchCIO.com, 2007, p. 1). For more detailed information regarding video resumes, see Chapter 7.

### Web Resumes

When the term *Web resume* is used, it usually refers to the HTML (Hypertext Markup Language) version of a resume. With the increasing popularity of the Web, many job candidates are now creating a Web resume in addition to their traditional paper resume. To do this, candidates must have a basic understanding of Web page design principles and HTML coding or an HTML editing program such as Microsoft FrontPage or Macromedia Dreamweaver; the candidate must know how to transfer files on to the Web; and finally, the candidate must have the time to maintain and update their resume on the Web.

The Web resume is very similar to the traditional paper resume with the added benefit of many design enhancements, such as hyperlinks within the page or to completely different Web pages, links to e-mail, and universal browser compatibility. Like the

**Be Alert!**

Use proper netiquette . . . think before you send a message!

**Keys to Job Search Success**

Always keep a journal or log of when and to whom you posted your resume including Web address, your username and password, and any unique information you submitted.

paper resume, the Web resume is a synopsis of the candidate's career highlights. The Web resume should be easy to read, project the appropriate professional image, and engage the viewer. This can all be accomplished by using the appropriate fonts, color, backgrounds, graphics, and Web design.

To improve search engine results, keywords, as discussed earlier, should be inserted in the <meta> tags in the <Head> of the HTML file. Job seekers should always include the word *resume* in the file name and in the <Title> tags in the HTML. This will increase the chances of the file being included in a search. (See Figure 5.4.)

### ASCII Plain-Text Resumes (.txt)

The second type of electronic resume is known as the ASCII plain-text resume. ASCII text files are the most common file format used and are universally recognized by all computers from PCs to Macs. This electronic version of the resume is used most often when cutting and pasting into resume application forms on Web job sites.

Steps in creating an ASCII plain-text resume:

1. Open a Microsoft Word traditional paper resume file.
2. Save the resume file as an ASCII Plain Text (.txt) file.
   a. Click on File, Save As, Plain Text, and then click on Save (see Figure 5.5).
   b. Nothing appears to happen, but that is okay.
3. Close the file but remain in Microsoft Word.
4. Reopen this new .txt file and the following should have occurred:
   a. Formatting has disappeared.
   b. Bullets are now asterisks.
   c. Font is now Courier.
5. Now is the time to make some formatting changes to the ASCII .txt file:
   a. Add any extra lines between major sections.
   b. Use ALL CAPS for words that need special emphasis.

**Be Alert!**

Listing an incorrect e-mail address is like giving out an incorrect phone number or mailing address.

Figure 5.4

```
<html>

<head>

<meta event planner, sport tourism, personnel management, marketing experience>

<title>Craig Ross Resume</title>

</head>

<body>

This space is for the actual resume content....

</body>

</html>
```

Example Enhancements to Improve HTML Search Engine Results

Figure 5.5

Creating an ASCII Plain-Text File
*Microsoft® product screenshot reprinted with permission from Microsoft Corporation.*

**Job Coach Tip**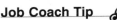

E-mail your electronic resume to yourself or a friend who has a different e-mail program so that you can open, review, and edit your resume before actually sending it to a prospective employer.

   c. Replace any bullet points with standard symbols such as *, +, or −.

   d. Use the space bar and *not* the Tab key.

   e. Don't indent any lines.

   f. Delete any reference to Page 2, Page 3, and so on that may have been in a header or footer section. The resume should appear as one long document.

   g. Clean up any extra white spaces or gaps caused by tabs and rearrange text if necessary.

**6.** Save the file again. It will be saved with a .txt file extension rather than the Word .doc or .docx extension used for Word files. Figure 5.6 illustrates the differences between the traditional paper resume and the ASCII plain-text version. Figure 5.7 is an example of a complete resume.

In addition, if candidates are asked to insert their entire ASCII plain-text resume into an e-mail message, the line lengths must be limited to no more than 60 characters per line. This is easily accomplished by clicking on File, Page Setup, and setting the left margin to 1" and the right margin to 1.7". Finally, save the .txt file as in step 6, but click Insert line breaks.

*When to Use Plain-Text Files*

If candidates follow the previous instructions on how to convert a paper resume to a plain-text (.txt) resume, they can use this newly created .txt file as their e-mail and online application resume. A common use for this resume file format is when candidates are asked to copy and paste a portion or all of the text version of their resume into specified fields located on a job board resume builder such as Bluefishjobs.com from the National Intramural-Recreational Sports Association.

Figure 5.6

**JOE SMITH**
joesmith@yahoo.com

_Campus Address_
1234 Anywhere St.
Anytown, USA 00000
(812) 111-1111

_Permanent Address_
5678 Somewhere Dr.
Yourtown, USA 11111
(317) 222-2222

**OBJECTIVE**
Desire an internship with a golf organization that will ~~~
and interaction with children and adults of all ages. Lo~~~
a golf resort/club that will utilize these event planning ~~~
the golf industry.

**EDUCATION**
Tim Buck Too University
Bachelor of Science in Recreation, Major in Sport Man~~~
Anticipated Graduation Date: May 2025

**KEY QUALIFICATIONS**
* Knowledge of the basic rules of golf through p~~~
  working at a golf club for many summers.
* Experience in communicating with children of ~~~
* Strong work ethic.
* Strong organizational skills.

**Paper resume**
Paper resume

```
***JOE SMITH
joesmith@yahoo.com

Campus Address
1234 Anywhere St.
Anytown, USA 00000
(812) 111-1111

Permanent Address
5678 Somewhere Dr.
Yourtown, USA 11111
(317) 222-2222

***OBJECTIVE
Desire an internship with a golf organization that will en
in event planning and interaction with children and adults
term goal is a position with the PGA or a golf resort/club
these event planning skills and practical work experiences

***EDUCATION
Tim Buck Too University
Bachelor of Science in Recreation, Major in Sport Managemen
Anticipated Graduation Date: May 2025

***KEY QUALIFICATIONS
* Knowledge of the basic rules of golf through playing vars
school and working at a golf club for many summers.
* Experience in communicating with children of all ages abo
* Strong work ethic.
```

**ASCII plain-test resume**
ASCII plain-text resume

Differences Between Paper Resume and ASCII Plain-Text Resume

Another use of this plain-text resume is when candidates are responding to a job announcement that states "no attachments." As shown in Figure 5.8, candidates can cut and paste the .txt resume into the body of the e-mail message.

**ASCII Rich-Text Resumes**

ASCII rich-text formatted (.rtf) resumes are compatible across different types of word processors while retaining the "richness" of a formatted document. Formatting such as bold, underline, italics, and so on can be saved. This type of electronic resume is used if candidates want to send their resume as an e-mail attachment or if an online resume builder allows an upload of a word-processed version of the resume. The process for saving a .rtf resume is the same as a .txt resume except that instead of clicking on Plain text in step 2, candidates should click on Rich Text Format.

_E-mailing a Resume_

Before e-mailing a resume to a prospective employer, it is wise to ask the employer for their preferred method of transmittal. Many employers would ask that candidates' resumes be included in the text of the e-mail while others may ask that candidates submit their resumes as an ASCII file, or they may offer further instructions.

In general, many employers are very skeptical about opening attachments and are requesting that candidates do not send attachments when responding via e-mail. The primary reason is that the attachment could be infected with a virus that could damage their computer system (Smith, 2000). Also, as discussed earlier, always submit a cover

Figure 5.7

```
***JOE SMITH

Campus Address:  1234 Anywhere St., Anytown, USA 00000
Campus Phone:  (812)111-1111
Permanent Address:  5678 Somewhere Dr., Yo
Permanent Phone:  (317)222-2222
E-Mail:  joesmith@yahoo.com

***OBJECTIVE
Desire an internship with a golf organization that will enhance current skills in event
planning and interaction with children and adults of all ages. Long-term goal is a
position with the PGA or a golf resort/club that will utilize these event planning skills
and practical work experiences in the golf industry.

***KEY WORDS
Customer service, golf experience, knowledgeable, responsible, strong work ethic, PGA,
organizational skills.

***EDUCATION
Tim Buck Too University
Bachelor of Science in Recreation, Majo                nor in Business
Anticipated Graduation Date:  May 2025

***KEY QUALIFICATIONS
* Knowledge of the basic rules of golf through playing varsity golf in high school and
working at a golf club for many summers.
* Experience in communicating with children of all ages about the game of golf.
* Strong work ethic.
* Strong organizational skills.
* An ability to bring energy and enthusiasm to the workplace.
* Ability to successfully communicate with parents and children.

***EMPLOYMENT HISTORY
Golf Center, Anytown, USA
Control Center Staff Coordinator
* Responsible for scheduling lessons and     times.
* Demonstrate great customer service skills.
* Complete many administrative duties.
* Interaction with      s and Women's Golf Traveling Teams coordinating practice times and
match time
* Responsible for financial transactions pertaining to memberships, clinics, lessons,
rentals, and various other programs.
* Train new employees.

Anytown Golf Foundation, Anytown, USA  May 2001-August 2003
Tournament Coordinator Internship
* Administered golf tournaments for the Anytown Junior Golf Program.
* Arranged tee-times, pairings, scorecards, scoreboards, registration, event results, and
awards.
* Acted as rules official, ranger, and event supervisor.
* Traveled throughout the state promoting the Golf Foundation.
* Fulfilled assigned administrative duties.
* Assisted with State Junior Qualifier.

Morningstar Golf Club, Anytown, USA  January 1998-May 2001
Golf Course Attendant
* Assisted Head Professional in organizing tournaments.
* Maintained all pro shop and clubhouse equipment and merchandise including purchasing,
inventory, and sales.
```

> Use *** and ALL CAPS instead of bold characters.

> Keywords can be grouped or placed throughout the text.

> All lines are left-justified.

Example of an ASCII Plain-Text Resume

**Job Coach Tip**

When using one of the free e-mail services such as Hotmail or Yahoo, create a professional sounding e-mail address.

letter in the text of the e-mail message with the electronic resume following. It is also helpful to add this statement to the end of your e-mail resume: "fully formatted hard copy version of this resume is available upon request."

One last concern with e-mailing resumes: It is never a good idea for candidates to mass e-mail their resume to employers they do not know. This is known as *resume blasting* and is comparable to *spamming*, which is very much frowned upon by all who use e-mail as a method of electronic communication. Most of the resumes received in this way are viewed as an annoyance and are consequently deleted by employers.

Figure 5.8

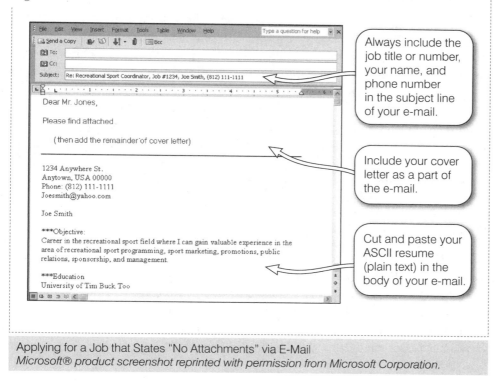

Always include the job title or number, your name, and phone number in the subject line of your e-mail.

Include your cover letter as a part of the e-mail.

Cut and paste your ASCII resume (plain text) in the body of your e-mail.

Applying for a Job that States "No Attachments" via E-Mail
*Microsoft® product screenshot reprinted with permission from Microsoft Corporation.*

## Phase V: Interviewing

The increasing use of technology in the job search process has resulted in the development and use of video technology for the interviewing process. This may include videoconferencing with a candidate or requiring candidates to tape interviews. These taped interviews are commonly referred to as *video resumes* because they offer job candidates an opportunity to describe their background, job skills, and interests. These recordings will not be placed on video cassette tapes, rather, they are written to a CD-ROM where administrators are then provided a chance to scan the top job candidates before spending a large amount of money to bring them in for an onsite interview.

Along the same line and similar to Web portfolios, electronic CD portfolios are gaining in popularity. Recreation and leisure service candidates can "burn" samples of their work onto a CD for distribution to a search and screen committee. Such samples can range from sport flyers, newsletters, and other publicity pieces to video clips of the candidate conducting participant meetings, pictures of bulletin boards, written manuals and rule books, and scanned letters of recommendation. This is also an excellent opportunity for candidates to demonstrate their computer expertise.

**Time Out**

Your Internet job search should represent only approximately 25% of the total time spent looking for a job.

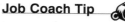

**Job Coach Tip**

Include the e-mail address (if available) for all references on your resume.

**Keys to the Job Search Success**

To improve their image and gain advantages over other applicants, job candidates today must become computer literate—and fast! Job candidates must have several versions of their resumes including the traditional paper resume, ASCII plain-text, ASCII rich-text, scannable resume, Web resume, and a Web portfolio to have a competitive edge over other job candidates.

### Phase VI: Job Offer

The final phase of the job search process consists of the actual job offer and is probably the phase least affected by technology. This is the point at which administrators evaluate the top candidates and then offer the job to their ultimate choice. Before this offer can be made, however, several steps must be taken to ensure all bases have been covered. Most of these tasks are accomplished through face-to-face interaction, thereby reducing the need for a lot of technology. For example, reference checks are usually made via telephone, and the search and screen committee will review and discuss the letters of recommendation. This step may also include a final videoconference or phone call to the candidate to answer any last-minute questions, comments, or concerns. Prior to the job offer being made, the employer must "tie up any and all loose ends" in an attempt to make the best possible choice of candidates for the position.

## Conclusion

The profound technological changes now under way are substantially altering the job search process, both for the employer and job candidate. The traditional job search process, with its dependence on the static printed job listing, the resume, and the face-to-face interview, is being replaced with a more dynamic electronic structure. The number of recreation and leisure services organizations using technology to search for prospective job candidates will significantly increase in the next decade (Lukow & Ross, 2001).

Job candidates, recreation and leisure services organizations, and staffs must all become familiar with the resources available to them to strategically merge new technology with the traditional job search process. Many organizations currently depend on traditional job search strategies. In the very near future, however, they will view technology as an integrated part of this search process.

This new organizational process will, in turn, force employers and job candidates to reevaluate their approach in this process. Employers will be forced to create and update departmental Web pages with mission statements, annual reports, department information, and agency resources, as well as post jobs online and use some form of technology in the interview process. Job candidates, on the other hand, need to know how to search the Web for job opportunities, revise and rewrite a traditional resume so that their electronic resume can be transmitted over the Internet and Web, understand how to professionally network via the Internet, and know how to successfully interview using videoconferencing.

## References

Angelfire.com. (n.d.). Science. Retrieved April 19, 2009, from http://www.angelfire.com/ca6/uselessfacts/science/002.html

Bolles, M. E., & Bolles, R. N. (2008). *Job-hunting online* (5th ed.). Berkeley, CA: Ten Speed Press.

Burns, K. (2009). Win at work. *U.S. News &World Report*, May 2009, 32–35.

Farr, M. (2004). *The very quick job search*. Indianapolis, IN: JIST Publishing.

Farr, M. (2006). *Seven-step job search* (2nd ed.). Indianapolis, IN: JIST Publishing.

Farr, M. (2007). *Same day resume* (2nd ed.). Indianapolis, IN: JIST Publishing.

Fogarty, K. (2009). *Can you Facebook your way to a new job?* Retrieved June 6, 2009, from https://cdn.theladders.net/static/pdf/socialnetworkingThree.pdf

**Did You Know...**

A 50-MB CD business card can store the following approximate content:

- 5000 pages of text
- 800 Web pages
- 500 photos
- 5 minutes of video
- 10-minute multimedia presentation

Lukow, J., & Ross, C. M. (2001). Technology's impact on the job search process in collegiate recreational sports. *NIRSA Journal, 25*(1), 42–56.

Nielsen Online. (2009). *Global faces and networked places: A Nielsen report on social networking's new global footprint.* Retrieved May 30, 2009, from http://74.125.47.132/search?q=cache:W_3n1xNi7nUJ:blog.nielsen.com/nielsenwire/wp-content/uploads/2009/03/nielsen_globalfaces_mar09.pdf+global+faces+and+networked+places&cd=1&hl=en&ct=clnk&gl=us

Rivera, P. (2009). *Can you blog your way to a new job?* Retrieved June 6, 2009, from http://www.philly.com/philly/jobs/CTW_jobs_20090428_Can_you_blog_your_way_to_a_new_job_.html

SearchCIO.com. (2007). SearchCIO definitions: Video resume. Retrieved June 7, 2009, from http://searchcio.techtarget.com/sDefinition/0,,sid182_gci1279042,00.html

Smith, R. (2000). *Electronic resumes and online networking.* Franklin Lakes, NJ: Career Press.

# Definition of Technology Terms

- **ASCII:** ASCII (pronounced "ASK-ee") is the acronym for American Standard Code for Information Interchange. It is the universal standard for text that all computers use to represent upper- and lowercase letters, numbers, and punctuation. It is the simplest of text formats that does not use formatting specific to any particular computer platform or application.

- **ASCII – hypertext (.html) resume:** HTML (or Hypertext Markup Language) is another ASCII file format that "marks up" or preserves text appearance for Web pages. Not all Web browsers present HTML files in the same way.

- **ASCII – plain-text (.txt) resume:** This is a plain-text resume that strips most formatting enhancements such as underline, bold, italics, horizontal or vertical lines, color, and special fonts. Text is left-justified and usually Courier font. These resumes are also referred to as e-resumes or electronic resumes.

- **ASCII – rich-text (.rtf) resume:** This format can be viewed by most word-processing software and retains most page and character formatting. However, not all computers and e-mail programs support this format.

- **Attachments:** Document files that are linked or attached to an e-mail message so that they arrive together. Attachments are usually formatted as Microsoft Word (.doc) or Adobe Acrobat (.pdf) documents.

- **Electronic classified ad:** Help wanted and classified ads that appear in printed newspapers are now available on the Web.

- **Electronic resumes:** Resumes that are formatted specifically for online job searches and include ASCII plain-text and rich-text formats as well as Web resumes and portfolios.

- **E-mail:** Short for electronic mail, e-mail is the most widely used business communication tool for sending and receiving text-based messages over the Internet.

- **E-networking:** Networking that combines traditional networking with the power and speed of the Internet and creates contacts and possible job leads.

- *Internet:* A network of computer networks used to transfer information from one user to another.

- *Posting resumes:* The job searcher sends an electronic resume on the Web that is usually stored in a job database where prospective employers can retrieve and review the candidate's information.

- *Resume blasting:* Process of sending a resume to thousands of prospective employers or resume databases. Blasting is comparable to spamming and is not recommended.

- *Scannable resume:* These resumes are a version of the traditional paper form resumes and are formatted to be scanned into a computer database as an image.

- *Search agents:* These are job search tools used to search job database postings on the Web that meet predefined search criteria identified by the job searcher.

- *URL:* URL, or Universal Resource Locator, is the address for a particular Web site or Web page.

- *Video resumes:* A way for applicants to introduce themselves to potential employers by highlighting or showcasing skills, talents, or abilities that might not be possible to show with a traditional paper resume.

- *Web portfolio:* Web portfolios are very similar to the traditional paper portfolios. They are a collection of visual and interactive documentation about an individual's knowledge, skills, abilities, and achievements. Web portfolios can contain many media types such as audio, video, graphics, and text.

- *Web resumes:* Resumes created using the same formatting as Web pages. These resumes, accessible 24 hours a day, 7 days a week, can include sound, pictures, graphics, and interactive hyperlinks.

# Assignment: Keywords and Resumes

1. **Find five job ads in a major online newspaper:**

   Include three that you could apply for today and two that you would like to be able to apply for in 5 years. (Attach them to this assignment.)

2. **Make a list of 10–15 keywords that highlight and describe your qualifications for these five jobs.**

   _____
   _____
   _____
   _____
   _____
   _____
   _____
   _____
   _____
   _____

3. **Now list these keywords as nouns, not verbs.**

   _____
   _____
   _____
   _____
   _____
   _____
   _____
   _____
   _____
   _____

4. **Prepare two versions of your resume for any one of these five jobs:**

   Include one traditional paper resume and one ASCII plain-text (.txt) resume. Format the ASCII version so that it can be used in the body of an e-mail message.

Assignments

82

Assignments

## Assignment: Job Search Timeline

1. **A successful job search is a result of careful planning and organization.**

   For this assignment, you must develop and organize all of your individualized job search plans (both traditional and electronic) and include an estimated timeline. You are encouraged to use calendars, charts, diagrams, or any additional material that will help you develop this timeline.

   _____

   _____

   _____

   _____

   _____

   _____

   _____

   _____

   _____

   _____

   _____

   _____

   _____

   _____

   _____

   _____

   _____

   _____

   _____

   _____

   _____

   _____

# Cover Letters and Other Letters

Effective communication plays a significant role in the job search process. Although much of the communication in this process is verbal, effective written communication is just as frequent and valuable. Written communication usually takes the form of a letter in the job search process and reflects a candidate's writing skills and professionalism. All letters should be prepared in a professional manner using proper format, content, and grammar. Candidates should be able to write different types of letters when involved in the job search process. This chapter examines these different types of letters along with their purpose, tips on how they should be written, and samples of each. The types of letters that are considered in this chapter are cover letters, reference request letters, job acceptance letters, job declination letters, and resignation letters.

Visit the Web site for this book to learn more about the organizations and topics covered in this chapter. http://health .jbpub.com/recreationjobs/2e

# Cover Letters

When applying for a position, the hiring organization almost always requests that candidates submit a resume. Some agencies also request candidates submit a letter of application or cover letter. Regardless of whether an employer requires a cover letter or not, all application packets in recreation and leisure services should include both a cover letter and a resume (Adams, 2001; Beggs & Elkins, 1997). Applications received without an accompanying cover letter indicate to the employer that applicants are not very interested in the job, lack professionalism, or are simply mass mailing applications. Because the primary purpose of sending a cover letter and resume to a potential employer is to obtain an interview, not sending a cover letter will gain applicants no favor in accomplishing this purpose.

A cover letter can be the difference between obtaining the job interview and landing in the reject pile, so it behooves applicants to devote the necessary time and effort to writing effective cover letters. Many employers will not even consider applicants who are not perceived to be qualified at first glance. That first glance at the cover letter is the applicants' one opportunity to make a good impression and progress through the screening process. There are three types of cover letters (Doyle, n.d.) applicants typically write:

1. The application letter responding to a known job opening
2. The prospective letter inquiring about possible positions
3. The networking letter requesting information and assistance in the job search process

An application letter for a known job opening takes some time for applicants to write because they should match the criteria listed in the job announcement with their own qualifications. A cover letter should complement, not duplicate, the resume it accompanies, with its goal being to interpret the more factual resume as well as add a personal touch. The prospective letter is an uninvited inquiry to an employer regarding possible job opportunities. This letter might be easier to write because candidates focus on their strengths and what they have to offer the organization, rather than focusing on specific job criteria. Although the disadvantage of sending this letter is the lack of a job opening, the advantages for applicants sending prospective letters include gaining early consideration for a position not yet advertised, and not having their resume buried in a pile of many others. Finally, the purpose of the networking letter is to expand an applicant's network of contacts by asking for job leads, career advice, referrals, and introductions. The focus of this letter is not to ask the contact for a job, but to request assistance in the applicant's job search process. Job search expert K. Isaacs (2005) states, "Thousands of positions are created and filled without ever being advertised, and a networking letter will help you uncover these hidden job opportunities" (p. 1).

## Writing the Cover Letter

When writing a cover letter, the two most important criteria for applicants to keep in mind are the format of the letter and the content of the letter. Additionally, candidates should follow some basic guidelines:

- *Keep the length to one page:* Applicants do not want to bore their readers. Be concise, but compelling and respectful of readers' time.

- *Address the letter to a specific person:* Sending the letter to the wrong person shows that applicants did not do their homework, or that they may just be mass

**Job Coach Tip**

The cover letter may be your only opportunity to provide the hiring agency a writing sample. Make sure your grammar is perfect!

**Did You Know...**

There are more than 28.6 million people that play golf in the United States.

National Golf Foundation

mailing letters. Avoid use of "Dear Sir or Madam" or "To Whom It May Concern" as well. If applicants do not know the specific person's name to send their letter to, then use "Dear Search Committee" or "Dear Human Resources Director."

- *Spell names correctly and use proper titles:* Incorrect spelling of names or addressing a woman as "Mr." will most likely lead to the applicant's resume being filed in the trash.

- *Use high-quality paper:* The paper the cover letter is typed on should match the paper used for the resume and should be at least 25% cotton, 16 lb–25 lb white paper (About.com, 2009).

- *Do not send out form letters or mass mailings:* This indicates applicants are interested in any job, and not necessarily with this specific agency. Cover letters should be customized for specific jobs allowing applicants to highlight skills and experiences that are appropriate for each specific job. It is a good idea to keep copies of all cover letters sent. For applicants applying for similar positions, they may be able to save time by editing an existing letter rather than creating a new one (Doyle, n.d.).

- *Do not send a picture:* Physical appearance cannot legally play a role in the hiring process in recreation and leisure services. It is not considered professional to send a photo, and the agency may choose not to interview the candidate because of legal concerns.

- *Do not get too personal:* Applicants should stay away from including personal information such as hobbies or interests in their cover letters. This type of information shifts the reader's focus away from the professionalism of the letter and is generally unacceptable in a cover letter (Kennedy, 2009).

- *Emphasize top selling points:* Applicants should focus on skills, talents, and top accomplishments they possess that compel the employer to call them for an interview.

## Format and Content of the Cover Letter

The cover letter should follow accepted business writing principles and reflect a conservative, professional appearance (see Figure 6.1). Some general guidelines to follow are these:

- Left-justify the document.
- The letter should be single spaced.
- Use 1-inch margins on the sides and top of the paper.

**Be Alert!**

Form cover letters will hurt your chances of getting an interview. Cover letters should be unique for each job you apply for.

**Did You Know...**

There are more than 4 million special events throughout the world every year.

International Festival and Events Association

**Keys to Job Search Success**

The cover letter is just as important as your resume. You should spend a considerable amount of time crafting the letter to match the job. In addition, be sure to keep it less than one page, know your reader, keep it professional, and highlight your strengths.

Figure 6.1

Candidate address
Candidate city, state, and zip code
Candidate phone number

Date

Agency contact person
His or her title
Agency name
Agency address
Agency city, state, and zip code

Salutation (such as "Dear Mr. Jones"):

Paragraph 1 should introduce the candidate, the current status of the candidate, and the purpose of writing. The primary function of this paragraph is to create a good impression and for the candidate to express interest in a specific position with the organization. Often, this paragraph also includes a statement of how the candidate learned about the job opening.

Paragraph 2 should provide the reviewer with a brief background of the candidate's experiences, why the candidate is qualified, special interests, and skills of the candidate. A good rule of thumb is for the candidate to highlight two or three skills he or she has that other candidates may not. This paragraph should also reinforce that the candidate has some knowledge of the organization and has done research on the organization. This is accomplished by mentioning certain services or characteristic of the organization. This paragraph is really the heart of the cover letter.

Paragraph 3 should refer to the candidate's enclosed resume (don't forget to enclose one!) and the candidate's availability for an interview. The candidate should indicate his or her enthusiasm to interview with the agency and also state how he or she will follow up the application. This paragraph should close by thanking the reviewer for his or her time and consideration of the candidate's application.

Closing (such as "Sincerely"),

Candidate signature

Candidate typed name

Enclosure: Resume

Format and Content of a Cover Letter

**Time Out**

A cover letter written for a known job opening takes time to write. Make sure to match your skills to the position.

**Job Coach Tip**

Always show enthusiasm during the interview, in your cover letter and thank-you letter, and subsequent follow-up communication.

- List return address, phone number, and e-mail address first. In some instances, this information is listed after the applicant's typed name on the bottom of the page. Formatting the letter in this manner helps to balance the cover letter.
- Provide the date that the letter is written below the return address.

The body of the cover letter should consist of three paragraphs, each with a specific purpose. The first paragraph of the cover letter serves as an introduction as to why the applicant is writing. The primary function of this paragraph is to create a positive impression of the candidate and to communicate the position for which the candidate is applying. Applicants should also mention how they became aware of the position. This can be very beneficial if the applicant was encouraged to apply for the position by someone connected to the agency or by a colleague connected to the interviewer.

The second paragraph highlights key skills and experiences applicants have that are related to the position. Applicants should include a brief statement indicating why they are qualified for the position along with statements indicating some knowledge of the organization. Along with qualifications, applicants should emphasize achievements and problem-solving skills as well as illustrate how their education and work skills are transferable and relevant to the position. This paragraph is considered the heart of the cover letter and is the point at which applicants really sell themselves.

In the third and final paragraph applicants should reiterate their enthusiasm for the position as well as refer to the enclosed resume. Applicants should state boldly their desire to interview for the position and how they intend to follow up in the application process. Close the paragraph by thanking the reader for his or her time and consideration.

See Figures 6.2 through 6.6 for samples of cover letters, a prospective letter, and a networking letter.

## Reference Request Letters

In the job search process, candidates are commonly asked to provide letters of recommendation from references. The number of recommendations requested varies by position, but for the most part, recreation and leisure service organizations ask for three references. In preparation for this phase of the job search, candidates should have a list of people who can serve as references. Most often candidates ask current and former employers to serve in this capacity, but recommendations on behalf of candidates can also come from college professors, internship supervisors, coworkers, and professional colleagues. Regardless of the relationship, those individuals serving as a reference should know the candidate well, both in terms of their work performance and character.

**Job Coach Tip**

In the closing of the cover letter, be sure to state how you will follow up, and don't forget to say "Thanks."

**Job Coach Tip**

A face-to-face or phone conversation is the best place to initially request a letter of reference. That should be followed up with a letter.

**Keys to Job Search Success**

Although you are writing the cover letter from a leisure services perspective, it should follow accepted business writing principles.

Figure 6.2

123 Cover Letter St.
Candidate, IL 34567
(123) 345-5678

July 12, 2009

Brendan Davis
Director
Riverside Park District
410 Johnson Rd.
Riverside, IL 30904

Dear Mr. Davis:

Please consider this letter a formal application for the Aquatics Facility Supervisor position. My supervisor, John Robinson, recommended that I apply for this position with your agency. I feel that upon review of my credentials, you will find that my experience and training in aquatics are a good complement for this position.

During the past two years I have been involved in all aspects of aquatics. In addition to the numerous aquatics responsibilities listed on my resume, one of the greatest contributions that I could make to your district and to this position is my ability to effectively conduct lifeguard training. I understand fully the importance of the duties and responsibilities of a lifeguard, and feel very confident in my ability to convey this importance to the staff that I train. I am also very knowledgeable in the practices of the National Pool and Waterpark Lifeguard Training Program, which are utilized by your agency.

I feel that my experience in aquatics and as a lifeguard, along with my professional attitude and strong work ethic, make me an excellent candidate for the Aquatics Facility Supervisor position. I would welcome the opportunity to speak with you regarding this position and would be happy to provide you with any additional information that you might need. I will contact you within two weeks to follow up on this application. Thank you for your time and consideration.

Sincerely,

*Sydney Jackson*

Sydney Jackson

Enclosure: Resume

Sample Cover Letter 1

Figure 6.3

November 3, 2009

Chad Hacker
Manager of Golf Operations
Great Acres Resort and Spa
200 Beachfront Ave.
Hollow Pines, FL 98765

Dear Mr. Hacker:

I recently read about your new executive golf course and was excited to see your job announcement in the October 2009 edition of *Golf World Today*. Please consider this letter a formal application for the Special Event Coordinator at the Hollow Pines Golf Club.

During the past seven years, I have had the opportunity to gain a wide variety of experiences in special event management with the Midland Hills Country Club in Lawrenceville, Florida. As you can see from the enclosed resume, I have conducted golf tournaments, clinics, and outings for a variety of age groups and skill levels. As part of this experience, I have established multiple partnerships with businesses in town and enhanced the reputation of the Midland Hills Country Club. I know that Great Acres Resort and Spa would like to reach out to the Hollow Pines community and establish similar relationships, and I know I have the experience to create this type of interaction.

I am confident that my experiences, along with my educational background and strong work ethic, would be a match for the Special Event Coordinator position. I would appreciate meeting with you to discuss this position further and will contact you next week. Thank you for your consideration.

Sincerely,

*Heather Smith*

Heather Smith
123 Cover Letter St.
Lawrenceville, FL 94567
(123) 345-5678

Enclosure: Resume

Sample Cover Letter 2

Figure 6.4

October 31, 2009

Ms. Martha Mullins
Assistant Manager
New Jersey Aquatics
4989 N. Eastside Dr.
Branchville, NJ 07826

Dear Ms. Mullins:

Thank you for sending me the internship information. After reviewing my objectives for an internship and the opportunities available through New Jersey Aquatics, I would like to apply for an internship in the summer of 2010 with your organization.

As you can see from my resume, I have been very active in athletics at Southern Kansas University. Through my involvement with the Student Athletic Board, I have had extensive experience in recruiting and managing volunteers. Along with my activities with the Student Athletic Board and academic requirements, I have also maintained a part-time job through my past three years of college. This has helped me to develop many useful organizational skills.

Feel free to contact me if you need any further information. I will contact you on November 15 to discuss in more detail the goals of the internship with your agency, as well as the enclosed resume. Thank you for your time, and I look forward to speaking with you soon.

Sincerely,

*Jacob Malone*

Jacob Malone
123 Cover Letter St.
Applicant, KA 84568
(123) 345-5678

Enclosure: Resume

Sample Cover Letter for Internship

Figure 6.5

123 Cover Letter St.
Jobless, WI 64567
(444) 888-9999

September 16, 2009

Mr. Cletus Whitaker
Recreation Manager
Senior Sunset Resort
3300 Resort Rd.
Luther, KY 11229

Dear Mr. Whitaker:

After recently reading of your senior citizen programs in *Recreation Today*, I am eager to join your recreation staff. I am excited about the prospects of implementing fitness programs and one-day outings in your senior citizen activities. As you can see from my resume, my credentials working with senior citizens would enable me to successfully promote the growth of such programs.

This December I will be receiving my Senior Fitness Instructor certification through Wisconsin State University. In addition to this certification, I have over five years of work experience planning and supervising trips for senior citizens. I know my training and experience would be an excellent fit with the direction of the Senior Sunset Resort.

Given the opportunity, I would be pleased to meet with you and discuss implementing these programs into your service offerings. I will contact you on October 1 to determine your interest and, if appropriate, to arrange for a personal meeting. I am looking forward to meeting with you. Thank you for your consideration.

Sincerely,

*Pamela Johnson*

Pamela Johnson

Enclosure: Resume

Prospective Letter

Figure 6.6

December 13, 2009

Mr. George Stallard
Sports Director
Chicago Sport and Social Club
625 N. Michigan Ave., Suite 1600
Chicago, IL 60611

Dear Mr. Stallard:

I was referred to you by Mr. Scott Hunter of Southwest Sports in Phoenix, Arizona. He recommended you as an excellent source for information about the sports club industry in the Chicago area.

My goal is to take my 10 years of experience in club sports and bring it to the Chicago area. I would appreciate hearing your advice on career opportunities in the club sport industry, on conducting an effective job search, and on how best to uncover job leads in the Chicago area.

Thanks so much in advance for any insight and advice you are willing to share. I look forward to contacting you early next week to set up a time that we can get together.

Sincerely,

*Kelly Martin*

Kelly Martin
123 Cover Letter St.
Candidate, AZ 54567
(222) 339-5355

Enclosure: Resume

Networking Letter

**Did You Know...**

The travel and tourism industry employs more than 200 million people internationally.

**World Travel and Tourism Council**

Before listing a person as a reference it is essential that candidates obtain permission to do so. It is a professional courtesy toward a reference for candidates to ask if that individual will serve in this role. The most common way to obtain this permission is by writing a letter requesting a reference from that person (see Figure 6.7). Additionally, candidates should provide their references with some idea of the types of positions being pursued and why. This information helps the person serving as the reference to more accurately communicate the candidate's potential for success in a specific position. Candidates should also provide their references with a current copy of their resume, as this allows the reference to more precisely link key job responsibilities in the desired position with the candidates' past experiences. Finally, as specific positions come available for candidates, they should inform their references and supply them with the

Figure 6.7

123 Cover Letter St.
Candidate, WA 74567
(123) 345-5678

August 1, 2009

Tristan Barnes
Superintendent of Parks
National Park Service
2525 Gambell St., Room 107
Anchorage, AK 99503

Dear Mr. Barnes:

Thank you for your willingness to write a reference letter for my application for the Parks Planner position with Jackson County Recreation District. As you know, I am interested in relocating to that area and excited about the prospect of developing a high ropes course.

My resume reflects my experiences working with the Kansas State Park System. I would like to remind you of my experiences developing a high ropes program, establishing an interpretation program, and a youth adventure program. I believe that these experiences will make me an attractive candidate for this position.

I have enclosed a copy of my resume and a copy of the job description, which includes the name, title, and address of the person that the reference letter should be sent to in the next two weeks. If you have any questions, please let me know. Thank you again for your help.

Sincerely,

*Matt Hardy*

Matt Hardy

Enclosures: Resume, Job Announcement

Reference Request Letter

correct address of the hiring agency as well as the name and position title of the person to whom the letter should be sent. If candidates have the job announcement and/or job description for the position, sending this to their references will provide all the necessary information their reference needs to write the letter of recommendation.

As a follow-up, candidates should send a thank-you note to the individuals providing the letters of recommendation within a couple of days of making the initial reference request. This action will not only serve as a reminder to their references to write and send the letter, but also shows the candidate's appreciation for their support.

# Job Acceptance Letters

Most job offers are made via a telephone conversation between employers and candidates, and in accepting the offer, candidates will most likely phone the employer. Once candidates have accepted a job however, they should confirm their acceptance in writing (see Figure 6.8). The majority of recreation and leisure services organizations will prepare a job acceptance letter for the new hire to sign formalizing the terms of employment. When the organization does not take the initiative to do this, candidates should write a letter of acceptance and send it to the person who officially offered them the position. The purpose of the letter is to formally accept the job offer and

Figure 6.8

123 Job Ave.
Beenhired, CA 12567
(123) 345-5678

December 1, 2009

Kate Bruso
Club Manager
Oceanfront Health Club
22 Sand St.
Granger, CA 92667

Dear Ms. Bruso:

As we discussed on the phone, I am very pleased to accept the position of Fitness Coordinator with the Oceanfront Health Club. I truly appreciate the opportunity, and I am looking forward to making a positive contribution to the agency and members of the club.

As we discussed, my starting salary will be $30,000, and health and life insurance benefits will be provided after the 90-day probationary period.

I look forward to starting the job on January 1, 2010. If there is any additional information or paperwork you need before then, please let me know. Thanks again for this exciting opportunity.

Sincerely,

*Kristen Mutters*

Kristen Mutters

Job Acceptance Letter

outline the agreed-upon terms and conditions of the position. Although brief, the contents of the job acceptance letter should include the following:

- *Thank-you:* A brief introductory statement thanking the agency for the excellent opportunity

- *Official acceptance:* A brief statement of the candidate's official acceptance of the position

- *Terms and conditions:* A key element of the acceptance letter, an outline of specific terms agreed upon such as salary, benefits, and primary job responsibilities

- *Starting date:* Formalizing the official start date of the candidate

The letter should conclude by reiterating appreciation for the job offer. Although the candidate has already secured the job by the time this letter is written, it is just as important as any other piece of correspondence that the letter is professionally written and error free.

## Job Declination Letters

When candidates receive job offers, but decline the offer, they must not only inform the agency by phone, but they must put it in writing as well. A letter of declination should be polite, brief, and to the point (see Figure 6.9). Generally, only two paragraphs in length, the letter should open with the candidate thanking the organization for the job offer. Following this statement, candidates should concisely and politely state their declination of the offer. Obviously, candidates should refrain from making derogatory comments about their interview visit. The second paragraph simply restates the candidate's appreciation for the opportunity.

## Resignation Letters

For some candidates accepting a new position, their decision means resigning from their current position. As a result, candidates/employees must provide their current employer with an official written notice of their resignation (see Figure 6.10). The resignation letter can be difficult for some employees to write, especially if they have been unhappy in the work environment or forced to resign. Regardless of whether employees leave a position on good or bad terms, the resignation letter should be a professional document that objectively addresses three major points:

1. *Date of resignation:* The exact date that the employee will be resigning should be included in the letter. It is a common practice for employees to give at least two weeks notice of their departure. However, organizational policies may dictate otherwise, with some agencies requiring immediate resignation while others may allow a more lengthy departure date.

2. *Explanation of resignation:* Employees must provide in a sentence or two their general reason for leaving. Typical reasons for resignation include changes in career direction, a decision to further one's education, a desire to investigate other opportunities, or personal circumstances. The explanation for leaving should never include derogatory statements toward the organization or any specific individual within that organization. Former employees certainly do not want to ruin any professional rapport or relationships by making inappropriate

**Did You Know...**

Boys and Girls Clubs of America serve 4.8 million boys and girls.

Boys & Girls Clubs of America

Figure 6.9

6700 Walnut St.
Lackojob, MN
(223) 777-5675

October 27, 2009

Jeff Campbell
Manager
Big Lake Amusement Park
1 Big Lake Rd.
Big Lake, WI 99503

Dear Mr. Campbell:
Thank you very much for offering me the position of Special Events Coordinator with Big Lake Amusement Park. It was a difficult decision to make, but I have accepted a position with another organization that more closely matches my career goals.

I sincerely appreciate you taking the time to interview me and to share information about the position and your organization.

Again, thank you for your consideration.

Sincerely,

*Rebecca Bergmann*

Rebecca Bergmann

Job Declination Letter

statements. Finally, the explanation for leaving should be brief and concise, avoiding long, drawn out statements.

3. *Positive aspects of the organization:* By mentioning positive aspects of working with the organization, employees emphasize their departure is on good terms. Discussing the positive attributes of the organization's relationship to the employee as well as the quality of the staff and/or services is a good method of leaving on a positive note.

# Conclusion

Successful job seekers never underestimate the importance of composing a cover letter and other letters that effectively convey their message and capture the reader's interest. The cover letter is one of the most important components or documents in the job search process and must be dynamic, creative, well written, and well prepared to communicate and market the candidate's skills and abilities. It is an excellent

Figure 6.10

876 Record Rd.
Rockwood, OK 57575
(123) 345-5678

September 15, 2009

Kirsten Horton
Executive Director
Rockwood Event Planning
77 McKelvey Rd.
Rockwood, OK 57575

Dear Ms. Horton:

It is with regret that I submit this letter of resignation effective September 30, 2009. I have accepted an event planning position with an organization closer to my family in Suncoast, Florida.

It has been a great pleasure to work with the outstanding staff at Rockwood Event Planning over the last few years. I will miss working for such a fine organization and wish Rockwood Event Planning continued success. If I can be of any assistance searching for a replacement for my position, please let me know.

Thank you for allowing me the opportunity to be a part of the Rockwood Event Planning team. I wish you the best.

Sincerely,

*Steven Tornow*

Steven Tornow

Resignation Letter

opportunity for candidates to distinguish themselves from others by building a relationship and a positive first impression with a prospective employer. Remember, in many instances, a cover letter is the first (and sometimes only!) written document that is reviewed by the employer. Candidates writing solid letters give themselves a competitive edge!

 **Keys to Job Search Success**

When writing a job declination letter or resignation letter, it is important to be professional and not make any derogatory comments about the job, agency, or staff. These people may play a future role in your career, so don't burn any bridges.

# References

About.com. (2009). Guide pick: Resume paper. Retrieved June 6, 2009, from http://jobsearch.about.com/od/toppicks/l/aatpresume.htm

Adams, B. (2001). *The everything job interview book.* Avon, MA: Adams Media.

Beggs, B. A., & Elkins, D. J. (1997). *Marketing yourself for the first job and portfolio development.* The John Allen Symposium. Carbondale: Southern Illinois University.

Boys and Girls Clubs of America. (2008). Retrieved May 2, 2009, from http://www.bgca.org

Doyle, A. (n.d.). *Your guide to job searching.* Retrieved May 12, 2009, from http://jobsearch.about.com

International Festival and Events Association. (n.d). Retrieved May 1, 2009, from http://www.ifea.com

Isaacs, K. (2005). Networking letters 101. Retrieved January 30, 2005, from http://resume.monster.com/archives/coverletter

Kennedy, J. L. (2009). *Cover letters for dummies* (3rd ed.). New York: Wiley.

National Golf Foundation. (2009). Retrieved May 2, 2009, from http://www.ngf.org

World Travel and Tourism Council. (2009). Retrieved May 2, 2009, from http://www.wttc.org

World Waterpark Association. (2005). Retrieved May 2, 2009, from http://www.waterparks.org

# Assignment: Mock Cover Letters

Chapter 6 identifies three different types of cover letters that a candidate may write, depending on the situation. This assignment requires you to write a mock cover letter of each kind.

## Scenario 1

You have just decided to relocate to another geographic region, but are not aware of any job openings in the area. Your current supervisor gives you the name of a friend that currently works in the recreation field in that area. Write a networking cover letter to this person.

## Scenario 2

You have always wanted to work for the Chesterfield Sports Academy, but they never seem to have an opening when you are in the job market. Write a prospective letter to the director of this organization.

## Scenario 3

Find an actual job announcement that matches your career interests. Write a cover letter that you would send with your resume to apply for this job.

### How are these letters similar? How are they different?

_____

_____

_____

_____

_____

_____

_____

_____

_____

_____

_____

_____

_____

_____

_____

_____

Assignments

Assignments

# Resumes

A personal resume is one of the most important tools used in the job search process today. Although there are other important aspects discussed in this textbook, the resume is generally the first formal document a prospective employer receives from candidates. It often plays an integral role in the employer's decision to include or exclude candidates in their pool of qualified applicants. Because of its importance to candidates seeking positions in recreation and leisure services, creating and designing an effective resume is a crucial step in the job search process. Employers generally look for three items in a resume: (1) the applicant's ability and capability; (2) experience, both volunteer and work; and (3) skills, both actual and transferable.

Visit the Web site for this book to learn more about the organizations and topics covered in this chapter. **http://health .jbpub.com/recreationjobs/2e**

The purpose of producing the resume is to assist candidates in obtaining an interview, not the job. It is the foundation for interview preparation (Schuman, 2008). Reed (1998) sums up the purpose of the resume by stating, "Resumes don't get jobs. Resumes get interviews. And interviews get jobs. You won't get an interview without a resume. And you won't get a job offer without an interview. But the resume is the first step to a job" (p. 9). Depending on the quality of the resume in terms of both content and presentation style, the chances for a job interview are enhanced or diminished.

The resume is used by employers as a screening device to evaluate the potential qualifications of applicants and to serve as a blueprint for the interview (Whitcomb, 2007). From candidates' perspectives, the resume is a reflection of their professional image. It is a very organized, professional profile or summary that showcases applicants' strengths, accomplishments, interests, skills, and work-related experiences. To be effective, the resume must be flexible, adaptable, and capable of illustrating change as one increases responsibilities, accomplishments, and job-related experiences and transitions from college to professional life. Above all, honesty is the best policy. Be truthful when listing job responsibilities. Never lie on the resume! In addition, because the resume is a direct reflection of the applicant's image, the document must be impeccable in terms of spelling, grammar, and format. The slightest error (i.e., typographical, grammatical, content, or format) contained in a candidate's resume could result in the application being eliminated.

Writing a resume can be a daunting task. Although most professionals agree resumes are vital, recommendations about what content to include and how it should be presented are often mixed and even contradictory. "Your resume is probably the most important document you will ever create because it helps you understand and package yourself appropriately as a commercial commodity" (Yates, 2008, p. 1). Due to the importance placed on resumes by employers in recreation and leisure services, it is essential that applicants prepare resumes in a way that best portrays their skills and qualifications while at the same time meeting the needs and expectations of the employer.

There has been a considerable amount of popular literature written about resume preparation including content, format, and presentation. Yet, most of this information is subjective, opinionated, and written for individuals pursuing jobs in general trade or business-related occupations. Combined with the fact that there are few standards for writing a resume, the result can be confusing for recreation and leisure services students attempting to develop their most important tool for the job search process. The purpose of this chapter is to provide information on resume content and format that is most appropriate for students entering the recreation and leisure services field. Much of the literature on resumes shares a different perspective for successful resumes in terms of content areas and format. The majority of information provided in this chapter is specific to recreation and leisure services and is based upon research involving the preferences of recreation professionals who review the resumes of candidates entering this field.

## Key Resume Content Areas

To develop an effective resume, it is important for job seekers to know exactly what type of content information should or should not be included in the resume. More important, when writing the resume, candidates should use the KISS approach: Keep it simple, stupid! "Your resume must reflect in quantifiable, real, specific terms what you have done before, who you have done it for, how long you did it, and how well you did it (Beshara, 2006, p. 95).

What follows are suggested content areas for applicants seeking positions in recreation and leisure services. Each content area contains a description of the appropriate information applicants should include as well as an example of how the information might be formatted.

## Heading and Contact Information

At the top of the first page of the resume, contact information should be listed including the applicant's full name, mailing address (both current and permanent if a student), phone number (cell number if this is the primary contact number), and e-mail address (see Figure 7.1). If applicants are using a personal Web site to highlight and support their skills and experiences, the URL address should be listed with the contact information.

## Career Objective

One area of resume content that is often addressed in the popular literature is the career objective. The career objective is a clear and concise statement providing the prospective employer with an immediate sense of who applicants are and the type of work or internship experience they are pursuing. Its primary purpose is to give employers an indication of the applicants' career goals and interests. The key for applicants in writing a career objective is to state what they have to offer employers, not what applicants expect to gain from employers or the job! Candidates should include an objective only if it is clearly stated and consistent with skills and accomplishments (Rosenberg, 2008). The other sections in the resume such as education, work experience, and professional involvement are then written to support this career objective statement in the most effective manner possible. Although many applicants develop career objectives for their resumes, there are some reasons not to include one. For example, if applicants are uncertain of their exact career path or desired position, it is not recommended they include a specific career objective on their resume. If the career objective is too specific, applicants may be eliminating themselves from consideration for some positions, particularly at the entry level. Fournier and Spin (2006) contend that the career objective is far too general and broad and takes up crucial space on the resume. In this case, it is best to omit the career objective statement and instead, incorporate the information into the cover letter. Figure 7.2 lists two examples of career objectives.

**Be Alert!**

Professional references should not include clergy, family doctors, friends, or relatives.

**Job Coach Tip**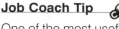

One of the most useful things you can do when you are writing your resume is to think like an employer.

Bolles & Bolles

---

Figure 7.1

**Mr. Joe Smith**

| **Current Address** | **Permanent Address** |
|---|---|
| 1000 Anywhere Dr. | 9999 Somewhere St. |
| Anytown, USA 00000 | Somewhere, USA 99999 |
| (000) 000-0000 | (111) 111-1111 |
| jsmith@yahoo.com | |

Example for Listing Heading and Contact Information

Figure 7.2

### Career Objective

- "Recreational sports professional seeks responsibilities in structuring and programming innovative and traditional sport tournaments and events."
- "Desire a fast-paced, challenging work environment in the tourism industry where hard work and creativity are encouraged."

Examples of Career Objectives

## Collegiate Education Record

Information pertaining to an applicant's collegiate educational experiences is an essential component of a good resume and should be a priority for inclusion. The name of the college or university attended, type of degree received (written out completely), dates degrees were conferred, and fields of study and majors should be included under the education section in reverse chronological order (see Figure 7.3). Applicants attending more than one institution should list the most recently attended first. Although many students fret over grades, research shows information such as grade point average, class rank, and courses taken are relatively unimportant to employers in recreation (Young & Ross, 2003). Although both overall and major grade point averages (GPA) are commonly included in the resume, the general rule of thumb is the GPA should only be included if greater than 3.25 on a 4.0 scale.

Professional certifications, honors, and awards (e.g., dean's list and scholarships) can be included in this section or in a separate section entitled "Honors and Award" toward the end of the resume. It should be noted that the Certified Therapeutic Recreation Specialist (CTRS) certification was rated the single most essential item by employers to include in a resume when applying for therapeutic recreation positions (Ross & Zabriskie, 2001). There is little value in listing high school education and related activities in the resume unless this represents the applicant's last educational experience or is directly related to the position opening (Banis, 2000; Graber, 2000).

Figure 7.3

### Education

ABC University, Anytown, USA          May 2005

Bachelor of Science in Recreation

Overall GPA: 3.5/4.0      Major GPA: 3.8/4.0

Course emphasis in Tourism Management

Examples for Listing Education

 **Keys to Job Search Success**

When choosing to develop a video resume, keep it as natural as possible to let the real you shine through, and remember, talk to the person on the other side of the camera, not the camera itself.

Hussain

## Related Work Experience

Related work experiences including full-time and part-time jobs, internships, and volunteer hours should be listed along with agency name and location (city and state), dates of employment (month and year), position titles, and several key responsibilities and achievements of the applicant while in that position. (There is no need to indicate salaries for these positions.) This section serves as the primary focus of the resume. For applicants still in college, work experiences not only enhance the education process, but they are likely to play a vital role in young professionals' resumes and in their abilities to be hired in recreation and leisure services.

The following are general guidelines for developing and describing key duties and accomplishments of related work experiences:

- Include the most important and relevant responsibilities first.
- Describe job responsibilities using action verbs and power words. Start each phrase or sentence with action verbs such as *planned*, *designed*, *supervised*, *created*, and *produced*. (See Figure 7.4.) Avoid using pronouns, especially *I*.

Figure 7.4

Resumes (and cover letters) are one way employers assess how successful an applicant has been. Words can reflect how positive of an image you have of yourself as well as the confidence you have in your abilities to perform. Focus on action phrases. Words that demonstrate action on your part convey an image of success to an employer.

| | | | | |
|---|---|---|---|---|
| accelerated | authored | converted | displayed | examined |
| accomplished | automated | coordinated | distinguished | executed |
| achieved | balanced | corresponded | distributed | exhibited |
| acted | cataloged | counseled | diversified | expanded |
| adapted | chaired | created | doubled | expedited |
| added | changed | critiqued | drafted | explained |
| addressed | clarified | cut | dramatized | expressed |
| administered | classified | decided | earned | extracted |
| advanced | coached | decreased | edited | fabricated |
| advised | collected | delegated | educated | facilitated |
| allocated | compiled | delivered | effected | familiarized |
| analyzed | completed | demonstrated | eliminated | fashioned |
| appraised | conducted | derived | emphasized | focused |
| approved | conferred | designed | enabled | forecasted |
| arranged | confronted | determined | encouraged | formulated |
| assembled | consolidated | developed | engineered | founded |
| assigned | constructed | devised | enlisted | gained |
| assisted | contracted | directed | established | generated |
| attained | contributed | dispatched | estimated | guided |
| audited | controlled | dispensed | evaluated | halved |

(continues)

*(continued)*

| | | | | |
|---|---|---|---|---|
| handled | located | programmed | revamped | structured |
| identified | made | projected | reversed | succeeded |
| illustrated | maintained | promoted | reviewed | summarized |
| imagined | managed | proposed | revised | supervised |
| implemented | marketed | provided | revitalized | surveyed |
| improved | measured | publicized | saved | systemized |
| increased | mediated | published | scheduled | tabulated |
| indoctrinated | moderated | purchased | screened | taught |
| influenced | monitored | raised | selected | tested |
| informed | motivated | realized | served | traced |
| initiated | narrated | recommended | serviced | tracked |
| innovated | negotiated | reconciled | shaped | trained |
| inspected | operated | recorded | simplified | transferred |
| installed | organized | recruited | sketched | transformed |
| instituted | originated | redesigned | skilled | translated |
| instructed | overhauled | reduced | sold | traveled |
| integrated | oversaw | referred | solidified | trimmed |
| interpreted | participated | regulated | solved | turned |
| interviewed | performed | rehabilitated | sparked | uncovered |
| introduced | persuaded | reinforced | specified | unified |
| invented | pinpointed | remodeled | spoke | updated |
| investigated | planned | reorganized | staffed | upgraded |
| launched | predicted | repaired | started | utilized |
| lectured | prepared | represented | stimulated | validated |
| led | presented | researched | strategized | verified |
| | prioritized | restored | streamlined | visualized |
| | processed | restructured | strengthened | widened |
| | produced | retrieved | stretched | won |

**Action Verbs and Power Words**

- Avoid using passive phrases such as: "responsible for...," "duties included...," or "worked as a...."
- Develop a reader-friendly resume by using bulleted lists with plenty of white space.
- Quantify duties and accomplishments when appropriate by using percentages, numbers, dollar values, or other measurable values for emphasis. For example, employees supervised, dollar amounts raised, participation figures increased, and/or number of sports scheduled, and so on.
- Pay particular attention to the proper use of verb tenses. When describing responsibilities in a current job, use present tense and past tense for previous jobs.
- Emphasize results and performance by showing *proof* of knowledge, skills, and abilities to do the job. In other words, candidates should describe accomplishments, not duties.

Figure 7.5 illustrates examples of related work experiences.

Figure 7.5

**Related Work Experience**

*Sample 1*

XYZ Sport Agency, Anytown, USA                    6/2001–present
*Recreation Supervisor*
Managerial position with nonprofit organization responsible for overall operation of recreation programs serving community population of over 800,000. Programs included Therapeutic Recreation, Seniors Programming, Adult Sports, Youth Sports, Family Events, Fitness Programming, Martial Arts, and Indoor Climbing.

- Managed $650,000 operating budget. All program revenue covered operating costs of programs.
- Managed five full-time staff and 80 part-time employees.
- Researched and created proposal for a 6-court, $900,000 indoor tennis facility at Northridge. Proposal was presented and accepted by Board of Directors. Worked with architects, contractors, and project managers throughout all phases of project.

*Sample 2*

*Camp Counselor*                    8/2005–7/2009
Have Fun Camp, Farmland, USA

- Provided instruction and supervised the canoe lessons for a group of 100 children ages 6–12.
- Created and established a system for organizing the first comprehensive pictorial database of 5000 pictures for the camp.
- Supervised eight employees.
- Trained five new employees on camp operations.
- Prepared and distributed food and drinks to up to 100 campers daily.

*Other Sample Descriptions*

- Stimulated a $100,000 increase in the recreation budget through innovative sales and marketing efforts.
- Coordinated the areas of finance, marketing, operations, programming, and sponsorship, including holding weekly and biweekly tactical meetings.
- Responsible for directing 40 student leaders and managing a budget of $50,000.
- Organized and conducted captain meetings for assigned sports, including: 181 teams for volleyball, 196 teams for soccer, and 435 teams for basketball.
- Interviewed, hired, and trained 15 new front-desk employees for spa operations.
- Managed a staff of 17 full-time professionals and over 200 part-time staff including front-desk staff, fitness leaders, instructors, and contract employees.
- Managed 15-acre outdoor facility including four softball fields, six flag football fields, and one club sports field.
- Developed a new promotion and selection process for the Park Ranger-Interpreter position.

**Job Coach Tip**

Include industry-specific buzzwords to focus your resume to a particular job or industry in the most effective manner possible.

**Job Coach Tip**

If you are hired somewhere, remember to remove your resume from the job boards where you posted it.

Examples for Listing Related Work Experiences

### Nonrelated Work Experience

Although the importance of including related work experience is obvious, it is also essential to include nonrelated work experience in the resume. Employers want to know all the candidate's work experiences, not just the experiences related to the current job opening. Nonrelated work experiences have merit because they can illustrate pertinent adaptive and transferable skills such as honesty, enthusiasm, reliability, patience, flexibility, ability to write clearly, organization, and time management. Nonrelated work job functions, achievements, accomplishments, positions, and titles should be included.

**Job Coach Tip**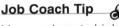

Use numbers to highlight your accomplishments and achievements.

### Internship Experience

The existence and importance of internships in recreation and leisure studies are supported by many curricula requiring this practical experience and have emerged as important considerations in the hiring decision. Furthermore, the internship experience can be an extremely important credential for an applicant without much professional work experience. Carefully selecting and successfully completing an internship can be a stepping stone to full-time employment.

### Professional Involvement

Professional involvement is an investment in time and energy for candidates, but one that is definitely a competitive advantage during the job search process. Recreation and leisure services employers value applicants who show an early commitment to get involved in professional organizations and activities while in college. Membership in professional organizations, attendance at professional conferences and workshops, delivering presentations at conferences, and writing articles in professional recreation journals (see Figure 7.6) are all perceived as very important by recreation employers in terms of hiring candidates. As a result, any professional involvement should be included in the resume. These are activities that students can get involved in throughout their college years and then continue into their professional careers.

**Job Coach Tip**

Create multiple resumes for multiple job applications.

Whitcomb

### Honors and Awards

This section is optional but should be included for candidates with significant honors and awards. Include the name of the award, sponsoring organization or agency, the date of the award, and, if possible, the total number who might have applied for the award or are eligible for the honor. (See Figure 7.7.)

### Activities

The activity section (see Figure 7.8) provides not only an opportunity for candidates to list key professional activities that are related to their career goals and interests, but it also allows candidates to demonstrate transferable skills and abilities. Activities could

**Keys to Job Search Success**

Think of yourself as a product and potential employers as consumers. A resume serves as a marketing tool or advertisement showing employers why they should interview you!

Figure 7.6

**Professional Involvement**

_Professional Memberships_

- National Parks and Recreation Association, 2003–present
- Resort and Commercial Recreation Association, 2004–present
- National Intramural-Recreation Sports Association, 2009

_Presentations_

- _Leadership andYOU_, XYZ National Association, April 24, 2009
- _The Role of Leadership in Tourism_, XYZ National Association, June 18, 2008

_Publications_

- _Event Planning at a CVB_, _XYZ Journal_, Winter, 2008

Examples for Listing Professional Involvement

Figure 7.7

**Honors and Awards**

- Outstanding Senior Recreation Major, XYZ University, Department of Recreation and Park Administration, December 2009.
- Dean's Senior Scholar Award, XYZ University, School of Health and Leisure Services, May 2008.
- Dean's List, XYZ University, School of Health and Leisure Services, May 2008.
- Outdoor Recreation Leadership Award, Backpacking Gear, Inc., October 2007.
- Volunteer of the Year, Walk for Life, September 2006.

Example for Listing Honors and Awards

Figure 7.8

**Activities**

- Vice President, Recreational Sports Management Club, 2006–2009
- Volunteer at Boys/Girls Club, 2006–2009
- Intramural Sports Head Supervisor, 2008
- Phi Gamma Delta fraternity member, 2002–2008
- Student Athletic Board, 2007

Example for Listing Activities

**Job Coach Tip**

When posting your resume online, there is nothing wrong with having a keywords line at the bottom of the page where you list words, appropriate to your experience and skills, designed solely to snag the site's search engine when an employer is doing a resume search.

**Job Coach Tip**

Don't use lower-level verbs for higher-level activity—"I administered" instead of "I directed." Power verbs are critical.

Simpson

include: membership in Greek organizations, academic societies, campus groups, volunteer or work experiences with agencies, and leadership responsibilities.

## References

One of the most asked (and debated) questions of job seekers in recreation and leisure services is whether or not to list references on the resume or insert the familiar *References available upon request* statement. The popular literature strongly recommends that references not be included on the resume (Banis, 2000; Farr, 2002; Graber, 2000; Nichols, 2001; Perrett, 2000; Smith, 2002). These authors indicate that employers prefer the *References available on request* notation be included at the end of the resume or no mention of references at all. However, results of several recreation studies revealed just the opposite. Recreation employers indicated they wanted to see a list of three to four references (preferably current or former employers or college professors) on a separate sheet attached to the resume (Ross & Zabriskie, 2001; Young & Ross, 2003). Although this finding is in direct disagreement with many resume publications, it appears to be the preference of those making the hiring decisions in recreation and leisure services settings. Relevant contact information (see Figure 7.9) including reference name, title, agency, mailing address, phone number, and e-mail address should be obtained for each reference, organized alphabetically into a reference list, and submitted along with the resume. Candidates must always make sure to ask their references for permission before listing them on their resume. (See Chapter 6.) Interviewers will eventually want to talk to references on the phone so that they can ask questions and hear their voice tone when asked about potential problem areas regarding a candidate.

Figure 7.9

**References**

| | |
|---|---|
| Dr. Joe Smith | Ms. Mary Jones |
| Professor | Director |
| ABC University | Parks and Recreation Dept. |
| Department of Recreation | 111 Anywhere Ave. |
| HPER Room 000 | Suite 111 |
| Anytown, USA 00000 | Anytown, USA 00000 |
| | |
| (000) 000-0000 | (111) 111-1111 |
| jsmith@abc.edu | mjones@prd.gov |

Examples for Listing References

## Keys to Job Search Success

Never exaggerate or lie about any aspect of your resume. Employers will eventually discover any false information.

# What *Not* to Include

Content items perceived as not important for entry-level professional recreation resumes are personal information such as birth date, birth place, marital status, race, age, health, gender, and religious/political affiliation (nor are they legal to ask!). Candidates should never include a picture of themselves with their resume because this could create problems for the employer. In addition, salary needs, reasons for leaving other jobs, and an educational record of high school performance and activities are not necessary.

# Organizing the Resume

Resume design and format encompass areas of sharp differences among disciplines. However, proper presentation, layout, and appearance of the resume can dramatically add to its effectiveness as well as to its efficiency and ease of reading. Employers, in general, want a resume that is easy to read and attractive in appearance. Although there is no single correct resume format, there are three accepted styles of formats: chronological resume, functional or skills resume, or the combination/hybrid resume.

- Chronological style lists experiences in reverse chronological order. The list includes dates of employment, names of agencies, and titles of jobs and functions performed at each agency. The chronological format is most often recommended because many employers prefer it and most students use it.

- Functional style lists the functions performed by category. Functional categories could include tournament scheduling, budgeting, event planning, personnel management, or others rather than presenting a complete work history. This style focuses on functional categories and skills that relate to the candidates' stated career objectives rather than on the jobs they have had. If the candidate does not have much work experience, this would be the format to use.

- Hybrid style is a combination of the first two and uses elements of both styles. The functional section appears near the beginning of the resume and the chronological (which merely lists dates, names of agencies, and job titles) appears near the end. This format is most effective if at least some of candidates' work experiences are related to their career objective, or if candidates want to highlight specific work responsibilities.

## Resume Length and Review

There are many different opinions in the popular literature regarding the length of a resume. Most experts (Farr, 2001; Hoheb, 2002; Ireland, 2002; Ledford, 2000; Lovelace, 2001; Mendels, 2001; Monroe, 2002; Nichols, 2001; Shim, 2002) consistently support the unwritten rule requiring resumes be limited to one page in length. Although a 1-page resume may be just the ticket for other disciplines and professions, studies in recreation and leisure services (Ross & Zabriskie, 2001; Young & Ross, 2003) indicate otherwise. More than 70% of recreation employers indicated that an applicant's resume should be two or more pages in length or determined by the amount of information. This finding suggests that candidates seeking a professional position in the field of recreation and leisure services should not be subject to the restrictions of the business field that traditionally prefers a 1-page format. The applicant's information (i.e., work experiences, accomplishments, etc.) should determine the length of the

**Job Coach Tip**

When describing responsibilities, it is best to use a diverse selection of power verbs.

**Did You Know...**

A job posting is all about tomorrow, and a resume is all about yesterday. Make your resume future-focused. Ask how you can honestly, ethically, and professionally marry yourself up with what the employer is looking for.

Gandel & Sterne

resume and not any particular predetermined page limitation. In recreation and leisure services settings the relevance and importance of the applicant's information are far more significant than the number of total pages on which they are typed. This is good news for those candidates who, because of space restrictions, have previously been forced to eliminate pertinent, although not crucial, information or revert to using a smaller font size. For candidates who do develop resumes more than one page in length, their name, phone number, and page number should be included in the header on each page (except the first) in case these pages get detached from the first page (see Figure 7.10).

One of the main arguments for having a short, 1-page resume is that employers in business and other related fields allow very little time to read each resume. Typically, employers in business only spend between 5 and 45 seconds reviewing applicants' resumes. In contrast, recreation employers reported spending 2 to 4 minutes or more reading each resume! This may be because of the fact that recreation and leisure services agencies have fewer applicants per job than do most business positions. Whereas major business corporations may have between 500 and 1000 applications for a particular position vacancy, the recreation and leisure services setting typically may have between 50 and 150 applicants per position. Overall, these findings indicate that recreation employers are interested in the valuable information provided on a resume, spend a considerable amount of time and energy examining that information, and are likely to question whether sufficient information can be placed onto a single page.

## Resume Design and Layout

When typing the resume, it is best to use simple fonts such as Times New Roman for text and Arial for headings. Fonts should not be smaller than 10 points (text) or larger than 14 points (headings). Emphasize key information by using a larger font size, all caps, bold, italics, or alignment rather than using more than three different font

Figure 7.10

Mike Smith  Page 2
(000) 000-0000

**XYZ Sport Agency, Anytown, USA**          June, 2006–present
*Recreation Supervisor*

Managerial position with nonprofit organization responsible for overall operation of recreation programs serving community population of over 800,000. Programs included Therapeutic Recreation, Seniors Citizens, etc.

Examples of Contact Information in Header

families (i.e., Times New Roman, Garamond, Comic Sans, Gothic, Arial, etc.). Limit use of underlining and bold fonts.

Avoid using abbreviations or ampersands (&) in the text of the resume, and always spell out agency names and professional associations. Although candidates may know what an acronym stands for, the reader may not. For example, rather than identifying the National Intramural-Recreational Sports Association by its acronym, NIRSA, write out the full name of the organization. Other general resume information preferred by recreation employers includes the following:

**Job Coach Tip**
A resume should only list relevant information that will help you secure a job interview. It is not an autobiography or history of your life.

- Chronological style over functional style, or the hybrid
- Bulleted lists for listing content information related to experience
- No preference for the color of paper containing the resume, but candidates should use high-quality, white or off-white color bond paper
- Resumes longer than one page be stapled
- Short sentences and short words rather than long ones
- Narrow columns rather then wider ones
- Plenty of white space rather than all text
- Mailing the resume in a flat envelope rather than folded in a #10 envelope

The resume was the most important of all the written application materials when compared to the application cover letter, letters of recommendation, or transcripts (Ross & Zabriskie, 2001; Young & Ross, 2003).

## Video Resumes: Good or Bad Idea?

An innovative trend in the job search process within the last few years is the use of video resumes, or what Nale (2008) refers to as "vesumes." To set themselves apart from other qualified applicants, some job seekers create short videos featuring a self-description of their skills and qualifications for the job. Not unlike the traditional paper resume, the quality, content, and length of the video resume can either help or hinder the candidate's chances of landing the job. If the video is well done, it can serve as a great way to market the candidate. However, "done poorly, it can, at best hinder your chances of getting an interview. At worst, it can knock you out of contention and embarrass you" (Doyle, 2009).

The advantages of using a video resume include showcasing a candidate's communication skills and creativity, as well as serving as an effective way in selling the candidate's intangible characteristics that a standard resume cannot. Curtis (2007) supports this notion by suggesting "Whereas a hiring manager may spend 10 seconds scanning a resume looking for a reason to reject a candidate, a video resume is something different, and therefore could hook a hirer's attention." The primary disadvantage of the video resume is that many organizations do not have the high-speed Internet connection or compatible browsers to view the video clip. Another disadvantage is that because video resumes are new, they are still considered risky (Richter, 2007) in that the candidate is taking a chance on how it will be received. A final disadvantage is the legal ramification of managers practicing subtle and unintentional discrimination when watching a candidate's video (Heathfield, 2009). Whereas many organizations discourage applicants from attaching photographs or including personal information on their resumes, the video resume can clearly communicate age, gender, race, national origin, and disabilities. Some organizations are fearful "that video resumes will invite lawsuits by candidates who could claim bias based on race, gender or age—indiscernable on paper, but not on video" (Cullen, 2007).

If candidates decide to use the video resume as a supplement to their standard resume, some technical considerations are to keep it short, produce a video with high resolution and sound quality, and carefully edit it for content and clarity. Professional dress is recommended along with practicing enough to sound prepared, but not so much that the resume sounds scripted (Doyle, 2009). Nale (2008) recommends that a video resume cover the same content areas as the paper resume with an introduction, history of experience, objectives, knowledge or special skills, education, and a summary. Finally, candidates must be cognizant to utilize the video resume to show potential employers who they really are, along with their creativity.

## Conclusion

Because of the increased number of applicants and competition for recreation and leisure services positions, candidates must naturally obtain the appropriate work experiences and educational background as well as the necessary qualifications, certifications, and credentials. During the job search process, however, it is essential for applicants to present this information as favorably as possible to potential employers to create a lasting impression. Applicants must remember that the only part of the job search process over which they have 100% control is the resume—from content to format. Knowing what specific resume content preferences recreation employers seek can be extremely valuable information when preparing an effective resume.

Recreation and leisure services professionals in general may have substantially different resume preferences than those commonly recommended for candidates from other disciplines. It is important to understand that different occupations require different approaches on how resume content is presented. Recreation and leisure service candidates should not attempt to follow the dictates of other occupations, but tailor their resumes to the preferences of recreation employers who will be reviewing their resumes and making the hiring decisions.

## References

Banis, W. (2000). How to win the resume battle. *The job guide: The student's guide to top companies.* Toronto, Canada: Simplicity Corporation.

Beshara, T. (2006). *The job search solution.* New York: American Management Association.

Big Brothers Big Sisters. (2009). Who we are. Retrieved May 24, 2009, from http://www.bbbs.org/site/c.diJKKYPLJvH/b.1539759/k.2640/Who_We_Are.htm

Bolles, M. E., & Bolles, R. N. (2008). *Job-hunting online* (5th ed.). Berkeley, CA: Ten Speed Press.

Boys and Girls Clubs of America. (2009). Who we are: The facts. Retrieved May 24, 2009, from http://www.bgca.org/whoweare/facts.asp

Cullen, L. T. (2007). It's a wrap. You're hired! *Time.* Retrieved May 31, 2009, from http://www.time.com/time/magazine/article/0,9171,1592860,00.html

**Did You Know...**

Municipal parks and recreation departments offer approximately 3000 positions in sports programming.

Curtis, R. (2007, February). Video resume: The future of job applications, or just a fad? Dice. Retrieved May 31, 2009, from http://career-resources.dice.com/technical-resume/video_resume.shtml

Doyle, A. (2009). Video resume tips: How to create a video resume. Retrieved May 31, 2009, from http://obsearch.about.com/od/videoresumes/a/videoresume.htm?p=1

Farr, J. M. (2002). *Getting the job you really want*. Indianapolis, IN: JIST Works.

Farr, M. (2007). *Same day resume* (2nd ed.). Indianapolis, IN: JIST Publishing.

Fournier, M., & Spin, J. (2006). *Encyclopedia of job winning resumes* (3rd ed.). Franklin Lakes, NJ: Career Press.

Gandel, C., & Sterne, S. (2009, March). Your next job. *Readers Digest*, 98–115.

Graber, S. (2000). *The everything resume book*. Holbrook, MA: Adams Media Corporation.

Heathfield, S. M. (2009). Video resumes: Do employers want video resumes? Retrieved May 31, 2009, from http://humanresources.about.com/od/recruitingandstaffing/qt/video_607_rs8.htm?p=1

Hoheb, M. (2002). Resume writing. *Scholastic Choices*, *18*(3), 19–23.

Hussain, A. (2007, June 26). Do video resumes help or lead to discrimination? DiversityInc. Retrieved May 31, 2009, from http://www.diversityinc.com/public/2028.cfm

Ireland, S. (2002). A resume that works. *Searcher*, *10*(7), 98–110.

Ledford, T. (2000). The truth about resumes. *Air Force Times*, *60*(41), 7–8.

Lovelace, H. W. (2001, May 7). Would you interview you? Informationweek.com. Retrieved September 14, 2009, from http://www.informationweek.com/836/uwhl.htm;jsessionid=T2YWP2JAAI3VFQE1GHPCKHWATMY32JVN

Mendels, P. (2001, August 13). When it's time to refresh your resume. *Business Week Online*. Retrieved September 14, 2009, from http://www.businessweek.com/careers/content/aug2001/ca20010813_566.htm

Monroe, M. S. (2002, December 22). Resume do's and don'ts: What to leave out is as important as what's in. *San Antonio Express-News*, 1G.

Nale, M. (2008, February 8). *10 things that make up a good video resume*. Ere.net. Retrieved May 31, 2009, from http://www.ere.net/2008/02/08/10-things-that-make-up-a-good-video-resume

National Park Service. (2009). Quick facts. Retrieved May 24, 2009, from http://www.nps.gov/aboutus/quickfacts.htm

Nichols, J. (2001). Building the perfect resume. *Careers & Colleges*, *21*(3), 41–43.

Perrett, J. L. (2000). United States. In M. A. Thompson (Ed.), *The global resume and CV guide* (pp. 221–247). New York: Wiley.

Reed, J. (1998). *Resumes that get jobs* (9th ed.). New York: ARCO Publishing.

Richter, H. (2007). Lights, camera, hired! *Newsweek*. Retrieved May 31, 2009, from http://www.newsweek.com/id/35063

Rosenberg, A. D. (2008). *The resume handbook* (5th ed.). Avon, MA: Adams Media.

Ross, C. M., & Zabriskie, R. B. (2001). An examination of resume preferences among therapeutic recreation professionals. *Annual in Therapeutic Recreation*, *10*, 33–44.

Schuman, N. (2008). *The everything resume book* (3rd ed.). Avon, MA: Adams Media.

Shim, G. (2002, November 18). You gotta look good on paper. *Omaha World-Herald*, 1D.

Simpson, C. (2009, March). Re: Finding a job. In C. Gandel & H. Sterne (Eds.), Your next job. *Readers Digest*, 98–115.

Smith, P. G. (2002). Creating the perfect resume. *Career World, 31*(3), 18–21.

Whitcomb, S. (2007*). Resume magic* (3rd ed.). Indianapolis, IN: JIST Publishing.

Yates, M. (2008). *Knock 'em dead resumes* (8th ed.). Avon, MA: Adams Media.

YMCA Canada. (2009). YMCA jobs. Retrieved May 24, 2009, from http://www.ymca.ca/en/who-we-are.aspx

Young, S. J., & Ross, C. M. (2003, December). Teaching resume effectiveness: Results from a recreation administrators' study. *LARNet: The Cyber Journal of Applied Leisure and Recreation Research*. Retrieved September 14, 2009, from http://www.larnet.org/2003-3.html

# Assignment: Developing Your Resume

Use the following worksheets as a foundation for building your resume. By accurately completing each section, you are well on your way to developing a winning resume. After completing all of the worksheets, the information that you record can be transferred to your resume.

## Education

*High School Attended:* _____

    City, State, Zip: _____

    Dates of Attendance From: _____ To: _____

    GPA: _____

*College Attended*

    City, State, Zip: _____

    Dates of Attendance From: _____ To: _____

    Overall GPA: _____ GPA in Major: _____

Major: _____ Minor: _____

Degree Earned: _____

*College Attended:*

    City, State, Zip: _____

    Dates of Attendance From: _____ To: _____

    Overall GPA: _____ GPA in Major: _____

Major: _____ Minor: _____

Degree Earned: _____

## Work Experience

*Agency 1:* _____

    City, State, Zip: _____

    Phone: _____

    Dates of Employment From: _____ To: _____

    Job Title/Department: _____

    Job Description: _____

    _____

    Job Duties and Responsibilities: _____

    _____

    _____

    _____

    _____

Assignments

Assignments

*Agency 2:* _____

City, State, Zip: _____

Phone: _____

Dates of Employment: From _____ To: _____

Job Title/Department: _____

Job Description: _____

_____

Job Duties and Responsibilities: _____

_____

_____

_____

_____

*Agency 3:* _____

City, State, Zip: _____

Phone: _____

Dates of Employment From: _____ To: _____

Job Title/Department: _____

Job Description: _____

_____

Job Duties and Responsibilities: _____

_____

_____

_____

_____

## Professional Development Experience

*Practicum:* _____

Agency: _____

Supervisor: _____

City, State, Zip: _____

Dates From: _____ To: _____

*Practicum:* _____

Agency: _____

Supervisor: _____

City, State, Zip: _____

Dates From: _____ To: _____

*Practicum:* _____

    Agency: _____

    Supervisor: _____

    City, State, Zip: _____

    Dates: From: _____ To: _____

## Seminar/Workshop/Conference/Certification

*Title:* _____

    Location of Training: _____

    Dates of Training: _____

    Skills Learned: _____

    Accomplishments: _____

*Title:* _____

    Location of Training: _____

    Dates of Training: _____

    Skills Learned: _____

    Accomplishments: _____

*Title:* _____

    Location of Training: _____

    Dates of Training: _____

    Skills Learned: _____

    Accomplishments: _____

## References

*Name:* _____

    Title: _____

    Agency: _____

    Address: _____

    City, State, Zip: _____

    Phone: _____

    E-mail: _____

    Relationship: _____

*Name:* _____

    Title: _____

    Agency: _____

    Address: _____

    City, State, Zip: _____

    Phone: _____

    E-mail: _____

    Relationship: _____

Assignments

Assignments

*Name:* _____
    Title: _____
    Agency: _____
    Address: _____
    City, State, Zip: _____
    Phone: _____
    E-mail: _____
    Relationship: _____

_____
_____
_____
_____
_____
_____
_____
_____
_____
_____
_____
_____
_____
_____
_____
_____
_____
_____
_____
_____
_____
_____
_____
_____
_____

# Interviewing

The interview is one of the most important aspects of the job search process. Although a good cover letter and resume are keys to getting the interview, the interview is the means by which the candidate actually lands the job (Darlington & Schuman, 2008). It is through the interview that both candidates and employers are afforded the primary opportunity to exchange job-relevant information. Additionally, the interview provides employers the opportunity to assess the knowledge, skills, and abilities of potential employees, while candidates should be using the interview to gain a realistic overview of job duties, responsibilities, and issues (Edginton, Hudson, & Lankford, 2001). Needless to say, performance during the interview by both candidates and employers is very important, yet how candidates prepare for an interview is equally as important as stepping into the interview room and performing. This chapter provides essential information regarding the steps candidates should take in preparing for the interview, what can be anticipated during the interview, and what candidates should do once the interview is completed.

Visit the Web site for this book to learn more about the organizations and topics covered in this chapter. http://health.jbpub.com/recreationjobs/2e

## Preparing for the Interview

Once a candidate has been offered the opportunity for an interview, it is important to determine the tasks that must be completed to make the interview happen. Issues such as date(s), travel and lodging arrangements, and the itinerary are necessary logistics that must be considered in setting up the interview. The hiring agency generally determines the preferred date(s) for the interview. In some instances, an interview may be scheduled for only a couple of hours; at other times, interviews may be scheduled over the course of several days. Regardless of the length of the interview, the agency generally works with the candidate to schedule the interview time.

Travel arrangements are another logistic needing consideration once the opportunity to interview has been extended. In some cases, the agency will assume responsibility for making travel arrangements for the candidate. Yet, in many situations, candidates will arrange their own travel with agencies reimbursing them for travel expenses. The first consideration concerning travel is determining whether the candidate should drive or fly. Based upon the average amount of time necessary to pass through most airport security systems, if candidates can drive to the interview site in less than five hours, they should drive rather than fly. If a flight is necessary and candidates are making their own arrangements, they should try to schedule their flight as soon as they have received their itinerary. By booking the flight early, candidates have a better chance of getting the flight they want, the seating they desire, and possibly to save money. Airlines often give discounts for flights booked at least 21 days in advance. Candidates can make airline travel arrangement through a travel agent, through the Internet, or by contacting an airline directly.

The costs of air travel vary based on the day of the week, time of day, number of stops, and type of seat. Traveling on a weekday is generally less expensive than traveling near or on weekends. Flights are generally less expensive later in the day and in the very early morning hours. Flying direct is usually more expensive than indirect flights with a stop or layover. Finally, traveling in coach is the least expensive, although candidates may be able to upgrade if they are members of a frequent flyer or other travel program.

In addition, when scheduling a flight, candidates should take into consideration arrival and departure times. Plenty of time should be allowed for arrival in case there are travel or weather delays. Candidates should also allow time between the end of the interview process and scheduling a return flight in the event the interview lasts longer than expected. Airlines recommend that passengers arrive at least 1 hour prior to their scheduled domestic flight time and 2 hours before an international flight. In addition to airline requirements, candidates arriving early at the airport will have a greater selection of seats and will ensure their luggage is on the same flight.

Packing is another issue candidates should consider when traveling by air. If the interview process is only one day, then candidates need not pack much and may consider packing a carry-on bag. Most airlines limit the size of carry-on bags to a range of 14–16 inches in height, 21–24 inches in width, and 8–9 inches in depth. Carry-on bags usually have a limit of 40 pounds, and checked luggage has a limit of 70 pounds, but the exact limits vary from airline to airline. In addition, some airlines charge fees for checked luggage or luggage exceeding 50 pounds. Knowing this information can save candidates time when arriving at an airport as well as getting out of the airport and on to their destination.

A second consideration in travel is lodging. For some interviews, lodging will not be necessary. However, if the candidate is traveling a long distance or the interview process is scheduled to take a full day or more, it is common for agencies to arrange lodging for the candidate at a local hotel. If candidates must make their own lodging arrangements, they should select a hotel in close proximity to the interview site. This allows more convenience not only to the hiring organization, but also affords the candidate access to neighborhoods and areas surrounding the agency.

If the interview is within driving distance, it is important for candidates to determine the best route to the agency prior to the interview. Additionally, candidates should determine the amount of time necessary to arrive 10 to 15 minutes early. The best way to do this is to drive the actual route noting the time it takes. One important factor to consider in estimating travel time is the day of the week and time of the day the interview is scheduled. If the interview is scheduled early in the morning, candidates may face traffic issues that can possibly delay travel. So, in conducting a practice trip, candidates should drive to the agency on a weekday at the same time of day they will arrive for their interview. Regardless of how long it takes to drive to the agency, the candidate should build in extra time to allow for unexpected delays.

Once the travel arrangements have been set, most hiring organizations will provide the candidate with an itinerary. Learning the itinerary is very useful to candidates not only for them to gain insight into the interview schedule, but also to help them familiarize themselves with the names and job titles of the different individuals they will be meeting in the organization. If an organization does not send an itinerary, it is perfectly acceptable for candidates to request one.

Agencies vary in the time allowed between scheduling the interview and actually conducting the interview. There are many factors influencing this time frame such as the agency's urgency to hire, length of the interview, number of candidates invited on-site, program schedule of the hiring organization, and issues related to scheduling air travel. A candidate can expect to have at least 1 week before the interview, and in most cases organizations will allow 2–3 weeks lead time. It is this lead time that becomes very valuable to prospective candidates in preparing for their interview.

## Researching the Agency

The importance of interview preparation cannot be overemphasized. In many ways, it is similar to studying for a college exam. If students do not study or do their homework, the chances of earning a good grade are not high. The same holds true for an interview: if candidates do not do their homework, the chances of making a good impression and consequently earning consideration for the job are not high. Before candidates engage in the interview, they must research the organization. Conducting research as a part of interview preparation will increase the candidate's knowledge about the organization, interviewers, and position as well as provide a boost of confidence. If possible, it is always wise for candidates to know a little about the people that will be interviewing them. This not only shows that candidates have prepared for the interview, it can also be flattering for the interviewer. Chapter 3 provides extensive information on the steps candidates should take in conducting research prior to the interview.

**Time Out**

Take time to practice your travel route to the interview site. By knowing the route and how long it takes to get there, you can determine what time you should leave for the actual interview. You should always arrive to an interview 10–15 minutes early.

**Be Alert!**

Seventy percent of job descriptions fail to specify the industry. Go to the corporate website and check. You'd better know before you go to the interview whether it's a job in real estate or transportation.

Worthington (as cited in Gandel & Sterne, p. 109)

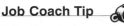

**Job Coach Tip**

Take time to research an agency, job, and employees thoroughly. Not only will this help prepare you for the interview, it will also boost your confidence during the interview.

# Candidate Self-Assessment

As candidates prepare for the interviewing process as well as position-specific interviews, it is essential to take a realistic self-assessment in terms of skills, abilities, knowledge, experience, strengths, and weaknesses. By engaging in this assessment and documenting the results, candidates will have a greater awareness of what they can offer a potential employer as well as contribute to a specific job. A self-assessment worksheet can be found in Chapter 1 along with a detailed description of the process candidates should follow.

Beyond simply listing strengths, candidates should pinpoint their strengths that match the qualifications and specifications listed in the job announcement. These strengths should then be emphasized by the candidate in the agency visit and actual interview. Weaknesses are more difficult to address and doing so can become a "moment of truth" for some candidates. In addressing weaknesses, it is crucial to recognize that no one is perfect and that everyone has areas upon which they need to improve. The key question for candidates to ask themselves in considering weaknesses is "Are my weaknesses surmountable?" In many cases, weaknesses can be overcome if candidates are willing to spend the time to learn more about a topic or deliberately practice a skill. So, after listing weaknesses in terms of a specific job, candidates should consider their answers to the following questions:

1.  What are the skills I would definitely have to improve to be successful in this job?

2.  How hard will I have to work to improve?

Employers recognize there are no perfect candidates for their positions, and they do appreciate those candidates who know what they do well along with their limitations. The purpose of the assessment is to identify how well the candidate matches up with the primary responsibilities of the position.

# Interview Practice

For those candidates new to the question-and-answer portion of the interview process or who have not participated in many interviews, practicing for the interview can be quite valuable. By practicing, candidates can review anticipated questions, rehearse answers, develop their own questions, and fine-tune their body language and nonverbal cues. Based upon the job announcement and after researching the organization, candidates should be able to anticipate questions specific to the position. There are also numerous sources listing standard interview questions from which candidates can rehearse answers. Candidates can practice answering questions on their own or solicit the assistance of a friend, colleague, or family member. By obtaining feedback from another person, candidates can obtain a different perspective of how their responses are articulated and perceived.

If another person is not available to assist in practicing the interview, candidates can practice on their own by videotaping themselves responding to questions. The feedback provided by the video recorder may be even better than that provided by another person. By videotaping the practice session, candidates will be able to hear every *um* and *ah* uttered as well as see every fidget, hand movement, and slouch. Although viewing the tape may be uncomfortable, candidates can gain valuable information on behaviors and responses needing improvement.

Nonverbal cues occur in many different forms, and many times candidates are not even aware of exhibiting these cues until it is brought to their attention. A candidate who slouches in his chair or does not maintain eye contact during the interview will likely leave a negative impression with the interviewer. Head nodding is a nonverbal way for candidates to convey to the interviewer their agreement or understanding of what is being stated. Nodding may also be used by the interviewer when the candidate is speaking and the candidate should pick up on this cue. Some people are more comfortable using their hands to make their point when speaking. However, too much hand movement can distract from the candidate's answers. Nonverbal cues illustrating restlessness or nervousness, such as tapping feet, shaking legs, twirling hair, or tapping a pen, should be controlled by the candidate. These movements are even more magnified in an interview when the primary focus is upon the candidate for a lengthy period of time. The best way to control these behaviors is by practicing the interview with another person, video taping, or in front of a mirror. Once candidates are aware of these behaviors, it is easier to control them through practice.

How much time should be spent practicing? The answer to this question is based not only upon the amount of interview experience candidates have, but upon their personal comfort level for each interview. Although candidates must be well prepared for the interview, they should not be so practiced that their responses sound cliché or rote. Practice to be prepared, but not so much that spontaneity and genuineness are lost.

One final thought specifically for recreation students graduating soon. Often in recreation and leisure services internship preparation courses, students are required to participate in mock interviews. Although some students simply go through the motions of completing another assignment, it is important for those students to take advantage of this opportunity to practice answering questions. Participating in mock interviews may be uncomfortable for some students, especially those with no interview experience. However, it is much easier to identify poor body language, distracting nonverbal cues, or inarticulate responses and to correct those behaviors in a class situation than in the few weeks prior to the actual interview when a career is at stake. Practice, practice, practice!

## Planning What to Wear

What a candidate wears to an interview is vital to the first impression the candidate makes with the interviewer. Candidates should examine their wardrobes and make sure they have appropriate attire for an interview. Candidates should inspect their clothing for missing buttons, loose strings, dirt, or lint. If necessary, a candidate should have their clothes dry-cleaned and pressed prior to the interview. For those candidates who make the determination that they do not have appropriate interview apparel, they must go shopping and purchase clothing that will help them make the best impression possible. Visit top-notch clothing stores and ask for help from experienced salespeople in selecting a coordinated interview outfit. Remember, the investment will pay for itself when the candidate lands the job!

Candidates should take a conservative approach in selecting interview attire, remembering that the key is to look professional. For local candidates, they may be able to determine the appropriate interview attire while collecting research from an agency and observing the common attire of the current staff. However, although staff may

**Job Coach Tip**

Based on the job description and your research, you should be able to anticipate some of the questions that will be asked in the interview.

**Job Coach Tip**

Practice answering the question "Tell me about yourself." Include your experience, accomplishments, skills and abilities, and education.

Seidman (as cited in Gandel & Sterne, p. 109)

follow casual dress, this does not mean it is appropriate for the candidate to dress casually for the interview. In fact, a candidate is always better off to overdress than to underdress for the interview (Ross & Blackman, 1998).

For men, a suit (navy, black, or gray) with a neatly pressed solid white or blue shirt is a conservative professional look for an interview. A tie with a simple and conservative pattern and color should also be worn. Dark socks matching the suit and polished brown or black dress shoes are the final touches to the interview attire. Socks should go high enough up the leg (over the calf) so that when the candidate sits down and crosses his legs no skin is visible.

For women, a solid-colored conservative dress or suit should be worn. If a dress or skirt is worn, it should be knee length with no extreme slits. When choosing a suit, a tailored conservative blouse should be worn. Neutral colored hosiery should be worn along with polished, closed-toed shoes with medium or low heels. Accessories should lend to the professional look yet remain simple. If makeup is worn, be careful not to overdo it.

Color is the most dynamic tool for dressing to enhance appearance. As a result, candidates should learn which colors best complement their skin, eyes, and hair coloring. Both men and women should make sure their hair is neat and that cologne or perfume is kept to a minimum, or not worn at all. Although it is important for candidates to be themselves throughout the interview process, they must remember to follow the conservative approach. For this reason, bold statements in the form of men wearing earrings, women wearing dangling earrings, or candidates wearing nose or tongue jewelry should be avoided. Visible tattoos should also be covered. Remember, by the time a candidate walks into the interview room and sits down, the majority of interviewers will have decided whether or not the candidate will be considered for the position. The candidate's image and appearance, combined with the attitude projected, will determine this first impression. Candidates can never underestimate the importance of their image and appearance!

## Final Preparations

Finally, it is the day before the interview and the candidate has accomplished all the necessary preparations. As the candidate gets ready for a good night's rest, she looks at her briefcase and considers the documents and materials that should be taken along on the interview. Candidates should take different documents to the interview. Some of these documents can be used by candidates to browse one last time before beginning the interview, while others may actually be needed during the interview. Candidates should come to the interview with a folder containing the following documents:

- *Agency information worksheet:* Reviewing information about the agency will be helpful before the interview.
- *Resume:* It is always a good idea to take along extra copies of the resume in case a member of the interview team needs to review the candidate's resume. Candidates who have extra resumes demonstrate their preparedness for the interview.
- *References:* If candidates have not provided references with their resume, then bringing those references to the interview will help the agency expedite the reference check process.

**Job Coach Tip**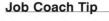

If you will be traveling for only one day, packing a carry-on bag will save you time when arriving and leaving the airport.

**Job Coach Tip**

Practice alone in front of a mirror or with a friend. Many very intelligent, highly successful people think they can go unprepared. Those who shoot from the hip usually shoot themselves in the foot.

Rosen (as cited in Gandel & Sterne, p. 109)

- *Self-assessment worksheet:* Having this information to look through one last time can be helpful and give the candidate something to do while waiting for the interview to start.
- *Portfolio:* If the candidate has a portfolio of work, this can help provide the interviewers an idea of the quality of work and experiences of the candidate.
- *Agency publications:* Agency brochures and flyers will give the candidate something to read while waiting for the interview.
- *Map to agency:* If candidates are not familiar with how to get to the agency, they should take along a map and directions to the interview.

## The Interview

The big day has finally arrived—the day of the interview! With hours of preparation and all the details behind them, candidates must be ready to step into the next phase of the process. There are a variety of methods used at this stage of the hiring process, but all with one primary purpose: the employer wants to get to know the candidate as a person. The different types of interview formats implemented are based upon the hiring agency's preference, level of the position, and the organizational structure of the agency. The types of interviews candidates in recreation and leisure services will generally participate in are screening, panel/board, one-on-one, interviews at conferences, telephone interviews, and assessment centers.

### Screening Interviews

An initial type of interview that many recreation and leisure service organizations use in the hiring process is the screening interview. The purpose of the screening interview is to make an initial contact with candidates who have progressed to the latter stages of the hiring process. Often organizations will narrow the pool of candidates down to a reasonable number (i.e., 5 to 10), yet this number is still too large to invite for on-site interviews. As a result, the hiring agency will contact each candidate to measure their interest in the position as well as to gain some insight into each candidate's personality. Usually conducted via the telephone, the format of screening interviews is brief and concise, with most interactions lasting no longer than 10 to 30 minutes.

Questions that can be anticipated during a screening interview are basic and usually directly related to responsibilities listed in the job description or the candidate's resume. In most instances, the screening committee is trying to get to know more about candidates, what they have done, and their personality. When discussing themselves, candidates should highlight experiences related to the position for which they are interviewing while being careful not to sound boastful. Bragging too much can convey an arrogant personality, while being too brief and not sharing adequate information may make the interviewer think a candidate has something to hide or lacks good communication skills. Maintaining the appropriate balance of providing information is a challenge, but can be successfully accomplished by practicing for the interview.

### Panel Interviews

When candidates are faced with a team of interviewers in the question-and-answer session, or when a variety of people within the organization meet and talk with candidates, a panel interview method is being utilized. The panel may comprise a wide

**Be Alert!**

Appearance matters! By the time you walk into the interview room, the interviewer may have already decided whether or not you will be considered for the position.

**Job Coach Tip**

In a panel interview, it is best to focus your attention and responses toward the panel member asking the question, but try to make contact with all of the panel members.

variety of people from the organization including subordinates of the position, colleagues of the position, the supervisor of the position, people from related departments within the organization, and upper-level administrators. The number of individuals involved in a panel interview vary widely depending upon the size of the organization and the level of the position, but generally range from two to nine members. Agencies use the panel interview format because it allows more than one person to be involved in the hiring decision, which results in a more balanced selection process. Although the involvement of several interviewers benefits the hiring organization, it can be somewhat intimidating for the candidate. In an attempt to reduce the intimidation factor, candidates should meet each panel member, shake their hand, and learn their name. Additionally, there are advantages of the panel format for candidates, in that they get to meet many people affiliated with the organization, they gain insight into the organizational structure of the agency, and they gain a better feel for the level of camaraderie among the people currently working in the organization. By fielding similar questions from different panel members throughout the visit, candidates are also likely to gain insight into the most important aspects of the position and values of the organization. This becomes particularly advantageous to candidates in determining whether or not the organization would be a good fit for their professional career.

One of the challenges for candidates in a panel interview is determining on whom they should focus their attention. In most cases, there will be one member of the panel who is leading the interview and often this is the immediate supervisor of the position. Candidates can focus slightly more attention on this person, especially when asking questions directed toward the panel in general. A good rule of thumb for candidates is to focus their attention and responses from direct questions on the panel member asking the question. It is appropriate to face the questioner and maintain eye contact with that person while occasionally looking at other members of the panel. Candidates should not forget about the other members of the panel while responding to direct questions and can maintain a nonverbal relationship with them by varying eye contact and occasionally shifting their body position. Panel interviews usually last between 30 and 90 minutes.

## One-on-One Interviews

Candidates meeting with only one representative from the hiring agency participate in the one-on-one interview format. The individual from the agency meeting with the candidate is not only likely to be the decision maker in the hiring process, but the person who would be supervising the candidate as well. The format of this type of interview involves questions and answers between the interviewer and candidate. In this situation, candidates should work at building a rapport with the interviewer while maintaining a good conversational flow in responding to questions.

The format of this type of interview involves questions and answers between the interviewer and candidate. The personal connection that the candidate makes with the interviewer is the most important element of this interview. Certainly, a candidate wants to provide good answers to questions and exhibit other good interview characteristics, but establishing a relationship with the interviewer is of the greatest importance. Often in a one-on-one situation, the final decision of interviewers is influenced subjectively by whether they like the candidate personally. This is different from a panel interview where there are multiple personalities and the panel tends to be more objective.

**Job Coach Tip**

When deciding what to wear to an interview, remember that the color of clothing plays an important role in enhancing appearance.

Candidates can build rapport with the interviewer and maintain good conversational flow by listening intently to the interviewer and responding professionally in a conversational tone. Most interviewers are aware of how stressful interviewing for a new position can be and will make an attempt at conversation with the candidate to put him or her more at ease. Candidates should take advantage of this opportunity to establish more of a personal relationship with the interviewer. If interviewers feel candidates are on the same page, then they are more likely to speak freely and create a situation where candidate and interviewer are exchanging ideas, as opposed to a question and answer forum.

Finally, showing enthusiasm will assist candidates in developing rapport. Candidates should leave no doubt about their interest in the job and agency, as well as their personal interest in the interviewer. Employers in one-on-one interviews, or any type interview for that matter, are looking for candidates who really enjoy what they do and are excited by the prospect of the job. Enthusiasm expressed by candidates can be contagious during the interview.

## Interviews at Conferences

If both the employer and the candidate plan on attending a professional conference near the time period of the hiring process, the conference can become an interview site. Interviewing at a conference can be beneficial to both the employer and the candidate. Employers are able to interview candidates without incurring candidate travel expenses, and candidates can use the opportunity to learn more about the interviewer and the hiring organization through conference presentations, conference socials, or informal conversations. Some professional organizations in recreation establish career centers with designated meeting rooms at the conference site for the express purpose of conducting interviews. Agencies may also schedule an interview at the conference on their own.

## Telephone Interviews

In situations where it simply is not possible for the interviewer and the candidate to meet at a common site, a telephone interview might be used. Although there are not many instances where a candidate is hired just on the basis of a telephone interview, it may be the only method to screen applicants or to interview candidates who are a great distance from the organization. The telephone interview can involve a panel in a teleconference format or a one-on-one interview. From the candidates' perspective, a telephone interview eliminates issues of what to wear to the interview, grooming, and issues related to traveling. An added advantage is that candidates are able to participate in the interview while in familiar surroundings and, as a result, may be more relaxed.

On the other hand, there are some challenges posed by a telephone interview that candidates must anticipate. Because candidates cannot see their interviewers, most of the nonverbal communication cues available in the face-to-face interview are eliminated. For example, the inability of candidates to make eye contact with interviewers makes it more difficult to get a feel for how their answers to questions are being received. Candidates must listen very closely for audible nonverbal cues and the way interviewers speak to gain a perspective of how their responses are received by the

 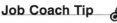

interviewers. Another challenge is caused by the location of candidates when they receive the interview phone call. Because they may be in their home for the telephone interview, it may be difficult to establish the "right frame of mind" for the interview. As a result of these challenges, candidates may find the following strategies helpful in making their telephone interview more successful:

- *Dress up:* If candidates dress as if they were going to a face-to-face interview, it may help them get in the right frame of mind.
- *Stand up:* Standing up while speaking and answering questions can make it easier to maintain a higher energy level in responding.
- *Stand still:* Pacing during the interview may distract the candidate as well as make some candidates sound as if they are out of breath.
- *Use notes:* Candidates can keep their notes nearby to refer to during the interview. Be sure notes are organized because candidates do not want to be shuffling through papers while their interviewers are waiting for a response.
- *Watch the ums:* It is very common for candidates to use *um* and *uh* when speaking. Although this is also something candidates should be aware of in a face-to-face interview, these speech patterns are much more obvious in a phone interview. Practicing can help to eliminate these crutch phrases.
- *Minimize distractions:* Candidates should turn off the television, stereo, computer, cell phones, or any other devices that may distract them during the interview. If possible, candidates should turn off call waiting on their own phone. The quieter the environment, the easier it will be for candidates to focus on the interview.

## Assessment Centers

The assessment center is often used in recreation and leisure services as a part of the interview process. The assessment center is a different component to the interview involving candidates demonstrating behaviors similar to those found in the work environment. Depending on the responsibilities of the position, candidates may complete written assignments or engage in exercises related to the job. Activities in an assessment center can include written assignments, simulations, and in-basket exercises.

- *Written assignments:* As part of the interview, candidates may be asked to write a press release, edit a brochure entry, or develop a promotional flyer. In addition, candidates may be asked to write a letter or memorandum to a staff member. These exercises allow for the agency to learn firsthand about a candidate's writing skills and communication skills.

 **Keys to Job Search Success**

Don't arrive for your interview empty handed! You should take a notebook that includes your resume, references, portfolio, job information, and agency publications. Not only will these be helpful to review before the interview, they will also give you something to do while you wait.

■ **Simulations:** Some agencies ask candidates to simulate or role-play a certain scenario that might be common to the position for which they have applied. Candidates may also be asked to simulate a presentation to the board. These simulations can be done during the question-and-answer phase of the interview, but more likely are conducted after the interview. Candidates are usually given time to prepare for the simulation and then perform before a video camera or a live audience in the presentation room.

■ **In-basket exercise:** The in-basket exercise is becoming more commonly used as an assessment center tool in recreation and leisure service organizations. The in-basket exercise consists of a scenario where candidates pretend they are on the job. The candidate comes into the exercise and may find 10 messages on his or her desk. Candidates must then determine the priority of these messages and how each will be handled, usually in a limited amount of time. In this exercise, candidates are given time to review the messages and develop their responses. At the end of the exercise, candidates come back to the interviewer, explain their priorities, and provide justifications for their answers. This exercise allows interviewers to gain an understanding of the thought process and logic of each candidate.

Regardless of the interview format, candidates should keep in mind general considerations related to the interview:

■ **Arrive early:** It can never hurt to arrive early, but arriving late will create a negative impression before stepping into the interview room. Arriving 10–15 minutes early allows candidates the opportunity to relax and gather themselves prior to the interview.

■ **Wait patiently:** A candidate who arrives early will have some time to wait for the interview to start. Candidates should use this time to review notes and agency information. If the interview does not start on time, candidates should continue to wait patiently. In most cases, starting an interview late is not intentional, but situations may exist where an interviewer wants to examine candidates in a stressful situation where things do not necessarily go as planned. Although candidates will not know if this is the case, they should not pace and check in with the support staff, but instead remain calm and casually continue to review materials about the agency and interview.

■ **Maintain eye contact:** When the interviewer greets the candidate, it is important for the candidate to maintain eye contact. This demonstrates the candidate is not intimidated or shy.

■ **Firm handshake:** While maintaining eye contact, a handshake is very common during initial introductions. It is important for candidates to offer a firm handshake with one or two shakes of the hand being appropriate.

■ **Small talk:** The interviewer will likely engage candidates in small talk after initial introductions. Candidates may be asked about the drive to the agency or weather-related issues. The interviewer is not really interested about traffic encountered on the drive or about the temperature outside, so candidates should not engage in long answers to these types of questions.

■ **Professionalism:** Candidates should not confuse small talk with informality and should respond to all questions in a professional manner.

**Job Coach Tip**

When waiting for the interview to start, sit patiently and review your interview materials. Pacing back and forth and checking in with support staff will make you more nervous and may leave a bad impression.

# Interview Questions

Candidates can expect to encounter different types of interview questions during the interview. Some of these questions will be very easy to answer while others will be more challenging. Regardless of the difficulty of the question, a candidate should be clear and confident when answering. This can be done by properly preparing and practicing for the interview. When practicing how to answer interview questions, candidates should prepare for personal questions, philosophical questions, knowledge-based or experience-based questions, situational questions, and think-on-your-feet questions. Finally, candidates should anticipate closing interview questions allowing them a chance to sell themselves one last time as well as being prepared to ask questions during the interview. These types of questions are discussed in the following sections.

## Personal Questions

An experienced interviewer will likely structure the interview beginning with easier questions followed by questions that gradually become more difficult. Easy questions asked by interviewers are usually more personal in nature. The purpose of asking personal questions is for the interviewer to get to know the candidate better.

- Why do you want this job?
- Tell me about yourself.
- What are your hobbies and interests?
- What are your short-term and long-term goals?
- How did you become interested in leisure services?
- What motivates you to perform?
- If we called one of your references, what would they say about you?
- What are three words that describe you?
- What accomplishments have given you the greatest satisfaction?
- What are your greatest strengths?
- What is your greatest weakness?

Questions of this general nature should be anticipated by candidates, they should have practiced answering these questions, and consequently should be well prepared to answer them. If candidates have properly prepared and are ready for these questions, their confidence will rise and help make the rest of the interview proceed more smoothly.

## Philosophical Questions

Another type of interview question likely to be asked is a philosophical question. These questions have a personal component to them, but primarily relate more to the personal philosophy of the candidate on issues related to the job.

- What is your philosophy about recreation?
- What is your management philosophy?
- What qualities should a good leisure service agency have?
- What is your customer service philosophy?
- What is your philosophy about youth sports?

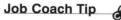

**Job Coach Tip**

When answering a philosophical question, keep in mind that your philosophy should be similar to the philosophy of the hiring agency.

- What is your philosophy about fitness programs?
- What is your philosophy about individuals with disabilities?

Questions about philosophy can be tricky. Although these questions are usually asked in a way to discover that which is most important to each candidate, this may not be the motivation behind asking the question. Often the interviewer wants to see if the candidate's personal philosophy matches the philosophy of the organization. Candidates who have researched the agency should know the organizational philosophy on many issues and be prepared to answer these types of questions in a way that reflects a commonality between their philosophy and the agency's.

## Knowledge-Based and Experience-Based Questions

Interviewers may ask questions that are knowledge based or experience based. These type of questions are relatively straightforward with no hidden meaning. By asking these questions, the interviewer wants to learn about the candidate's knowledge or experience with a specific issue:

- With what recreation management computer software are you familiar?
- What steps would you take in developing a youth arts and crafts program?
- Have you operated a tractor in the work setting?
- What are the measurements of a youth soccer field?
- What experience do you have in supervising youth programs?
- What experience do you have in facility management?
- Tell me about your experiences supervising staff.
- Have you ever had the opportunity to prepare a promotional brochure?
- Describe a work-related problem you have had and how you handled it.
- What experience do you have speaking in front of groups?

Answering these questions can be easy if candidates have experiences or knowledge matching the question. If candidates do not have the experiences or knowledge to answer the question, they should answer the question in a way that applies their related experiences. For instance, if candidates are asked about their experiences planning, organizing, and conducting adult sport programs, yet they have no experience doing this, they can focus on similar experiences that are appropriate for the position. In this situation, candidates could focus on their experiences supervising youth sports programs or their experiences with adult fitness programs in responding to the question.

## Situational Questions

A type of question that can be challenging for candidates is the situational question. Situational questions are questions where the interviewer creates a scenario, and candidates are asked to tell how they would handle it. Situational questions usually involve some type of scenario with a problem commonly found in the workplace, or a situation where something has gone wrong. Although it can be hard to anticipate the specific situational questions that will be asked, candidates should expect these types of questions and focus on problem-solving steps in responding to them. The questions generally focus on job-relevant situations (see list following) and will provide the interviewer some insight into candidates' thought processes and how they might actually perform in a difficult situation.

**Job Coach Tip**

The correct answer to a situational question may be included in company policies. You should acknowledge this prior to answering the question.

- If a child is injured during summer camp, how would you handle the situation?
- You receive a call from a participant in your adult softball program telling you one of your umpires used profanity while on the job. What steps would you take in confronting this problem?
- You have heard that one of your part-time staff persons is stealing supplies from the departmental storeroom. What would you do first?
- A parent calls and tells you that your youth dance class is terrible and wants a refund. How would you deal with this situation?

Answering a situational question can be tough. In some cases, the scenario may be addressed through agency policies. For example, when a child is injured at camp, there should be agency policies governing how the situation is handled. Although candidates could try to familiarize themselves with agency policies, they might acknowledge that a situation like this should be covered by a program policy, but then state how they would handle it. The best way to handle situational questions is to use common sense, and quite honestly, that is what interviewers are looking for when asking these types of questions.

### Think-on-Your-Feet Questions

The last type of question that a candidate may get in an interview is a think-on-your-feet question. These questions are designed to see how well and how quickly candidates respond to unexpected scenarios. These questions are supposed to catch the candidate off guard and are oftentimes humorous.

**Be Alert!**

The think-on-your-feet question is designed to catch you off guard. Take a moment and compose yourself. Keep in mind that there is no right answer to this type of question, so answer with confidence.

- If you were a cartoon character, who would you be? Why?
- Compare yourself to a thumbtack.
- If you were an animal, what would you be? Why?
- If you could only have one office supply, what would it be? Why?
- If you could have dinner with any one person, who would it be and why?
- Compare yourself to the chair you are sitting in.

Although these questions may seem a little absurd, they allow the interviewer to see how candidates respond under pressure as well as test their creativity. Obviously, there is no one correct answer to questions of this nature; rather, candidates should be prepared if one of these comes their way during the interview.

### Closing Questions

It is common for interviewers to wrap up the interview with a few closing questions or questions providing candidates one last opportunity to sell themselves. These questions give candidates an excellent opportunity to relate any additional information about themselves that did not come out in the interview. This is also an appropriate time for candidates to submit a portfolio if the opportunity did not occur during the interview. By answering these kinds of questions, candidates have the chance to summarize their strengths and state why they are a good fit for the position. Candidates should be prepared to answer these questions before coming to the interview:

- Why should we hire you?
- What do you bring to the position that other candidates don't?
- Is there anything else that you would like to tell us?

## Questions for the Interviewer

After the closing questions are answered, the interviewer will usually ask the candidate if he or she has any questions. Candidates should never pass up the opportunity to ask questions because this can indicate a degree of arrogance or lack of interest in the position and organization as well as leave a negative impression at the end of the interview. Candidates should use this time to show they have done their homework on both the position and the organization. Candidates can also use this opportunity to obtain answers to issues of legitimate concern that have arisen through the course of the interview process.

By conducting thorough research and taking time to prepare properly, candidates should come to the interview with a list of questions to ask throughout their time spent at the agency but not about information that could easily be found from the agency's Web site. It is important to have a variety of questions because there is a good chance that some of the candidate's questions will be answered before the candidate is given the opportunity to ask.

- Who will be my direct supervisor?
- Could you tell me a little about the typical schedule the person in this position should maintain?
- What process is used to evaluate employee performance?
- What are some of the biggest challenges facing this department?
- What type of orientation and training will be provided for this position?
- Are there opportunities for professional development?
- What is the start date for this position?
- What is your time frame for making a hiring decision?

One question candidates are typically not sure when it is appropriate to ask concerns salary and benefits. Research data from a study involving the interview preferences of recreation professionals (Ross & Blackman, 1998) indicated that employers believe it is appropriate for candidates to initiate a discussion regarding compensation, but only at the close of the interview. More specifically, employers indicated the best time for candidates to raise the salary and benefit question is after the job offer has been made. At which point candidates should ask and, if necessary, negotiate an appropriate salary.

## Illegal Questions

There is the possibility that during the interview process an inexperienced interviewer or an unethical interviewer will ask an illegal question. Interviewers should be cautious when asking questions in the areas of age, race, religion, ethnicity, citizenship, marital status, family status, physical appearance, health, disabilities, sexual preference, criminal record, nonprofessional affiliations, and military record (Edginton et al., 2001). In most cases, questions concerning these topics have no relevance to the job. However, if information from one of these areas is pertinent to the job, an interviewer should carefully word questions so that they are lawful. An interviewer can discuss the long hours and travel involved in the job along with whether that will be a problem for the candidate. But the interviewer cannot ask specific questions about children or family. The interviewer also cannot ask any questions about physical appearance unless

**Did You Know...**

Working can be fun. Forty percent of employees claim work is a fun place to be.

Leisure Trends Group

the candidate is applying for a position where height or weight requirements are involved for safety reasons (this will rarely be the case in recreation and leisure services).

When candidates are asked an illegal question during an interview, there are three actions they can take. Candidates can answer the question, refuse to answer the question, or examine the intent behind the question and then respond with an answer that might be appropriate for the job (Best-job.Interviews.com). Answering an illegal question is up to the judgment of the candidate. If candidates are not offended by the question or feel the question is being asked out of curiosity with no ill intent, then answering might be the best action to take. Candidates can avoid answering a question by tactfully evading it, providing an answer to another question, or answering the question humorously. Candidates may also choose not to answer the question, although the consequence of this option can possibly jeopardize any rapport the candidate has established with interviewers. This is especially true in a situation where the interviewer meant no harm in asking the question and is not even aware that it is illegal. If candidates do refuse to answer a question, they should do so tactfully. For example, in responding to an illegal question, candidates may simply reply, "I'm sorry, but I don't feel like that question is relevant to the position for which I am interviewing" (Resumagic.com).

## After the Interview

Once the interview is over, candidates should evaluate their performance. Evaluating a performance can be helpful in following up with the agency and can also benefit candidates in future interview situations. When evaluating their interview performance, candidates should focus upon the following questions:

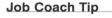

**Job Coach Tip**

You should evaluate your performance after the interview. This will help you focus on what you need to improve for future interviews.

- How well did I answer the questions?
- What questions did I have difficulty with?
- Did I speak clearly and concisely?
- How aware was I of my nonverbal cues?
- Was I confident?
- Was I enthusiastic?
- What points did I forget to make?
- Overall, how did I do?
- What did I do well?
- What could I have done better?

When evaluating the interview, the candidate should make notes of information learned during the interview along with concerns about the position, agency, or interviewer that developed during the course of the interview. This information may be useful in a second interview or in negotiating a job offer. The interview evaluation should also

**Keys to Job Search Success**

Take the time to write down questions to ask during the interview. Make sure you include several questions because there is a good chance that some of your questions will get answered during the course of the interview.

include information regarding the time frame for a hiring decision or any other issues related to the interview follow-up.

Another crucial step after the interview is sending follow-up correspondence to the agency. Candidates asked to provide additional information such as references or portfolio materials should send those to the agency immediately upon arriving home. It is also proper interview etiquette to send a brief thank-you letter to the organization. The thank-you letter should be sent within three days of the interview to each person involved in the interview process (Beggs, 2001). In the case where more than one person was involved with the interview, the candidate should prepare a slightly different letter for each person.

The thank-you letter should be typed following the accepted format for business letters and consist of three paragraphs (see Figure 8.1). The purpose of the first paragraph is to thank the individual for his or her time as well as the opportunity to learn more about the organization. The second paragraph should be used to restate the candidate's

Figure 8.1

June 1, 2009

Mr. Joe Johnson
Superintendent of Recreation
Smithville Parks and Recreation Department
123 Oak St.
Smithville, NY 55555

Dear Mr. Johnson:

Thank you for taking the time to interview me for the position of Recreation Supervisor with the Smithville Parks and Recreation Department. I was very impressed with your new athletic facilities and your plans to expand the youth sports programs.

As you know, I have five years of experience working with youth sports and athletic facilities. After meeting with you and visiting the facilities, I am excited about the opportunity to apply my experiences to the Smithville Parks and Recreation Department.

Thank you again for this opportunity. I look forward to hearing from you soon.

Sincerely,

*Jane Smith*

Jane Smith

A Sample Thank-You Letter Sent to the Employer Following the Interview

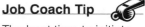

**Job Coach Tip**

The best time to initiate discussion regarding salary and compensation is after a job offer has been made.

interest in the position and to emphasize his or her greatest strengths for the position. The third paragraph is a final thank-you allowing candidates to mention the follow-up procedure, if appropriate. It is becoming an accepted practice to utilize e-mail as an avenue for sending a thank-you letter. Using e-mail can be more time efficient and may also open the door for informal communication with the interviewing agency. Although e-mail may be considered more informal than a letter, it should be prepared using the same three-paragraph format and should be professional and individualized if multiple thank-you e-mails are being sent.

The follow-up letter is important in helping the candidate once again to come to the attention of the interviewer. This is important because the interviewer may be conducting interviews with other candidates or may even be in the decision-making process. Writing a thank-you letter is not only exhibiting good manners and demonstrating professional courtesy, but it is another opportunity for the candidate to reiterate professionalism and writing skills.

## Second Interviews

In some situations, an agency may wish to conduct a second interview, although with budget dollars at a premium at most recreation and leisure service organizations, this does not occur frequently. If a candidate is invited back for a second interview, that means either the agency is very serious about the possibility of hiring the candidate or has narrowed their applicant pool to one or two final candidates.

In some respects, the second interview can be difficult to prepare for. Although candidates have already collected and reviewed information about the organization, they will need to review it once again. The second interview will likely be more job specific and additional job-specific questions may arise than in the first interview. For example, a candidate interviewing for a position running preschool activities may be asked advanced questions such as these:

- What is the normal motor skill development level of a 3-year-old?
- At what age should interactive play replace parallel play?
- At what age do children learn to negotiate during play?
- You have had the opportunity to review our preschool programs. What additional programs do you think we should be offering?

If candidates have done their homework about the position and the agency, they should do well in their second interview. Remember, candidates engaging in a minimal amount of preparation for their first interview will likely be exposed during the second interview.

## Conclusion

The interview serves as an information exchange between candidates and interviewers, and is usually the deciding factor in candidates receiving a job offer. Good interviews involve a great deal of preparation, research, and self-assessment. Additionally, practicing for an interview will help a candidate be prepared to handle different types of questions and interview situations. Candidates should also be prepared to ask the interviewer questions about the organization and the position. Regardless of the type of position for which candidates are interviewing, professional appearance and behavior are just as important as the answers to the interview questions. This chapter provides an overview of the three phases of the interview: preparation, the actual interview, and what to do after the interview. The interview is the opportunity for candidates to sell themselves, so being prepared and conducting oneself professionally is a must!

## References

Beggs, B. A. (2001). *Student internship manual: A guide to completing a professional internship.* Bloomington: Indiana University.

Best-Job-Interviews.com. (2009). *How to handle illegal interview questions.* Retrieved June 1, 2009, from http://www.best-job-interview.com/illegal-interview-questions.html

Darlington, J., & Schuman, N. (2008). *The everything job interview book* (2nd ed.). Avon, MA: Adams Media.

Edginton, C. R., Hudson, S. D., & Lankford, S. V. (2001). *Managing recreation, parks, and leisure services: An introduction.* Champaign, IL: Sagamore Publishing.

Gandel C., & Sterne, H. (2009). Your next job. *Reader's Digest, March,* 98–115.

National Park Service. (n.d.). Quick facts. Retrieved April 25, 2009, from http://www.nps.gov/aboutus/quickfacts.htm

National Sporting Goods Association. (n.d.). Consumer purchases of sporting goods by category. Retrieved May 9, 2009, from http://www.nsga.org/files/public/ConsumerPurchasesofSptGdsbyCategory.pdf

Reeves, E. G. (2009). *Can I wear my nose ring to the interview?* New York: Workman Publishing.

Resumagic.com. (2009). Illegal job questions. Retrieved June 1, 2009, from http://www.resumagic.com/interviews_illegalquestions.html

Ross, C. M., & Blackman, R. J. (1998). Interview preferences: An empirical study of collegiate recreational sport administrators. *NIRSA Journal, 22*(3), 32–37.

Assignments

## Assignment: Mock Interview

Partner with one of your classmates for this exercise and interview each other. Take the time to establish a list of potential job interview questions. Try to cover each of the categories of questions discussed in the chapter.

_____

_____

_____

_____

_____

_____

_____

_____

_____

_____

_____

_____

_____

_____

_____

_____

_____

_____

_____

_____

_____

_____

_____

_____

_____

_____

_____

_____

_____

Once you each have your set of interview questions, schedule a time to meet to interview each other. Prior to interviewing each other, arrange to videotape or audiotape the interviews.

After you have interviewed each other, play back the tape and critique your performance: Were there any surprises when you played back the tape? What would you do differently next time?

_____

_____

_____

_____

_____

_____

_____

_____

_____

_____

_____

_____

_____

_____

_____

_____

_____

_____

_____

_____

_____

_____

_____

_____

_____

_____

_____

_____

Assignments

# The Role and Value of the Internship

Internships have become the standard practical experience for many disciplines and fields, with nearly three quarters of all college students engaging in internships today as compared to 1 in 36 in 1980 (Vault.com, n.d.). Few within the field of recreation and leisure services would question the importance of internship experiences for students entering the field. Whereas in some fields internship experiences are viewed as optional or supplemental experiences, in curricula accredited by NRPA/AALR internships have been required for more than 35 years (Council on Accreditation for Recreation, Park Resources and Leisure Services, 2008). Although internships in recreation and leisure services may vary in terms of number of clock hours, credit hours, and remuneration, the most important dimension is choosing the one that best fits the students' career path. Choosing an internship matching individual strengths and allowing students to gain experiences in areas that are of interest to them will not only create a positive internship experience but will better prepare students for the job market (Huddleston, 2001).

Chapter 9

Visit the Web site for this book to learn more about the organizations and topics covered in this chapter. http://health .jbpub.com/recreationjobs/2e

Whereas many students complete an internship to fulfill their degree requirements, it is crucial for students to recognize the internship also serves an important role in the job search process. Internships provide access to job sources, the opportunity to learn and improve skills, and can even assist students in landing a full-time position (Gault, Redington, & Schlager, 2000). In a study of employment patterns of recreation graduates, Beggs (1995) found that graduates completing internships found their first job more quickly than graduates who did not complete internships. This research finding leads to the question of what is it about an internship that benefits students in landing their first full-time position? The internship in recreation and leisure services plays six key roles in the job search process:

1. Realistic expectations
2. Career goals
3. Competency development
4. Career direction
5. Establishing networks
6. Establishing employability

## Realistic Expectations

It is natural for students to begin their internship experience with expectations that may be far different from the expectations of the internship agency (Knemeyer & Murphy, 2002). The internship experience plays an important role in the transition from college to the professional environment of full-time employment by allowing students to learn first-hand the expectations of their professional colleagues. For example, although students may have proved themselves as outstanding in the classroom, they must still prove their worth when beginning their internships. Some students express disappointment when they are not asked to participate in important projects within the first couple weeks of starting their internship. Rubinstein (2002) provides some valuable advice by stating, "Remember, you're coming in with a blank slate, and you'll have to demonstrate that you're capable of handling the grunt work before you get to do the more substantive and interesting things" (p. 74).

Another expectation that may surprise some students involves the length of time tasks take to be completed. The professionals supervising interns expect interns to work as many hours as necessary to complete a task with quality. As a result, some interns will find themselves working more than 40 hours per week. Remember the expectations of an entry-level professional from Chapter 2: long hours can be expected.

## Career Goals

In preparing to select an internship agency, students should document a career vision statement as well as internship goals and objectives. The professional vision statement helps students to clarify the overall career picture of where they would like to be in the future. Additionally, documenting this vision allows students to determine goals, objectives, and strategies for realizing their vision as they experience professional growth. Students should use their imaginations in thinking about where they see themselves in 5 to 10 years in terms of job responsibilities, functions, and productivity. Although it can be fun to let one's imagination go, students should remain realistic in their vision. Following is an example of a professional vision statement for a student preparing for an internship:

> *I see myself five years from now as one of the professional staff at a community recreation facility in an urban area in the western United States. I will be responsible for developing and coordinating a variety of programs for youth. At the same time, I will be planning for my own nonprofit camp for inner-city at-risk youth.*

Statements of students' goals and objectives help them to clarify those dimensions they want to gain from their internship experience. Further, identifying goals and objectives allows students to communicate more clearly with the agency intern supervisor before and during the internship. Finally, it provides students with criteria to determine whether their needs are being met and indicates whether they are getting the most from their internship experience. The format of the internship goals and objectives statement should list specific goals. Beneath each goal, the specific objectives that must be met to reach the goal should be listed. For example:

1. To gain experience in public relations and promotions in a leisure service organization:
   a. Design and implement a promotion campaign for a special event.
   b. Write newsletters and bulletins for the Internal Relations Department of the organization.
   c. Work in the organization's information services.
2. To gain experience in agency management and administration:
   a. Observe a strategic planning meeting.
   b. Help in organizing the agenda for an agency staff meeting.
   c. Assist in the budget planning of an event.
3. To increase knowledge of agency support services:
   a. Observe and assist in front-line office staff duties.
   b. Observe and gain knowledge of maintenance operations.

Students should submit the professional vision statement and internship goals and objectives to the internship supervisors both on-site and at their institution.

## Competency Development

Students fresh from completing four years of coursework in a recreation curriculum may feel as though they are bursting with knowledge of programming, leadership, marketing, customer service, management, and budgeting. Granted, most recreation curricula provide fundamental knowledge, concepts, and theories related to recreation and leisure services. However, the internship experience provides students opportunities to mold that knowledge into professional competencies as well as develop them further. Based upon the discussion of the self-assessment in Chapter 1, students can identify those competency areas where they are strong as well as those still needing work. Students should then choose an internship experience that will help them to learn and grow in those competency areas where they still need work. The goal by the completion of the internship is for students to have fine-tuned competencies learned in their coursework and be better prepared to enter full-time employment (Cook, Parker, & Pettijohn, 2004; Knemeyer & Murphy, 2002).

**Time Out**

The vision statement allows students to think about where they want to be professionally in 5–10 years.

**Time Out**

Don't fall behind on your paperwork! Internship reports should be submitted the week they are due.

# Career Direction

By the time students select their internship they should have a fairly good idea of which area of recreation and leisure services they want to work in. Many students reaffirm the direction of their career through their internship experience. Between 60% and 70% of graduates in recreation and leisure services enter a career directly related to their internship and area of study (Beggs, 1995). Further, in several studies involving preferences of recreation professionals in a position to hire entry-level professionals, a majority indicated the candidates' internship site affected their hiring decision (Ross, 1998; Ross & Zabriskie, 2001; Young & Ross, 2003). This finding underscores the importance of the internship not only for students to gain experience, but also in the search for a job.

On the other hand, it is through their internship experience that some students realize the area of recreation on which they have focused is not the best career path for them. This is an equally important revelation and learning opportunity for students, and is not necessarily a cause for alarm. Students in these situations should still learn all they can from their internship agency. Once they have completed their internship, however, they will need to reassess and redirect their career path to the area of recreation and leisure services they find most interesting.

# Establishing Networks

Internships provide an excellent opportunity for students to build or expand their professional networks. Interns should get to know as many other employees as possible during their internship because this will extend their network and make their experience more enjoyable. If interns are invited to organizational social events or professional workshops and seminars, they should attend as a way to meet more people and show sincere interest in their agency. Rubinstein (2002) puts it this way, "You never know how the contacts you make will end up helping you later on" (p. 79).

# Establishing Employability

A good internship experience can help students establish their reputation as capable professionals suitable for full-time employment in the field (Jewel, 2001). A positive experience may even lead to a situation where the agency wants to hire the intern at the completion of the internship experience. Although most agencies will not have openings available for interns completing their experiences, if interns have established themselves as good employees, the agency may recommend them to other agencies that do have job openings. Former interns should make an effort to stay in touch with their site supervisor or other people at their internship agency just in case a full-time position does become available. Think of the competitive advantage this provides over

**Keys to Job Search Success**

Doing great work on your internship will do you no good if no one knows about it. Don't brag or flaunt, but make sure people know what you're working on, the skills you are gaining, and how you're creating value for the organization.

Mesh

unknown candidates because former interns understand the work and have already proven themselves to be reliable employees who can get along with others.

# Making the Most of Internships

By now students should recognize the importance of their internship to the job search process. Most of the steps necessary for landing a good internship are the same for landing a good full-time position. Students should complete a self-assessment prior to beginning their search for an internship followed up with thoroughly researching those agencies with which they would like to intern. Resumes, letters of correspondence, and interviewing skills are essentially the same for an intern candidate as for the full-time candidate. Even the considerations of accepting the offer are similar for the intern. So, not only does the internship provide students with professional experience, but the process of landing an internship provides students great practice in the steps of the job search process.

There are specific steps, however, that students can take to make the most of their internship experience and thereby enhance their search for full-time employment in recreation and leisure services.

## Have a Plan

Although the career vision statement and internship goals generally guide interns in the selection of their internship agency and site, interns should think specifically about what they want to get out of their internship. Students should take time to think about the kinds of projects or contributions interns can make to the agency, the skills they would like to gain, and specifically what they would like to learn about the organization. If it is possible, interns should visit their agency one or two times before starting work so that they can meet people and get a sense of the work environment. This is also a good time to discuss with the site supervisor in more detail what the intern will be doing over the next few months. In this meeting, students should share their internship goals and ask whether their aspirations are realistic. If an on-site visit is not possible, interns should set up a phone call with their site supervisor. This action sends the message that the intern is serious about the internship and wants to make the most of the experience.

## Make the Most of Menial Tasks

No matter how great the internship experience is, it is likely interns will be asked to accomplish "gofer-like" tasks. Rubinstein (2002) states: "Be prepared to develop intimate relationships with photocopiers, fax machines, and filing cabinets" (p. 75). Rather than viewing these tasks as mundane or degrading, interns should view them as opportunities to interact with a variety of people. Part of what is valuable about an internship is understanding what the day-to-day operation is like at the recreation agency. Accomplishing these menial tasks will help interns demonstrate that they are responsible and reliable. In turn, when more substantial projects come up, professionals are more likely to involve interns who they know will complete the project in a responsible and reliable fashion.

## Take Initiative

Once interns have been on-site for a couple of weeks, some may feel they have the basics handled and can glide through the rest of their internship fairly easily. Although

**Job Coach Tip**

When working with the agency to select a project, try to come up with an idea that will challenge your skills and improve your experience.

**Did You Know...**

The average attendance for a weekend special event is 222,000.

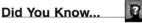
International Festival and Events Association

it is human nature to gravitate toward a routine, interns should fight that natural tendency and push themselves to learn as much as possible. To make the most of the experience, interns must take initiative, volunteer to help with more difficult projects, and even suggest ideas to their site supervisor. Although some interns may feel it is not their place to make suggestions, the worst that can happen is their supervisor says no. In the best-case scenario, however, they may find themselves in charge of their own project or program.

## Check In Often

Generally, professionals assigned as site supervisors for interns are in those positions because they want to be. These recreation professionals usually like their jobs and are willing to share their knowledge with interns wanting to learn. Interns should take advantage of this by making every effort to check in with their site supervisor on a regular basis. Discussions can focus upon progress of the internship, what the intern is working on, what the site supervisor is working on, and whether the intern can help in any way. If the pace of the organization is hectic, interns may want to take the initiative to schedule a regular meeting once a week or so. By suggesting this to their site supervisor, interns will be well on their way to gaining the respect of their new professional colleagues.

## Ask for Assistance

Although interns are often referred to as the "new kids" within the organization, they must not be afraid to ask for help when it is needed. Even when they make mistakes, interns cannot be reluctant to ask for help in learning what went wrong. Remember, the primary purpose of the internship is to learn, so the worst thing interns can do is refuse to admit to errors or ask for help. Everyone in the organization probably remembers when they were just beginning their careers, so they are prepared for the typical mistakes interns make. Interns should ask questions throughout their internship experience. In fact, the professionals working in the agency expect interns to ask questions. Most professionals in recreation and leisure services do not mind sharing their experience and knowledge with interns or young professionals. A word of caution, however—interns should not evolve into a nuisance. They should ask questions, but make sure the time is appropriate and convenient for the professional asked.

## Dress Appropriately

Students should determine the appropriate dress code for their internship agency. In some cases, interns may be given staff shirts or uniforms to wear and if that is the case, attire is not that big of an issue. In other cases, interns will be in an environment where professional dress is required. Dressing professionally establishes an image of credibility along with reflecting well upon both the organization and the intern. Regardless of the situation, interns need to learn the appropriate attire and then check to make sure their wardrobe reflects the appropriate look prior to the start of the internship. The internship agency may also have grooming policies. Again, prior to beginning the internship, students should check into these types of details and be prepared to meet the guidelines of any existing policies.

---

**Be Alert!**

Even if the internship agency doesn't have a job for you after the internship, don't burn bridges. They may keep tabs on you for future employment.

---

**Did You Know...**

The job outlook for hotel/lodging managers will provide average job growth and very good job opportunities because of steady growth in travel. Those seeking jobs at hotels with the highest level of guest services will face strong competition.

**Bureau of Labor Statistics**

### Manage Time

Students must be prepared to make adjustments to their schedule to account for the hours of the internship. The internship is just like a job requiring a full workday and a full workweek. It may involve starting at an early hour and/or working weekends. Habits interns may have grown accustomed to in college will likely require some adjusting. Managing time by keeping a schedule of activities and meetings becomes a necessity for interns to be viewed as a success.

### Find a Mentor

Finding a great mentor is not something that happens for every intern completing an internship. If interns do not form a close relationship with their site supervisor, they should not worry. Mentoring relationships do occasionally take root as the result of an internship, but certainly not frequently. A close mentorship is a lot about personalities, so to force that sort of relationship could end in disaster. Interns should enter their internship with an open mind, be accepting of advice from their site supervisor and simply see how the professional relationship grows. Some professionals stay in touch with their internship site and the people there long after their internships are over.

## Conclusion

The value of the internship cannot be underestimated in the job search process. Internships are not only a training ground for students, but they also provide access to job sources and the development of professional networks. By selecting an internship that matches their career interests, interns can gain greater insight into the realistic expectations of the workforce and better determine direction and goals. In addition, internships provide hands-on experiences to enhance coursework and provide confidence in an intern's abilities.

The job search process has been called a linear process because a candidate must complete each step before moving onto the next. Mastering and completing an internship is yet another step in the job search process, but also one that serves as a link between students' academic experiences and their professional careers. It has been said that the best way to make a future link is to build the current link as strong as possible so that it connects securely to the next link (Donovan & Garnett, 2001). This analogy applies directly to the internship as a crucial piece of the job search process. Students preparing for internships and students already in internships should make the most of their internship experience and grow from it. This chapter focuses on using the internship not only as a link to one's career, but also as a forerunner to the job search process.

**Job Coach Tip**

Make sure that you have the proper wardrobe for your internship. Dressing inappropriately will leave a bad impression.

**Did You Know...**

Turnover for many cruise positions is very high, but most cruise lines get thousands of applications weekly, so matching your skills to a ship's needs is one key to getting a job.

Garrison

 **Keys to Job Search Success**

Utilize all of your resources when researching internship opportunities. There are numerous Internet sites that list internship openings that are easy to access. However, the best source may be the internship files that your university internship coordinator maintains, so check with them as well.

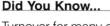

# References

Beggs, B. A. (1995). *A follow-up study of employment patterns of graduates of the Department of Recreation at Southern Illinois University.* Unpublished master's thesis, Southern Illinois University, Carbondale, IL.

Bureau of Labor Statistics, U.S. Department of Labor. (2007, December 18). Lodging managers. In *Occupational outlook handbook, 2008–09 edition.* Retrieved June 13, 2009, from http://www.bls.gov/oco/ocos015.htm

Cook, S. J., Parker, R.S., & Pettijohn, C. E. (2004). The perceptions of interns: A longitudinal case study. *Journal of Education for Business, 79*(3), 179–185.

Council on Accreditation for Recreation, Park Resources and Leisure Services. (2008, October). *Learning outcomes standards and assessment.* Retrieved June 13, 2009, from http://www.nrpa.org/coa/default.aspx?documentId=6161

Donovan, C. P., & Garnett, J. (2001). *Internships for dummies.* New York: Hungry Minds.

Garrison, L. (2009). Cruise ship jobs: The hotel department: Working in the hotel department of a cruise ship. About.com. Retrieved June 13, 2009, from http://cruises.about.com/cs/cruisejobs/a/hoteljobs.htm

Gault, J., Redington, J., & Schlager, T. (2000). Undergraduate business internships and career success: Are they related? *Journal of Marketing Education, 22*(1), 45–53.

Huddleston, E. (2001). Real-life lessons: Internship programs help put knowledge into practice. *Athletic Business, 25*(11), 34–36.

International Association of Amusement Parks and Attractions. Amusement park and attractions statistics. Retrieved May 2, 2009, from http://www.iaapa.org

International Festival and Events Association. (n.d.). *About Us.* Retrieved April 2, 2005, from http://www.ifea.com

International Health, Racquet and Sportsclub Association. (2009). Consumer research. Retrieved May 5, 2009, from http://cms.ihrsa/org

Jewel, D. L. (2001). *Professional practice manual: Experiential education in leisure services, recreation, parks, and tourism* (3rd ed.). Springfield, IL: Charles C. Thomas.

Knemeyer, A. M., & Murphy, P. R. (2002). Logistics internships: Employer and student perspectives. *International Journal of Physical Distribution and Logistics Management, 32*(2), 135–152.

Mesh, A. (2007). The 5 best pieces of job/internship advice you will ever get. *Cornell Business.* Retrieved June 13, 2009, from http://www.cornellbusiness.com/home/index.cfm?event=displayArticlePrinterFriendly&uStory_id=b0b1eaa0-1fe6-47ce-bf5f-555fd680943c

National Park Service. (2005). *National Park Service.* Retrieved April 2, 2005, from http://www.nps.gov

Ross, C. M. (1998). Resume content preferences: An empirical study of collegiate recreational sports administrators. *NIRSA Journal, 22*(2), 17–21.

Ross, C. M., & Zabriskie, R. B. (2001). An examination of resume preferences among therapeutic recreation professionals. *Annual in Therapeutic Recreation, 10,* 33–44.

Rubinstein, E. (2002). *Scoring a great internship.* Chicago: Independent Publishers Group.

Travel Industry Association of America. (2001). The shopping traveler. Retrieved May 2, 2009, from http://www.tia.org/pubs/pubs.asp?PublicationID=89

Vault.com (n.d.). How to take advantage of your internship. Retrieved June 13, 2009, from http://www.vault.com/wps/portal/asean/!ut/p/c5/04_
SB8K8xLLM9MSSzPy8xBz9CP0os3gzQ0u_YHMPIwN_E3dHA0-
LQHc3C19Pd69QE6B8JJI8UA6I3T2cnd1DXY1CTQwJ6A4H2YdfP0jeAAdw
NND388jPTdWP1I8yx22PqX6IfqSTfkFuhEGWSaIjADZisCo!/dl3/d3/
L3dJVkkvd0xNQUJvQWtnQSEhLzRCbjR0V0F5SUlBIS82XzYxOU5TN0gy
ME80R0EwSThRR0Y4TUlHM0k0LzNfQ0dBSDQ3TDAwTzJWMDAyTjVTU
TBVUzMwSDUvOnlkYWQzMDMzMDAwMQ!!/?WCM_GLOBAL_CONT
EXT=/wps/wcm/connect/Vault_Content_Library/articles_site/articles/
internships/how+to+take+advantage+of+your+internship

Young, S. J., & Ross, C. M. (2003, December). Teaching resume effectiveness: Results from a recreation administrators' study. *LARNet: The Cyber Journal of Applied Leisure and Recreation Research.* Retrieved June 1, 2005, from http://larnet.org/2003-3.html

## Assignment: Internship Search

Your assignment is to identify three internships that are of interest to you. However, before you can do that, you must determine what your priorities are in selecting an internship: quality experience, remuneration, or geographic location.

1. **Address your requirements for each of these criteria and determine which is of the greatest importance to you.**

   _____

   _____

   _____

   _____

   _____

   _____

   _____

2. **Use your job/internship search skills to find three actual internships that meet your highest priority.**

   _____

   _____

   _____

   _____

   _____

   _____

   _____

Assignments

Assignments

# Evaluating the Job Offer

After hours of researching organizations and positions, preparing cover letters, perfecting the resume, traveling, staying in hotels to interview the next day, and successfully completing the interview, the candidate finally receives a job offer. This is wonderful news; being offered the job is the goal for which all the preceding steps have been taken. Yet, with the job offer comes an entirely new set of considerations for candidates to take, and in some ways, this point in the job search process can be quite stressful. How do candidates know if this job is really right for them? What is really important in a job? Are the terms of the offer fair? Should negotiations for a higher salary and more benefits be the next step? Is the organization a good fit for the candidate? Quite often, these are the questions racing through candidates' minds when they finally receive an offer. Although these are tough questions deserving candidates' honest thought and consideration, solid preparation for this point in the job search process can make receiving an offer much less stressful. This chapter addresses the questions and issues candidates face when determining whether to accept the offer of a job. Although there are many questions demanding answers at this point in the process, there are three facets of evaluating the job offer candidates should contemplate:

- Establishing priorities
- Checking for a good fit
- Determining negotiable terms

**Chapter 10**

Visit the Web site for this book to learn more about the organizations and topics covered in this chapter. **http://health .jbpub.com/recreationjobs/2e**

Be prepared for the job offer! Establish your priorities prior to receiving an offer. It will make it easier to negotiate and you'll end up happier with the final offer.

# Establishing Priorities

When candidates receive a job offer, it can be very tempting to accept on the spot without taking time to think about all the aspects involved. Candidates should never feel pressured to accept an offer immediately because most employers want candidates to think about it for at least a day and expect them to take some time before responding. Although there are highly successful candidates who have accepted positions on the spot and been quite satisfied with their choice, an instantaneous decision like this is more likely to result in dissatisfaction later on for the employee. So, prior to accepting an offer, and actually before the offer is even received, candidates should determine what aspects of the job are most important to them. Establishing and understanding priorities will make it easier for candidates to evaluate their offer, decide whether negotiations are necessary, and decide whether they will accept the position (Tullier, 1999).

The range of features in a job offer varies widely and can be overwhelming at times. The following list reflects the most common features candidates should consider in establishing their priorities:

- *Salary:* Making a specific amount of money may be important if candidates are already employed or candidates know they will be incurring certain costs in accepting the position.

- *Insurance and retirement:* Most recreation and leisure services agencies provide a benefits package including health coverage, life insurance, and retirement. For most candidates these features are a high priority.

- *Job security:* Some politically sensitive positions or those based on high standards for performance do not always offer a high degree of job security. This is an aspect that deserves serious thought by the candidate.

- *Work schedule:* Candidates may want to work a certain schedule based on personal or job-related issues.

- *Job matching personal interests:* In most cases, candidates want a job they are good at and in which they have an interest. To some candidates this is even more important than salary.

- *Agency philosophy:* If agency and candidate do not share similar philosophies, the result will likely be dissatisfaction for both. For example, if the candidate has a different philosophical approach to customer service than the organization does, the differences may not be resolved easily.

When you receive a job offer, take some time to consider the offer before responding.

- *Organizational structure:* The level of the position within the organization, to whom the position reports, job supervision of the position, and how decisions are made within the organization are all important considerations.

- *Job scope:* Responsibilities accompanying the job are often motivating factors for seeking a specific position.

- *Challenging work:* In addition to matching a candidate's interests, a challenging position can be rewarding. Many candidates change jobs to find a more challenging position.

- *Opportunities for advancement:* Career advancement within an organization is appealing to many candidates. Not being able to move up can lead to dissatisfaction with the job or to higher employee turnover.

- *Opportunities for professional development:* Many candidates value opportunities to join professional organizations, attend professional conferences, and develop themselves through specialized training or certifications.

- *Current staff:* Having the opportunity to work with a well-known or respected professional can be an incentive to some candidates.

- *Matching career goals:* A position congruent with a candidate's career goals should be a higher priority than one that does not match future goals.

- *Future of the organization:* The prospect of working with a growing organization or one developing new facilities may be a priority to some candidates.

- *Geographic location:* Quite often, candidates apply for positions that have already met their geographic requirements. Location is almost always a high priority in accepting a job.

- *Facilities:* State-of-the-art offices, facilities, and equipment are like test driving a new vehicle—once experienced, it is hard to go back to driving an old clunker! Once candidates are accustomed to newer facilities, office environments, and technology, it can be difficult to settle for less.

- *Organizational culture:* Organizational culture can be difficult for candidates to measure. Regardless, all prospective employees would prefer to work in a positive environment and get along with coworkers.

- *Travel:* Some candidates may seek travel in a job, while others prefer to be in a position where travel is not required.

- *Degree of independence:* Being able to work independently and make decisions is important to many candidates. On the flip side, some candidates prefer more guidance and someone else making decisions.

- *Prestige:* The title of the position or the agency name can carry with it a certain amount of prestige, and may be important to some candidates.

- *Additional benefits:* Are there additional benefits available, such as tuition reimbursement for pursuit of higher degrees, or club memberships, or a company car? Many employers offer perks including casual dress code, flextime, on-site day care, and compensation time (National Association of Colleges and Employers, 2001).

In identifying those features of the job that are most important, candidates should develop a complete list for each job they have received offers for, or from which they expect to receive offers. Once this list has been established, candidates can determine the order of these priorities in terms of importance. There are three methods candidates can choose from in sorting their priorities for each job. Regardless of the method candidates choose, this exercise will help them prepare in responding to a job offer.

**Did You Know...**

In 2007, 54.5 million people visited a casino in the United States.

American Gaming Association

### Keys to Job Search Success

It's important that candidates conduct an extensive assessment of what is important to them. This may include personal and professional issues. Regardless, prioritizing this list is a priority!

One method of determining individual job priorities is to list the most important and least important priorities in the job. For instance, if geographical location and salary are of great importance to the candidate, those features should be listed on the most important list. If work schedule or opportunities for advancement are of little concern to the candidate, those features would be placed on the least important list. Establishing what is and is not important to the candidate not only determines if the job matches the candidate's priorities, it also assists the candidate in determining what terms of the offer may need to be further negotiated.

A second prioritizing method candidates can take is to rank all of the priorities on the list from most important to least important (Harris, 2001). If candidates identify 25 items they feel belong on their priority list, then they would rank the priorities from 1 through 25. This method provides candidates some differentiation between the priorities they consider most important.

Another method of understanding the priorities that are important to candidates is to rate each priority item on a scale of 1–10 (Tullier, 1999). This method will allow candidates to see all of the priorities they consider important (those rated at 7 or above) as well as the priorities of less importance (those at 4 or below). A challenge in using this method is when candidates rate all items high and therefore have difficulty determining the lesser priorities. To avoid this error it is important for candidates to be brutally honest with themselves in rating their priorities.

One final consideration candidates should take in establishing their priorities involves making sure there are no "red flags" surrounding the position or organization. This is a good time for candidates to reexamine their research on the organization and reflect on their interview. It is also the time to do a final research check on the organization by searching on the Internet or library databases. If candidates have not already done so, they should utilize their network or professional contacts to learn more about the reputation of the organization, its employees, and the position. In many instances, if an organization has had a difficult time keeping a position filled, it can raise concerns about the work environment and the organization in general. This can also create a situation whereby the organization has developed a negative reputation. If that is the case, the candidate would be wise to take this information into consideration. On the other hand, by doing this one final research step, candidates may discover the organization has an excellent reputation. Regardless of the outcome, engaging in this final check can play a crucial role in the candidate's decision to accept or decline the offer.

## Checking for a Good Fit

In evaluating a job offer, candidates want to obtain the best deal possible, as well as make sure the offer received is fair. This step in the evaluation process builds from the first step of establishing priorities and focuses specifically on checking the fair market

 **Keys to Job Search Success**

A wide variety of issues may be important to a candidate when interviewing for a job. If candidates conduct quality research and assess their priorities in the early stages of the job search process, then evaluating a job offer will be a much easier task.

value of the position. In this step candidates must not only determine whether the offer is fair, but that it also matches their priorities established in step 1.

The package offered will vary based on the level of the position, geographic location, job responsibilities, and type of agency. At this stage of the process, candidates should have a good idea of the fair market value for this type of job. If this information is not known, candidates can obtain greater insight by speaking with their professional contacts or by checking the lists of salaries in the *Occupational Outlook Handbook* published by the U.S. Department of Labor. Another dimension of determining the fairness of the offer is to calculate the cost of living for the particular geographic region or municipality of the position. A salary calculator is available on the Web; it compares the cost of living for most cities in the United States as well as Canada and some international cities. This measurement device helps candidates to determine the value of their salary in a particular geographic region as well as assists in developing a fair and objective salary request.

Based upon their list of priorities, candidates should also prepare a desired package for the position. The desired package is a listing of what the candidate wants in the job offer and can be accomplished by completing a job package worksheet (see Figure 10.1). This worksheet requires candidates to be objective and fair in determining what they are seeking in terms of salary, benefits, work schedule, job responsibilities, professional development opportunities, perks, and any other significant priorities specific to their needs. Candidates should complete the Desired column of this worksheet prior to receiving the offer. Once the offer has been made, then candidates should complete the second column of the worksheet including actual figures and information from the offer. The last column of the worksheet is a checklist for candidates to indicate whether the offer is acceptable in each priority category or whether they wish to negotiate that item.

The last dimension of determining a good fit of the offer to the candidate's priorities is to compare the offer to the list of important priorities. It is common for candidates to adjust their priorities as they critique the offer. Sometimes the reality of the offer makes candidates more aware of what is really important to them (Tullier, 1999). For instance, the candidate may have listed salary high on her priority list and work schedule at the bottom of the list. In the instance where the salary is actually higher than what the candidate expects, but the hours include weekends and evenings, she may decide that salary is of lesser importance and work schedule is of greater importance. If the actual job offer fails to meet the candidate's priorities or is below the desired package created, the candidate will then want to consider negotiating for a better offer.

## Determining Negotiable Terms

It is rare that a job is accepted without any discussion or negotiation taking place, but this does not mean that all job offers in recreation and leisure services are negotiable. With many government-funded leisure service agencies, there may not be flexibility in salary and benefit packages, yet there may be some flexibility in regard to job responsibilities or work schedule. For recreation positions in commercial and nonprofit settings, employers might have more flexibility in negotiating salary, benefits, and additional perks. Negotiating can feel somewhat risky, especially for candidates who really want the job, but to gain the best possible package candidates must be willing to try. Like any other situation in the job search process, there are pros and cons to negotiating a job offer. The disadvantages seem obvious in that the employer might reject any attempts at negotiating, or in the worst-case scenario, withdraw the offer. For candidates with

**Did You Know...**

It is an important fact to note that many of the personnel on board a cruise ship are not working for the cruise line directly but for concessionaires, or subcontractors, whose company contracts with the cruise line to provide certain services for a percentage of the profits.

Garrison

**Job Coach Tip**

When discussing the start date of your new job, negotiate a reasonable amount of time necessary to help you make a smooth transition into your new position.

Figure 10.1

Job Title: _____

|  | Desired | Actual | Negotiate |
|---|---|---|---|
| Salary | _____ | _____ | _____ |
| Vehicle | _____ | _____ | _____ |
| Laptop | _____ | _____ | _____ |
| Schedule | _____ | _____ | _____ |
| Start date | _____ | _____ | _____ |
| Vacation | _____ | _____ | _____ |
| Relocation package | _____ | _____ | _____ |
| Professional development | _____ | _____ | _____ |
| Perks | | | |
| _____ | _____ | _____ | _____ |
| _____ | _____ | _____ | _____ |
| _____ | _____ | _____ | _____ |
| Job Scope | | | |
| _____ | _____ | _____ | _____ |
| _____ | _____ | _____ | _____ |
| _____ | _____ | _____ | _____ |
| Other Priorities | | | |
| _____ | _____ | _____ | _____ |
| _____ | _____ | _____ | _____ |
| _____ | _____ | _____ | _____ |

Job Package Worksheet

**Job Coach Tip**

Perks such as casual dress code, day care, and flextime have become important tools in negotiation.

**Be Alert!**

An employer is expecting you to negotiate your salary, so they may make an initial offer that is low. Be prepared to counter with a dollar figure that is higher and fair.

a tendency to settle for whatever is offered, the disadvantage of not negotiating could lead to feelings of resentment toward the organization later on. This is especially true if after they are hired candidates learn they could have negotiated a better package, or new hires after them negotiate better starting packages. The advantage to negotiation is also obvious in that candidates might be surprised at what can be gained simply by asking.

Candidates do not want to attempt negotiation of every item in the offer, rather they should focus on the items of greatest priority and the package as a whole. The question most people think of when negotiation is mentioned deals with salary. Is the salary negotiable? This is a common question and one the employer is probably expecting (Adams, 2001). Although candidates want the highest salary possible, they must remain objective and realistic. Candidates should be prepared to provide a fair salary figure that they can justify should the employer ask them. Related to salary, there may be an opportunity to negotiate overtime or compensation pay as a part of the offer.

Salary is not the only part of the offer that can be negotiated. Candidates may seek to negotiate the days of the week or the times of the day they work. Professional development is another area that could be addressed in negotiations. If candidates want opportunities to attend professional conferences, or to maintain their professional membership affiliations, they could negotiate that the agency covers their expenses in lieu of a higher salary.

Beyond those items previously identified as negotiable, other aspects of the job that may be negotiated are the following:

- *Start date:* The job start date is negotiable with almost any job. If the candidate is finishing an internship, taking classes, or is leaving another position, most likely the hiring agency understands that a later start date may be necessary. Candidates should be reasonable and in most cases their request will be accepted by the agency.

- *Relocation expenses:* Relocation packages range from candidates paying up-front expenses and getting reimbursed (or partially reimbursed) to all-inclusive packages where the agency handles everything. The all-inclusive packages are usually provided for senior-level executives. Even if a relocation package is not offered, candidates may wish to negotiate it into the deal. Typical negotiable components of relocation are:

  - Cash relocation allowances for miscellaneous expenses

  - Food allowances or per diems

  - Moving expenses (cash or professional packers and movers)

  - Storage of household goods

  - Travel expenses to new location (including air fares, mileage, meals, hotels)

  - Hotel expenses

  If the agency offers a relocation package, but the candidate does not need it, then he or she may be able to negotiate other issues such as salary or professional development expenses.

- *Merit raise:* A merit raise is usually paid out annually as compensation for a job well done. Sometimes, these raises are discretionary, and sometimes there is a well-defined scale. As with salary, merit raises are sometimes negotiable and sometimes not.

- *Job scope:* There are some agencies where jobs are highly structured and the scope of the job is restricted. In many leisure service agencies, there is some flexibility in job responsibilities. If candidates have strong preferences for certain responsibilities that are reasonable for the position, they should be discuss them during negotiations.

**Job Coach Tip**

It's a mistake to focus only on base salary when negotiating the job offer.

**Time Out**

Negotiate a start date that will allow you the time you need to get your affairs in order.

 **Keys to Job Search Success**

When negotiating salary it is important to have an understanding of fair market value. By using resources available in the library and on the Internet, a candidate can determine what a fair salary is and use this information in negotiation.

**Time Out**

The responsibilities of the position may require you to work evenings and weekends. Make sure you negotiate your work schedule if this is an issue.

- *Vacation time:* Vacation time is sometimes negotiable. Larger public agencies tend to have more rigid policies that are nonnegotiable. Be cautious requesting additional vacation time as it may indicate to the agency that candidates are more interested in time off than the job.

- *Vehicle:* Based on the nature of the position, a vehicle is an item that can be negotiated. If candidates are negotiating for a position where travel is required, then negotiating a vehicle or travel allowance is reasonable. If the agency has already offered a vehicle as part of the package, candidates may be able to negotiate the type of vehicle. Vehicle negotiation rarely takes place for entry-level positions.

- *Work schedule:* Leisure service agencies are often flexible when it comes to work schedules because many programs and activities take place in the evening and on weekends. As a result, candidates may be able to negotiate the start of their workday at noon or to have certain weekdays off.

- *High-tech equipment:* Today, electronic gadgets are often part of the job. If high-tech equipment is not included in the job offer, candidates can negotiate the use of a cell phone, laptop computer, home computer, personal digital assistant, and any other type of equipment that can be justified to assist them in the job.

- *Tuition reimbursement:* Many agencies will reimburse employees for taking college courses. Some agencies have an annual limit, and others require a commitment to stay with the agency for a specific length of time after completing a course. Furthermore, some organizations require employees to earn a minimum grade before authorizing reimbursement. If the agency does not offer a tuition reimbursement plan, candidates can negotiate this benefit.

**Job Coach Tip**

Make sure you understand the total package involved in the job offer. This will make it easier to negotiate and help you get the benefits and perks you desire.

There are some issues that are not negotiable and candidates are wasting their time requesting changes to these items. For example, retirement is not negotiable as most agencies have a retirement system that applies to all full-time employees. Medical and life insurance are two other nonnegotiable items. Although employees may have flexibility in the options they choose for both their medical and life insurance, organizations offer the same basic packages to all employees.

## How to Negotiate

Candidates can easily identify and consider the items they would like to negotiate, but it can actually be more difficult to embark on the negotiations. Before negotiating, it is very important to make sure the complete offer is understood. It is perfectly acceptable to ask the employer for some time to review the offer or discuss it with family, and in most situations the employer will grant that time. The amount of time varies by position, with some candidates receiving as little as 24 hours, while in other cases candidates may have up to a week to respond. If the employer does not provide a time frame, it is in the best interest of candidates to review the offer and get back to the employer within 24 hours or as soon as possible after the offer is made (Beggs & Elkins, 1997).

Negotiating is a skill that requires candidates to do the following:

1. *Be prepared:* Know the offer, understand priorities, and aim for negotiating the items that are of the greatest individual importance.

2. ***Remain calm and patient:*** Do not get too excited or upset during the process and jump at the employer's first response.

3. ***Be fair:*** Know what the position should pay and what the package should include while remaining objective and reasonable in making requests.

4. ***Be flexible:*** Candidates should be willing to give in order to get what is most important to them, recognizing they are not likely to get everything requested.

Once the terms of the offer have been successfully negotiated, and both sides feel they are receiving the best end of the deal, it is typical for candidates to accept the offer. However, it is possible at this point in the process that there are a few items upon which agreement cannot be reached. If these items are of enough importance to candidates, and they feel unable to accept the job, then they should inform the employer that they must decline the offer. This should be done over the phone and with a letter. When corresponding to reject a job offer, a candidate should be polite, professional, and to the point. If possible, the candidate does not want to burn any bridges when declining an offer.

The process is nearly done when candidate and employer have negotiated the deal successfully. However, just because there is a verbal agreement on the offer does not mean the deal is complete. To avoid any disputes about the offer, it is important for the employer to confirm the negotiated offer in writing. If employers do not take the initiative to do this, then it is perfectly acceptable for candidates to request it. This is a common practice and candidates should not be timid about making this request (Adams, 2001; Tullier, 1999). Once candidates have the offer in writing, they can congratulate themselves on their new position!

**Job Coach Tip**
Successfully negotiating the offer may be valued by the agency as a skill you bring to the job.

## Conclusion

Receiving a job offer can be an exciting moment in the candidate's life. However, before accepting that offer, it should be evaluated to determine if it meets the priorities and requirements of the candidate. If it does not, a candidate may wish to negotiate some of the terms of the offer. By being prepared, patient, fair, and flexible, candidates can work through the negotiation process in a professional manner. Once terms of the offer have been successfully negotiated and agreed upon by both the organization and candidate, it is necessary to confirm the offer in writing. When candidates have the offer in writing, they officially have a new job!

**Job Coach Tip**
Get it in writing! The deal is not done until you have the offer in writing.

 **Keys to Job Search Success**

Be patient when negotiating the deal. The employer would like you to jump at their first offer. Take some time to digest the offer before responding.

## References

Adams, B. (2001). *The everything job interview book.* Avon, MA: Adams Media.

American Gaming Association. (2008). 2008 state of the states, the AGA survey of casino entertainment. Retrieved May 9, 2009, from http://www.americangaming.org/survey/index.cfm

Beggs, B. A., & Elkins, D. J. (1997, April). *Marketing yourself for the first job and portfolio development*. Paper presented at the The John Allen Symposium. Southern Illinois University, Carbondale, IL.

Garrison, L. (2009). *Working in the hotel department of a cruise ship*. About.com. Retrieved June 13, 2009, from http://cruises.about.com/cs/cruisejobs/a/hoteljobs.htm

Harris, M. B. (2001). *Choosing among job offers*. Job Choices, Diversity Edition 2001, 80–83.

National Association of Colleges and Employers. (2001). *The job market for graduates with nontechnical degrees*. Job Choices in Business 2001, 7–9.

Themed Entertainment Association. (2008). Themed Entertainment Association/ Economics Research Associates' attraction attendance report 2008. Retrieved April 25, 2009, from http://www.themett.com/TEAERA2008.pdf

Tullier, M. (1999). *The unofficial guide to acing the interview*. New York: Wiley.

# Assignment: Let's Make a Deal

Listed below are two job offers that you have just received after completing your internship. After reviewing each one, determine what terms you need more information about and items that you want to negotiate. Be sure to use the job package worksheet (Figure 10.1) while doing this exercise. What item is your highest priority to negotiate for each offer?

## Offer 1

You have been offered a Recreation Supervisor position with your hometown parks and recreation department. The starting salary is $27,500 and includes a standard benefits package. In addition, you will get a laptop computer and $1000 a year toward professional development. They have also offered you the opportunity to start immediately following your internship.

_____

_____

_____

_____

_____

_____

_____

_____

_____

_____

## Offer 2

You have been offered a Recreation Supervisor position in Big City, USA, which is about an 8-hour drive from your family. However, the scope of the position is exactly what you have been looking for. The salary for the job is $25,000 and includes standard benefits. There is no money for professional development, and you will have a desktop computer in your office (no laptop). The position starts approximately 3 months after the completion of your internship.

_____

_____

_____

_____

_____

_____

_____

_____

_____

**Chapter 10** Evalutating the Job Offer

Do you think you'll end up working in your hometown or Big City, USA?
Explain your reasoning.

_____

_____

_____

_____

_____

_____

_____

_____

_____

_____

_____

_____

_____

_____

_____

_____

_____

_____

_____

_____

_____

_____

_____

_____

_____

_____

Assignments

# Navigating the Transition from College to Professional Life

One of the toughest transitions in most people's lives is from the schoolroom to the workplace. High school and college graduates are primed for this jolting change with lofty well-meant speeches projecting bright hopes for the future and spouting wise counsel about how to make it in the business world and what pitfalls to avoid. They are, in effect, given a healthy dose of inspiration, a hearty pat on the back, and then encouraged to go out into the world and make it—on your own—because that's what it boils down to in the end.

No question about it. Of course, there's no other way. Venturing out into the world is just that. But no amount of preparation, however well intended, could achieve a smooth and easy transition from the accustomed routine of regularly scheduled classes and class work to the hard competitive world of job seeking and, once that is achieved, beating out coworkers for the promotions, preferred assignments, and other perks associated with getting ahead. (Dreyer, 1992, p. 17)

Every year, hundreds of thousands of students graduate from college and begin their first professional position. For many, it is a dream come true. Suddenly, the last 16 years of sitting in a classroom studying for exams and quizzes are gone; worrying over assignments, research papers, grades, and internships while juggling a social life is over. It is a tremendous feeling of achievement in one's life (and rightfully so!). Students in this phase of their lives may feel like they have finally made it! Yet, in reality, they are really getting ready to confront their biggest challenge yet—becoming a professional. Becoming a professional is a journey upon which graduates embark and travel for the rest of their careers. This journey takes graduates into totally new and different environments and destinations than what they have been accustomed to in college. New destinations call for new maps, new skills, and new navigational strategies for being successful in a new work and living environment.

Chapter 11

Visit the Web site for this book to learn more about the organizations and topics covered in this chapter. **http://health .jbpub.com/recreationjobs/2e**

Getting started on the journey is the most critical step down a successful path and takes place throughout the first year on the job. This first year is an extremely important time, in any career or new job, and to be successful requires graduates to learn and exhibit a number of personal and organizational skills. It is a time of many changes and learning that can be an emotional and stressful experience, yet challenging and exciting. Many individuals go through a period of uncertainty as they find themselves between being a college student and a budding professional. This period is often referred to as a transitional stage and is one of the most challenging employment stages that an individual will experience. The fact that 60% of new college graduates plan to leave their first job within two years may be due to problems inherent in the college-to-work transition and is especially true for those students who have limited practical work experience while in college (Leonard, 2001).

It is important for the students in recreation and leisure services, or in any career field for that matter, to understand this transition as they begin their careers. Basically, two phases of transition occur at the same time.

One phase is the candidate's professional transition (learning the ropes of a new job) and the other phase is the candidate's personal transition (adjusting to life after college in a new community and surviving financial and social independence). Demands on recreation managers, supervisors, activity leaders, and sport programmers are changing—with the expectations of doing more with less. Times are changing. The changes in the workplace (and society!) after the tragic events of September 11, 2001, have imposed new demands, responsibilities, and strategies on how recreation programs and facilities are managed. No amount of preparation can *guarantee* a smooth transition from life as a student to life as a professional. However, awareness and preparation can at least help reduce the stress experienced and hopefully give new professionals a greater sense of control over their personal and professional lives. This chapter describes both of these transitions as well as shares employers' and new hires' expectations of that first year on the job.

## Realistic Assessment

The first step in preparing for the transitional period in this new journey is for new professionals to take a realistic assessment of who they are and how they will likely be viewed by a new employer. For most, the first 30–60 days is a blueprint for their immediate future. This taste of realism is essential to gain a better insight into the expectations to be imposed by a new employer. The assessment may consist of the following items:

1. *Professional reputation:* Just starting out, most individuals embarking on their new career do not have a professional reputation yet. When graduating from

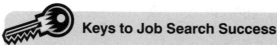 **Keys to Job Search Success**

*Congratulations! You've landed the job.*
During the first few days at the job, you will be introduced to many people. It is very important that you remember their names and positions in the organization. Jot down names until you remember them. Whereas they have only one new name to remember, you may have scores!

college and beginning that first job, new hires have no professional track record, no proven full-time experiences, no previous accomplishments—they really are starting from scratch! It is important for new hires to recognize this and work hard at building a solid professional reputation.

2. *Negative stereotypes:* Because of the actions and reputations of some previous college graduates, many organizations expect new hires to be naive and unrealistic in their expectations. Other employers have learned to expect a "know-it-all" who will come across as arrogant, condescending, and may not be willing to learn the ropes of their new organization. The type of new hire these employers fear most is one who will want to make changes from the very first day and talk about "better ways" to do things based upon their limited experiences without having knowledge of the organization. Many people feel threatened by change, especially from a new, young, and inexperienced hire. One of the first hurdles for new hires to clear is proving to the organization that these stereotypes do not fit them. Beat the negative stereotype and embrace learning with open arms. Although this may not feel comfortable at first, this type of attitude and behavior will serve the new hire best in the long run. Remember, acceptance in the workplace has to be earned and evolves over time.

3. *Job performance:* The job performance of new hires is all that really counts to their employer. A high grade point average, offices held in college, previous job experiences, and outstanding internship experiences are for the most part left at the front door when new hires walk into their first job. New hires must understand, it is not that these accomplishments are not important; in fact, they served their purpose very well: they are what attracted the employer in the first place! Yet, now is the time for new hires to shift their focus and to earn their employer's respect and confidence through diligent homework, appropriate actions, and exceptional performance on the job. It is through this performance in that first year that new hires can demonstrate to their boss and coworkers that they made a good hiring decision.

4. *Prove productivity:* New hires' first year on the job should be spent proving to their employer and colleagues that they are a hard-working, dependable, responsible, mature, and productive member of the team. Although most new professionals know they can be productive, it is important that this is demonstrated to those with whom they work. Some behaviors designed to demonstrate productivity are as follows:

- Get started on assignments right away and submit completed assignments before the deadline.

- Learn what is important to your supervisor and communicate with him or her regularly on priorities for assignment completion.

**Job Coach Tip**

Ask for any relevant reading material (program manuals, annual reports, organizational charts, etc.) even before you officially start work. This will definitely impress your new employer.

**Job Coach Tip**

Consider building your professional wardrobe as an investment rather than an expense.

Salisbury University Career Services Office

**Be Alert!**

Avoid making (and receiving) personal telephone calls. Limit your personal calls to emergency situations.

**Keys to Job Search Success**

Seek out mentors. Whether your organization has a formal or informal mentoring program, mentors can be extremely helpful during your first year. Having a terrific mentor as you begin your new job can make all the difference in the world!

- Be inquisitive and ask questions to learn more about your new place of employment.

- Submit drafts of assignments prior to the due date for review and to gain feedback. This not only helps new professionals to know whether or not they are on the right track, but it also shows their boss their desire to be accurate and efficient in the use of their time.

- Show that tasks can be accomplished by working alone as well as being a productive member in a team effort.

5. *Fair chance:* In most organizations the young professionals will be given an opportunity during that first year to prove themselves while learning the details of their job. Many opportunities will arise where new hires will have a chance to impress the rest of the recreation staff. New professionals should recognize and capitalize upon these opportunities to show their potential.

A key component in new hires being successful with this realistic assessment is to take charge of their careers by accepting full responsibility and accountability for their success or lack thereof. Indeed, help will be obtained from colleagues and supervisors, but the real responsibility must come from within!

## Professional Life Begins with a Winning Attitude and Positive Results

One of the most frequent problems cited by employers concerning new employees deals with attitude—attitudes about new employees' roles in the department, their expectations, job assignments, work ethic, and organizational policies and procedures. The following are suggestions for the new professional in developing a winning attitude that will lead to positive results and a smoother transition period:

1. *Expectations:* A common mistake of many young professionals is to believe that they were hired to change the organization and to make a big impact upon their career field. It is quite natural for the young professional to have such high expectations during their first year on the job and to want to show their boss that they are competent and talented. One important step for new professionals attaining a winning attitude is to lower their high expectations. A far better strategy than wanting to make a lot of changes is to be content with the many challenges of learning specific duties and responsibilities. New hires should seek to understand the new work paradigm and what is expected while developing skills that will allow them to make a contribution to the organization at their current level. New professionals should not worry about moving up the career ladder at this point in their careers because there will be plenty of opportunities to do that later.

2. *Contentment:* Young professionals generally bring a lot of energy and enthusiasm with them into the workplace. Along with this energy is the misconception

**Time Out**

If your employer provides the option, have your paycheck directly deposited into your bank account. This will save you the time and trouble of depositing a paycheck each pay period.

**Time Out**

If your employment is subject to certain pre-employment health and/or drug tests, get them completed as soon as possible to prevent payroll delays.

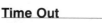

**Keys to Job Search Success**

During your first few weeks at the job, follow the 80/20 rule. Listen 80% and talk 20%. And, by all means, avoid those who talk 100%!

that professional work is always fun, glamorous, and exciting. The reality of the workplace reveals that work is not fun all of the time, and that no job is perfect. In learning to be content, young professionals in recreation and leisure services must accept that during their first year they will find themselves doing a number of routine and, sometimes, boring tasks. Failure to recognize this reality can lead to an unhappy professional who moves frequently from one position to another. To avoid this pitfall and gain contentment with their job choice, new professionals must learn the program (yes, even the grunt work!) and build on these experiences. This is a great way to earn respect from colleagues. Whereas new professionals might have been "star honor students" in college, they are rookies in their new careers. Unfortunately, the often-used phrase of "paying your dues" is a reality.

3. *Amenable to new ideas:* Even though new professionals have most likely just graduated from an institution of higher learning they still have a lot to learn and in many instances will start from the ground floor level. It is acceptable not to know everything there is to know about recreation and leisure services when just starting out. Pretending to know it all is not the best way for new professionals to build respect and a solid reputation. Such behavior only displays cockiness, naïveté, and immaturity on the new professional's part. Rather, a display of respect to those who do have the knowledge and experience is very important. In being amenable to new ideas, it is essential for new professionals to come to the workplace with a willingness to learn and work on developing a "watch-listen-observe-learn" posture while around other professionals before making any suggestions. By implementing this strategy, new professionals will gain a lot and learn from their experience in the organization.

4. *Mind your manners:* It has been said "Manners maketh man." Whereas most individuals may have practiced good manners during the interview process to land the position, it is just as important to practice proper etiquette in the workplace on a daily basis. Minding one's manners can be practiced by answering every phone call politely and by greeting every participant with a smile and a "can help" attitude. Although barging into a college friend's fraternity, sorority, or dormitory room without knocking first may have been fun and acceptable in college, barging into the boss's office without knocking is not! New professionals should treat both colleagues and participants as they would like to be treated.

5. *Strong and determined work ethic:* During the first year, new professionals must be willing to work hard and often long hours. Overtime is just a part of the job in the field of recreation and leisure services. Expect it! Recreation programming is not a nine-to-five job and new professionals in the field must accept this fact. Rather than focusing upon the hours they must do whatever it takes to get the job done and done *right* the first time and on time.

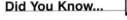

**Did You Know...**

Despite occasional dips in the annual growth curve, the last decade has seen a rapid rise in travel and tourism and expects a 4% annual growth rate over the next decade.

**World Travel and Tourism Council**

## Keys to Job Search Success

Make it a point to notify all of your references and network contacts that you have accepted a new position. Give them your new office and home telephone numbers and thank them again for their help. Stay connected with your key contacts.

**Job Coach Tip**

Stay away from office gossip and office politics, and by all means never contribute to it! Associate with winners and not whiners.

6. *A pleasant personality:* Professionals like to be around other colleagues who are friendly, have pleasant personalities, and who smile a lot. Therefore, it is essential in establishing a positive attitude not to be labeled as a complainer or one who criticizes all the time. Courtesy should be displayed to all of the employees in the organization, from the custodial staff to the director.

7. *Time management:* A successful career in the recreation field depends, to a large degree, upon effective time management skills. Interpersonal communication skills along with technical skills will allow the new professional to handle a demanding schedule along with multiple, and sometimes, competing priorities. Because it is the digital age, taking advantage of the Internet, handheld PDAs, electronic calendars, and prioritized daily task lists will assist new professionals in staying on top of their commitments. New professionals must always arrive at work on time, if not a little earlier than required. (Hint: It's not like the 8 a.m. class that they skipped because they hit the snooze button too many times on the alarm clock.) It they arrive late for work too many times, new professionals will likely find themselves looking for a new job.

8. *Develop patience:* While it will be tempting at first for most new professionals, they should not be overly anxious to prove themselves. The exuberance brought into the work environment must be tempered with an appropriate amount of patience. This type of balanced approach will give new professionals a chance to learn and grow into their new position. A harmonious work relationship with one's supervisor and coworkers should be the goal. The essentials of the job must be learned to achieve success in the eyes of the boss, not to mention providing a quality recreation program for the participants.

9. *Understanding:* In understanding the job and knowing what the young professional is hired to do, many individuals find themselves reading through their job description. To feel comfortable with the new position, it is important for new hires to know and understand what the mission, goals, and objectives of the organization are and to realize where they fit into the big picture of the organization. Meeting with supervisors and colleagues can assist new professionals with understanding their roles and responsibilities. Initiating conversation as well as being open to learning are key attributes for the new professional to model. They must remember that learning does not end just because they are no longer sitting in the classroom!

**Did You Know...** 

The National Park Service has approximately 16,000 permanent employees and hires up to 10,000 temporary and seasonal employees each year with additional support provided by 125,000 volunteers annually.

National Park Service

10. *Professional involvement:* An easy way to maintain a winning attitude toward a career and that first job is for new professionals to get actively involved in local, state, and national recreation and leisure services associations. Developing professional relationships early on will help new professionals maintain a positive and refreshed attitude as well as assist in their professional growth and development.

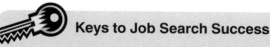 **Keys to Job Search Success**

During your first few months on the job, become known as either the employee who is the first in to work or the last one to leave...or both! However, although this approach is fine when starting a new job or career, don't do both forever—it's not healthy in the long run!

11. *Communication:* The ability to communicate skillfully with others and through others to achieve one's goals is essential in the workplace. Communication includes interpersonal or human relations skills as well as written communication such as e-mail and regular correspondence. The recreation and leisure services profession is a people-oriented profession and requires day-to-day interaction among people. Successful new hires must build strong relationships with their coworkers and program participants from day one.

12. *Performance appraisal:* The process of determining and communicating to an employee his or her performance on the job is critical to the professional development of all employees, but particularly for the new professional. Even if it is not the norm in their organization, new professionals can ask their supervisor for a 3-month or 6-month evaluation of their performance. A request of this nature demonstrates to their boss that they are committed to their position, the organization, and improving their performance. Finally, asking for this feedback helps new professionals to stay on top of knowing and meeting the expectations of their boss and the organization.

## Performance Standards of Success

One of the most dramatic changes that college graduates report when beginning their first job is the standard by which performance is judged. The working world is a new environment with new strategies for being a success and one with which the young professional is generally not familiar. Listed in Figure 11.1 are a number of issues comparing how they are dealt with from a collegiate point of view and from the perspective of the workplace.

### What to Expect the First Year—Realistically!

In the first year on the job, the new professional can realistically expect the following:

1. *Benefits:* After living through those collegiate years on a shoestring budget, new professionals will receive a regular paycheck along with health insurance and retirement benefits. Compared to the wages earned in many part-time jobs or in an internship while going to school, new professionals will get paid a lot more money for doing some of those same jobs.

2. *Autonomy:* Although most college graduates have already experienced some degree of independence by living away from home during college, their first job provides total autonomy and independence. Many times this autonomy is in an unfamiliar town or new region of the country. In relocating for their first job, it is important for new professionals to get used to living in a new community by learning as much as they can about their new hometown. Although being new to a community can be very exciting and provide a plethora of new opportunities, it can also be scary, sometimes leading to feelings of loneliness. To ward off these lonely times, new professionals can join book clubs, participate

**Job Coach Tip**

Clearly, what you do on and off the job helps establish your identity as a young professional.

**Job Coach Tip**

Don't assume your boss knows what you're doing all of the time. Don't wait around—seek out feedback.

**Did You Know...**

Boys and Girls Clubs of America (BGCA) employs more than 50,000 trained professional staff in all 50 states, Puerto Rico, and the Virgin Islands and on U.S. military bases around the world.

BGCA

**Keys to Job Search Success**

The knowledge you acquired in college will be critical to your success, but the process of succeeding in school is very different from the process of succeeding at work.

Holton & Naquin

Figure 11.1

| Task | Student | Professional |
|---|---|---|
| **1.** Work assignments on syllabus | Receive detailed instructions | Receive usually vague instructions from boss |
| **2.** Initiative | Exams and assignment due dates trigger student action | Must be self-motivated |
| **3.** Job performance | "C" is passing; affects the individual not college or professors | A basketball tournament that is scheduled at 75% accuracy will not be accepted by the boss or participants; affects the organization, boss, and even coworkers |
| **4.** Exams | Tested on schedule | No formal exams; tested everyday. Open-book exam 40 hours a week |
| **5.** Philosophy | College encourages students to create new ideas and to think liberally | Organizations usually want the employee to do it the organization's way |
| **6.** Daily routines | Most students enjoy a free existence; college is a series of sprints from one break to the next; nap in the afternoon | Must put in at least 8 hours each day; arriving and leaving at the same time each day; no naps |
| **7.** Teacher vs. boss | Teacher helps the student to learn | Boss has goals/ objectives that must be accomplished |
| **8.** Deadlines | Usually given 2–3 months to complete | May be due tomorrow at the latest |
| **9.** Handling problems | If students do not like the professor or the assignments, they can simply drop the class | Must work through any problems with the boss |
| **10.** Control of one's agenda | Student controls | Organization controls |
| **11.** Individual vs. team | Students are in charge of their success or failure | The professional is dependent upon a team of colleagues |
| **12.** Solutions | There is usually a right or wrong answer | There is no right or wrong answer |
| **13.** Measuring success | Progress is measured continuously with grades | Lack of regular feedback given on performance |

*(continues)*

| | | *(continued)* |
|---|---|---|
| 14. Advancement | Fairly often, semester by semester; no limit to the number of degrees that can be awarded in college | Advancement is limited with a great deal of competition |
| 15. Assessment | Report cards | Performance evaluation reviews |

Being a Student vs. Being a Professional

in adult sport leagues, or enroll in classes, such as yoga or art. (Hint: Remember, the chosen career is in recreation and leisure services!) In an attempt to meet new people outside of the workplace, it is also possible for new professionals to volunteer or become active in community organizations and civic groups.

3. *Surprises and challenges:* Surprises are inevitable during that first year, and new professionals must be ready for unpredictable situations. Regarding challenges, new professionals have opportunities to be creative and make contributions to their organization as well as to their chosen field. They should make the most of these challenges encountered in that first year.

4. *Overwhelmed:* Because everything is so new and there are so many adjustments to make, names to remember, and policies to follow, it is natural for new hires to feel overwhelmed initially. A common cause of stress early in the career of new professionals is the feeling of having too much to do in too little time. Although the load of tasks to accomplish may appear insurmountable, things will begin to become routine within a matter of weeks or months. The best advice for those who do feel overwhelmed is to communicate this to your boss. Don't be a martyr—ask for help!

5. *Information overload:* There is so much to learn and absorb at a new job. To be successful without being stressed out, new professionals should attempt to prioritize the most important aspects that must be learned immediately and those aspects that can wait. Even though it is natural to want to know everything right away, that is simply unrealistic. One of the keys to navigating a successful transition is to learn to feel comfortable with being new rather than fighting it. As a result, new professionals should ask questions about anything they do not understand and try to learn something new everyday on the job.

6. *Fatigue:* Because new professionals spend a significant number of hours at the job during the first year, the stress, pressure, and long hours can sap their energy. It is guaranteed that new professionals will feel tired, but with time, they will get used to the routine and will learn how to pace themselves. A major change for many new hires is the partying and late hours enjoyed in college usually come to a halt as many individuals are unable to sustain enough energy to work all day and stay up into the early morning hours. Developing a disciplined lifestyle will help new professionals in maintaining their physical and emotional health.

7. *Dress:* What new professionals wore as students on the college campus will more than likely stay in the closet when they start working. Dressing for the workforce is much different from dressing for college. Even though many recreation organizations have relaxed their dress codes, new professionals should continue to follow a more conservative standard, at least for the first few

**Did You Know...**

There were more than 22,500 recreation therapists working in the United States in 2008 earning an average annual salary of $39,930.

Bureau of Labor Statistics

**Job Coach Tip**

When given a new project, ask for a deadline if one is not given to you.

**Job Coach Tip**

To alleviate stress, take a brief mental break, go for a 10-minute walk, listen to some relaxing music, and so on.

months. It is certainly acceptable to wear a professional-looking warm-up suit while conducting recreation programs and sport activities in a gym or on a ball field. However, inside the office, a business casual attire is expected at the least. Look around and see how others are dressed.

8. *Reading, reading, and more reading!* During the first couple of months new professionals find themselves doing more reading than most ever thought possible. Policy manuals, organizational literature (pamphlets, brochures, and newspaper articles), annual reports from previous years, program and event documentation from previous events, file after file on meeting minutes, complaint forms, accident reports, and so on, all have to be read and understood. The best advice in this situation is for new hires to try to learn as much as possible about the job, the recreation program, and the organization. In other words, they should try to be a "sponge" and soak in as much information as possible about the organization and the job.

9. *Learn the organization's corporate culture:* Every organization has a unique culture and set of rules just like each professor in college had a different teaching style and grading policy. In a new professional's first year on the job, he or she should take the time to learn and understand the organization's management philosophy and style of accomplishing work. Because an organization's culture guides the behavior of its employees, it is important that new hires learn what is and is not acceptable behavior in the workplace. For example, does the organization, and more specifically the boss, expect the new hire to attend all social functions, or are there some that are more important to attend than others? Knowing these details will help new professionals fit in, feel more comfortable, and get along better with their colleagues at the office.

10. *Being a freshman all over again:* Remember those nervous feelings of being new on the first day at college? New professionals will likely experience very similar feelings in their first days on the new job. Throughout this process it is important for them to understand that being new is a part of the transition, and the best way to handle being new is to embrace it with an open mind. New professionals will enjoy successes as well as failures in their first year on the job—guaranteed. The key to being successful in this transition to a professional is what is learned from those high and low points.

## Conclusion

There probably is no perfect way to transition from college to a career. Yet, this chapter shares a number of strategies that can be immediately implemented in attempting

---

**Be Alert!**

Just because you graduated from college does not mean you should stop learning! Take advantage of learning opportunities provided by your organization that will help you grow professionally and personally.

---

**Job Coach Tip**

Your long-term career success can depend on how well you do during your first year in the work world.

CampusCareerCenter.com

---

**Keys to Job Search Success**

Perform at the level of the job you want, not the job you have. As you delve into your first year on the job, you want to show management that you have a strong work ethic and that you take initiative. Prove this by volunteering for projects outside of your daily tasks, which shows your employer that you are a hard worker and you gain experience along the way.

eCampusTours.com

to overcome some of the difficulties generally encountered with a new job. New professionals should recognize their first job is usually viewed as a stepping stone in their career path, and more important, their first job does not predict where they will ultimately end their work career.

Most young professionals do not retire in their first position or at their first agency. Yet, from their first experience on the job, many young professionals establish a strong foundation for the future. Making a successful transition is the new professional's responsibility. The transition stage is an exciting opportunity to grow professionally and apply what has been learned in the classroom. Although the life of most new professionals has dramatically changed since college, if they have a positive mental attitude; are able, willing, and accepting of what has been shared in this chapter; and can anticipate the challenges ahead, little difficulty should be experienced in adjusting to the new challenges of their first job. They will be off to a great start in creating a new career in recreation and leisure services. Enjoy and have a great career in a fabulous field!

# References

Boys and Girls Clubs of America. (2009). *Who we are*. Retrieved May 17, 2009, from http://www.bgca.org/whoweare/facts.asp

Bureau of Labor Statistics. (2008). *Occupational employment and wages*. Washington, DC: U.S. Department of Labor. Retrieved May 25, 2009, from http://www.bls.gov/news.release/pdf/ocwage.pdf

CampusCareerCenter.com. (n.d.). The first year on the job. Retrieved May 24, 2009, from http://www.campuscareercenter.com/students/article.asp?news_id=912

Dreyer, R. (1992). Transition. *Supervision, 53*(5), 17–18.

eCampusTours.com. (n.d.). First year on the job. Retrieved May 24, 2009, from https://www.ecampustours.com/careerexploration/newjob

Holton, E. F., & Naquin, S. S. (2001). *How to succeed in your first job*. San Francisco: Berrett-Koehler Publishers.

Leonard, B. (2001, November). College graduates entering the workforce have lowered expections. *HR Magazine, 46*(11), 32.

National Park Service. (n.d.). Jobs with the National Park Service. U.S. Department of Interior. Retrieved May 25, 2009, from http://www.nps.gov/personnel/index.htm

National Park Service. (n.d.). Quick facts. U.S. Department of Interior. Retrieved May 25, 2009, from http://www.nps.gov/aboutus/quickfacts.htm

Salisbury University Career Services Office. (2008). Your first year on the job: Some job advice. Retrieved May 24, 2009, from http://www.salisbury.edu/careerservices/Students/FirstYearOnJob.html

U.S. Forest Service (n.d.). *General careers overview*. U.S. Department of Agriculture. Retrieved May 25, 2009, from http://www.fs.fed.us/fsjobs/jobs_overview.shtml

World Travel and Tourism Council. (2009). *Travel and tourism economic impact 2009 executive summary*. Retrieved May 17, 2009, from http://www.wttc.org/bin/pdf/original_pdf_file/exec_summary_2009.pdf

YMCA of the USA. (2009). *About the YMCA*. Retrieved May 17, 2009, from http://www.ymca.net/about_the_ymca

Assignments

## Assignment: Balancing a Personal and Professional Life

Even though most of you have been out on your own for several years now while in college, starting a career will mean a lot of changes for you in your personal life as well. As a new full-time professional, the biggest change you will experience is in your daily life and the routines that will have to be adjusted. For example:

| | |
|---|---|
| **8:00 a.m.** | Remember when you hated those 8:00 a.m. classes! Remember how hard it was to keep your eyes open, and how hard it was to get up when the alarm clock went off! Now, all of a sudden, you have to get up early every day, week after week, year after year! (What a depressing thought!) |
| **10:00 p.m.** | Not all jobs will be 8:00 a.m. to 5:00 p.m. There will be many occasions when you get to work at 7:00 a.m. and will not leave until 10:00 p.m. that night and be expected back at 8:00 a.m. the next day. That's life! You may not like it or agree with it, but there's not much you can do about it. |
| **Dress** | No more sweat pants, jeans, and T-shirts to work. You will find yourself having to dress up for work the majority of time. You will have to adjust to wearing more formal clothes that might not be as comfortable as the attire you wore to class everyday. |
| **Exercise** | Although you might be used to playing basketball, lifting weights, or playing golf whenever you wanted during college, finding time to exercise while working full time will be a challenge. First, finding the time during the day will probably be impossible with job assignments you will have. More than likely, the only time available will be at night and on weekends. The problem with nights is that you are so tired from work, you run out of energy for exercise. However hard, you need to find time to work out to keep in shape both physically and mentally. Believe it or not, you will have to schedule in leisure time! If you don't, you will never have the time. |
| **Free Time** | As we have been talking about, a professional career takes a lot of time and energy on your part. Even though you might feel that classes, homework, and class projects are taking a large portion of your time during the day, you will not appreciate how much free time you really have while in college until you start working full time. Just having the flexibility during the day to go to the bank, to the mall to buy some clothes, to see some friends, to go to the student recreation building, to drive to the lake or park to enjoy the scenery, or to just relax in your apartment and watch the television is something that you are going to miss. Usually some free time will be available in a job but certainly not like it used to be. |
| **The Weekend** | You will soon find out that the weekdays are primarily for work and work-related tasks while the weekend will be for you. You will start living for the weekends! TGIF! This will be a different routine |

for you. While in college, school work and leisure time were sometimes mixed together—weekday or weekend. You might find yourself playing basketball on a weekday afternoon and maybe studying in the library on the weekend.

**Burnout or Burn-In**

"Burnout" is when you get to the point that you are no longer productive in your work. You usually are not as effective as you once were and you basically have no energy to continue on. It's your body's way of telling you to slow down and relax a little. However, burnout usually does not occur during your first year. During that first year, you are going to approach your new job with a high level of energy, enthusiasm, and be eager to do a good job. It is not uncommon to start to wear down after about six months. But this isn't really burnout.

Most new professionals will experience what we refer to as "burn-in" during the first year. You will work long hours while trying to learn and do as much as possible during your first year. Be that "sponge" and absorb as much as possible from your supervisors and colleagues. Sometimes you will have to sacrifice your personal life to move to the top of your profession.

To be successful, however, you need to find a good, healthy balance between burnout and burn-in. Work at a pace that is comfortable for you to enjoy your job (and perform well) as well as your personal life. You can't always work at full speed and neither can you work all of the time. Find that balance. Work hard, but save a little for the next day, too!

How do you plan to balance your personal and professional lives?

_____

_____

_____

_____

_____

_____

_____

_____

_____

_____

_____

_____

Assignments

Assignments

## Case Study 1: Navigating the Transition

You just started to work for an agency on August 1. It is now November 1 and you receive a phone call from your mom in the morning before you leave for work. It seems like your dad is in one of those rare generous moods and has proposed a family outing. You say great, right? However, as your mom explains the outing you get more and more excited. Dad is proposing for their 25th wedding anniversary (December 1) that he will foot the bill for the entire family to fly to Hawaii for a 1-week vacation and celebration! Free air flight, condo on the main island, free food, and a couple of free outfits to wear while over there. To top it off, you can bring one friend along with you. Because of your dad's work schedule, this is the only time that he can go. This is the most excited you have seen your dad in years. You find out that he has been saving for this occasion for the last 5 years!

### Questions

1. What do you say to your mom? Dad?

_____

_____

_____

_____

_____

_____

_____

_____

_____

_____

_____

_____

_____

_____

_____

_____

_____

_____

_____

_____

_____

_____

2. What do you say to your director?

_____

_____

_____

_____

_____

_____

_____

_____

_____

_____

_____

_____

_____

_____

_____

_____

_____

_____

_____

_____

_____

_____

_____

_____

_____

_____

_____

_____

_____

_____

_____

_____

_____

_____

_____

Assignments

Assignments

## Case Study 2: Navigating the Transition

You had a great interview with this particular agency, an agency that you have been dreaming of. It is the number one ranked program in the country. The administration has a national reputation as being top in the field. You heard them make presentations at national conferences while going to college, and you agreed with everything they were saying. This would be a perfect career match for you—same philosophies, style, personality, work ethic, and so on.

Six weeks ago, your dream came true. You were hired by this agency to be their recreation coordinator responsible for adult sports programming as well as special events. Things were going really well, at first. After about 4 weeks on the job, you started to recognize some things that you didn't think were right. As an avid softball player, you were really looking forward to the start of your softball program as a recreation programmer *and* a player. However, you just heard through the grapevine that the director has an unwritten rule that says "employees are not allowed to participate in the sport programs that they are responsible for." In other words, you cannot play in the softball program, but you can participate in other recreation programs. You are devastated! You are angry, and you don't think it is fair!

### Questions

1. As a recreation programmer, why don't you think it is fair?

_____

_____

_____

_____

_____

_____

_____

_____

_____

_____

_____

_____

_____

_____

_____

_____

_____

_____

2. As a recreation administrator, why would you implement this kind of rule?

_____

_____

_____

_____

_____

_____

_____

_____

_____

_____

_____

_____

_____

_____

_____

3. How would you handle the situation as a first-year professional?

_____

_____

_____

_____

_____

_____

_____

_____

_____

_____

_____

_____

_____

_____

Assignments

**Assignments**

## Case Study 3: Navigating the Transition

As a new employee who has been working at the XYZ Parks and Recreation Department for only 3 months, you have been putting in 70-hour weeks, working week nights and weekends. Your social life has evaporated. You recently noticed that the only other person that seems to be working these same hours is also a recent college graduate. This individual has expressed that same sentiment that you have: all work and no play.

One night, while you were scheduling a basketball tournament, this other individual asked you to go to a local establishment and have a drink. It was late; you were tired and needed a break, and said, "Sure, what the heck." You had a pretty good time with this individual, but after a couple of hours you informed the individual that you had to get back to scheduling that basketball tournament. Nothing more was said or done about the break until a couple of weeks later.

This same individual asked you to go out to dinner. Seeing that you had no food in the refrigerator, you said sure. It seems that after that evening you were *really* starting to like this person. You shared the same goals, philosophy, work ethic . . . you know the line.

### Questions

1. Should you develop an "office romance" with this person? What if the department's policy is no office dating. What would you do?

_____

_____

_____

_____

_____

_____

_____

_____

_____

_____

2. Same scenario, but this individual happens to be the director's administrative assistant. Would this change your mind?

_____

_____

_____

_____

_____

_____

_____

# Appendix A

**Recreation and Leisure Services
Professional Organizations and Associations**

Visit the Web site for this book to learn more about the organizations and topics covered in this appendix. **http://health .jbpub.com/recreationjobs/2e**

# General

### American Academy for Park and Recreation Administration (AAPRA)

PO Box 1040
Mahomet, IL 61853
(217) 586-3360
http://www.aapra.org

### American Alliance for Health, Physical Education, Recreation and Dance (AAHPERD)

1900 Association Dr.
Reston, VA 20191-1598
(800) 213-7193
http://www.aahperd.org
Career Link: http://www.aahperd
.org/careerLink/main.htm

### American Association for Physical Activity and Recreation (AAPAR)

1900 Association Dr.
Reston, VA 20191-1598
(800) 213-7193
http://www.aahperd.org/aalr
/aalr-main.html

### American Zoo and Aquarium Association

7970 D. Old Georgetown Rd.
Bethesda, MD 20814
(310) 907-7777
http://www.aza.org
Career Link: http://www.aza.org
/JobListings

### Canadian Association for Leisure Studies

c/o Department of Recreation and
Leisure Studies
Faculty of Applied Health Sciences
University of Waterloo
Waterloo, Ontario N2L 3G1
http://www.cals.uwaterloo.ca

### Canadian Parks and Recreation Association

404-2197 Riverside Dr.
Ottawa, ON K1H 7X3
(613) 523-5315
http://www.cpra.ca/EN/main.php

### Canadian Parks and Wilderness Society

National Office
506-250 City Centre Ave.
Ottawa, ON K1R 6K7
(613) 569-7226
http://www.cpaws.org

### International Facility Management Association

1 E. Greenway Plaza Suite 1100
Houston, TX 77046-0194
(713) 623-4362
http://www.ifma.org
Career Link: http://www.ifma.org
/career/index.cfm

### International Federation of Park and Recreation Administration

Globe House, Crispin Close
Caversham, Reading, England, RG4 7JS
(44) 0 118 946 1680
http://www.ifpra.org

### National Correctional Recreation Association

Strength Tech, Inc.
PO Box 1381
Stillwater OK 74076
(800) 443-6543
http://www.strengthtech.com
/correct/ncra/ncra.htm

### National Recreation and Parks Association

3101 Park Center Dr.
Alexandria, VA 22302
(703) 858-0784
http://www.nrpa.org
Career Link: http://www.nrpa.org
/careercenter

**Parks and Leisure Australia**

15 Neale St.
PO Box 210
Bendigo Central Australia 3552
(61) 3 5444 1763
http://www.parks-leisure.com.au

**Physical and Health Education Canada**

301-2197 Riverside Dr.
Ottawa, ON
K1H 7X3
(613) 523-1348 or 1-800-663-8708
http://www.cahperd.ca/eng/about
/contact_us.cfm
Career Link: http://www.cahperd.ca
/eng/careers/index.cfm

**World Leisure Association**
**World Leisure Secretariat**

203 Wellness/Recreation Center
University of Northern Iowa
Cedar Falls, IA 50614-0241
(319) 273-6279
http://www.worldleisure.org

# Outdoor Recreation

### Adventure Travel Society

4555 Southlake Parkway
Birmingham, AL 35244
(866) 233-2053
http://www.adventuretravel.com

### American Camp Association

5000 State Rd. 67 North
Martinsville, IN 46151-7902
(765) 342-8456
http://www.aca-camps.org
Career Link: http://www.aca-camps
.org/jobs

### American Hiking Society

1422 Fenwick Lane
Silver Spring, MD 20910
(301) 565-6704
http://www.americanhiking.org

### American Recreation Coalition

1225 New York Ave. NW, Suite 450
Washington, DC 20005-6405
(202) 682-9530
http://www.funoutdoors.com

### American Trails

PO Box 491797
Redding, CA 96049-1797
(530) 547-2060
http://www.americantrails.org

### Association for Experiential Education

3775 Iris Ave. Suite #4
Boulder, CO 80301-2043
(303) 440-8844
http://www.aee.org
Career Link: http://jobsclearinghouse
.aee.org/home/index.cfm?site_id=619

### Association of Outdoor Recreation and Education

2705 Robin St.
Bloomington, IL 61704
(309) 829-9189
http://www.aore.org
Career Link: http://www.aore.org
/careers/default.aspx

### Canadian Parks and Wilderness Society

880 Wellington St., Suite 506
Ottawa, ON K1R 6K7
(613) 569-7226
http://www.cpaws.org

### International Ecotourism Society

733 15th St., NW, Suite 1000
Washington, DC 20005
(202) 347-9203
http://www.ecotourism.org

### Land Trust Alliance

1331 H St. NW, Suite 400
Washington, DC 20005-4734
(202) 638-4725
http://www.lta.org
Career Link: http://www.
landtrustalliance.org/about-us
/jobs/jobs

**National Association for Interpretation**

PO Box 1892
Fort Collins, CO 80522
(970) 484-8283
http://www.interpnet.com

**National Association of Recreation Resource Planners**

MSC-1777
PO Box 2430
Pensacola, FL 32513
http://www.narrp.org
Career Link: http://www.narrp.org
/clubportal/jobbank/joblist.cfm?clubI
D=1431&pubmenuoptID=23113

**National Association of State Park Directors**

8829 Woodyhill Rd.
Raleigh, NC 27613
(919) 676-8365
http://www.naspd.org

**National Forest Recreation Association**

PO Box 488
Woodlake, CA 93286
(760) 648-1091
http://www.nfra.org

**National Outdoor Leadership School**

284 Lincoln St.
Lander, WY 82520-2848
(800) 710-6657
http://www.nols.edu
Career Link: http://www.nols.edu
/alumni/employment

**National Park Foundation**

11 Dupont Circle NW, Suite 600
Washington DC, 20036
(202) 238-4200
http://www.nationalparks.org

**National Parks Conservation Association**

1300 19th St., NW, Suite 300
Washington, DC 20036
(800) 628-7275
http://www.npca.org

**National Ski Areas Association**

133 S. Van Gordon St., Suite 300
Lakewood, CO 80228
(303) 987-1111
http://www.nsaa.org

**Natural Areas Association**

PO Box 1504
Bend, OR 97709
(541) 317-0199
http://www.naturalarea.org
Career Link: http://www.naturalarea
.org/employment.asp

**North American Society for Environmental Education**

2000 P St. NW Suite 540
Washington, DC 20036
(202) 419-0412
http://www.naaee.org
Career Link: http://eelink.net/pages
/EE+Jobs+Database

**Outdoor Industry Association**

4909 Pearl East Circle, Suite 200
Boulder, CO 80301
(303) 444-3353
http://www.outdoorindustry.org
Career Link: http://www
.outdoorindustry.org/careercenter
.html

**The Student Conservation Association**

689 River Rd., PO Box 550
Charlestown, NH 03603-0550
(603) 543-1700
http://www.thesca.org
Career Link: http://www.thesca.org
/employment

**USDA Forest Service**

1400 Independence Ave., SW
Washington, DC 20250-0003
(202) 205-8333
http://www.fs.fed.us
Career Link: http://www.fs.fed.us
/fsjobs

**Wilderness Education Association**

900 East 7th St.
Bloomington, IN 47405
(812) 855-4095
http://www.weainfo.org
Career Link: http://www.weainfo
.org/en/cms/?1447

# Nonprofit Organizations

### Big Brothers/Big Sisters of America

230 North 13th St.
Philadelphia, PA 19107
(215) 567-7000
http://www.bbbsa.org
Career Link: http://www.bbbs.org
/site/c.diJKKYPLJvH/b.1755225/k
.B9CB/Careers.htm

### Boy Scouts of America

PO Box 152079
Irving, TX 75015-2079
http://www.scouting.org
Career Link: http://www.scouting
.org/careers.aspx

### Boys and Girls Clubs of America

1230 W. Peachtree St., NW
Atlanta, GA 30309
(404) 487-5700
http://www.bgca.org
Career Link: http://www.bgca.org
/careers/

### Girls Incorporated

120 Wall St.
New York, NY 10005-3902
(800) 374-4475
http://www.girlsinc.org
Career Link: http://www.girlsinc.org
/about/employment-opportunities
.html

**Jewish Community Centers**

520 Eighth Ave.
New York, NY 10018
(212) 532-4949
http://www.jcca.org
Career Link: http://www.jccworks
.com/

**United Way of America**

701 North Fairfax St.
Alexandria, VA 22314
(703) 836-7112
http://www.liveunited.org/about
/missvis.cfm
Career Link: http://www.liveunited
.org/jobs

**YMCA of the USA**

101 N. Wacker Dr.
Chicago, IL 60606
(800) 872-9622
http://www.ymca.net
Career Link: http://www.ymca.net
/careers

# Commercial Recreation and Tourism

### Adventure Travel Society

4555 Southlake Parkway
Birmingham, AL 35244
(866) 233-2053
http://www.adventuretravel.com

### American Hospitality Academy

PO Box 7832
Hilton Head Island, SC 29938
(843) 785-7566
http://www.rrtm.com

### American Hotel & Lodging Association

1201 New York Ave. NW, #600
Washington, DC 20005-3931
(202) 289-3100
http://www.ahla.com/
Career Link: http://www.ahla.com
/content.aspx?id=20378

## American Planning Association

122 S. Michigan Ave., Suite 1600
Chicago, IL 60603
(312) 431-9100
http://www.planning.org
Career Link: http://www.planning
.org/jobsandpractice/

## American Society of Travel Agents

1101 King St., Suite 200
Alexandria, VA 22314
(703) 739-2782
http://www.astanet.com
Career Link: http://www.asta.org
/Education/?navItemNumber=508

## Association of Collegiate Conference & Events Directors

419 Canyon Ave., Suite 311
Fort Collins, CO 80521
(970) 449-4960
http://www.acced-i.org
Career Link: http://careers.acced-i
.org

## Club Management Association of America

1733 King St.
Alexandria, VA 22314
(703) 739-9500
http://www.cmaa.org
Career Link: http://www.cmaa.org
/template.aspx?id=46

## Convention Industry Council

700 N. Fairfax St., Suite 510
Alexandria, VA 22314
(571) 527-3116
http://www.conventionindustry.org

## Cruise Lines International Association

910 SE 17th St., Suite 400
Fort Lauderdale, FL 33316
(754) 224-2200
http://www.cruising.org
Career Link: http://www.cruising
.org/shipboardEmployment.cfm

## Hospitality Management Society

1600 Holloway Ave.
San Francisco, CA 94132
(415) 338-1111
http://userwww.sfsu.edu/~hms

## International Association of Amusement Parks and Attractions

4230 King St.
Alexandria, VA 22303
(703) 671-5800
http://www.iaapa.org
Career Link: http://www.iaapa.org
/industry/careeropportunities

## International Association of Conference Centers

243 North Lindbergh Blvd.
Saint Louis, MO 63141
(314) 993-8575
http://www.iacconline.com
Career Link: http://www
.iacconline.org/resources/index
.cfm?fuseaction=JobBoard

## International Association of Convention and Visitor Bureaus

2025 M St. NW, Suite 500
Washington, DC 20036
(202) 296-7888
http://www.iacvb.org
Career Link: http://www.
destinationmarketing.org/Career_
Center/CVBJobOps.asp

## International Association of Exhibitions and Events

12700 Park Central Dr., Suite 308
Dallas, TX 75251
(972) 458-8002
http://www.iaee.com/
Career Link: http://www.iaee.com
/careers/career_center

## International Festivals and Events Association

2601 Eastover Terrace
Boise, ID 83706
(208) 433-0950
http://www.ifea.com

## International Institute for Peace through Tourism

685 Cottage Club Rd., Unit 13
Stowe, VT 05672
(802) 253-2658
http://www.iipt.org

## International Special Events Society

401 N. Michigan Ave.
Chicago, IL 60611-4267
(800) 688-4737
http://www.ises.com
Career Link: http://careers.ises.com
/home/index.cfm?site_id=553

## Meeting Professionals International

3030 Lyndon B. Johnson Freeway,
Suite 1700
Dallas, TX 75234-2759
(972) 702-3000
http://www.mpiweb.org/Home.aspx
Career Link: http://www.mpiweb
.org/Marketplace/Careers.aspx

## National Amusement Park Historical Association

PO Box 871
Lombard, IL 60148-0871
http://www.napha.org

## The Professional Convention Management Association

2301 South Lake Shore Dr., Suite 1001
Chicago, IL 60616-1419
(312) 423-7262
http://www.pcma.org
Career Link: http://www.pcma.org
/Careers.htm

## Resort and Commercial Recreation Association

PO Box 1564
Dubuque, IA 52004-1564
http://www.rcra.org
Career Link: http://www.rcra.org
/(S(d3kyuzj3ecz5ip55rs0rdufd))
/member_login.aspx?SID=d3kyuzj3ecz
5ip55rs0rdufd

## Trade Show Exhibitors Association

2301 South Lake Shore Dr., Suite 1005
Chicago, IL 60616
(312) 842-8732
http://www.tsea.org
Career Link: http://careercenter.tsea
.org

## Travel and Tourism Research Association

PO Box 2133
Boise, ID 83701
(208) 429-9511
http://www.ttra.com

## Travel Industry Association of America

1100 New York Ave. NW
Suite 450
Washington, DC 20005-3934
(202) 408-8422
http://www.tia.org

## Visitor Studies Association

PO Box 14375
Columbus, OH 43214
(614) 670-7379
http://www.visitorstudies.org

## World Tourism Organization

Capitán Haya 42
28020 Madrid, Spain
(34) 91 567 81 00
http://www.world-tourism.org

## World Travel and Tourism Council

1-2 Queen Victoria Terrace
Sovereign Court
London E1W 3HA
United Kingdom
(44) 0 870 727 9882
http://www.wttc.org

### World Waterpark Association

8826 Santa Fe Dr.
Suite 310
Overland Park, KS 66212
(913) 599-0300
http://www.waterparks.com
Career Link: http://www.waterparks
.com/careers.asp

## Fitness and Sports Management

### Aerobics and Fitness Association of America

15250 Ventura Blvd., Suite 200
Sherman Oaks CA 91403-3297
(800) 446-2322
http://www.afaa.com
Career Link: http://www.afaa
.com/205.afa

### American College of Sports Medicine

401 West Michigan St.
Indianapolis, IN 46202-3233
(317) 637-9200
http://www.acsm.org

### American Council on Exercise (ACE)

4851 Paramount Dr.
San Diego, CA 92123
(858) 279-8227
http://www.acefitness.org
Career Link: http://www.acefitness
.org/aboutace/careers.aspx

### Aquatics Resources Network

3500 Vicksburg Lane N #250
Plymouth, MN 55447
(800) 680-8624
http://www.aquaticnet.com

### Association of College Unions International

One City Centre, Suite 200
120 W Seventh St.
Bloomington, IN 47404-3925
(812) 855-8550
http://www.acui.org
Career Link: http://www.acui.org
/career

### IDEA Health & Fitness Association

10455 Pacific Center Court
San Diego, CA 92121-4339
(800) 999.4332
http://www.ideafit.com
Career Link: http://www.ideafit.com
/jobs-and-classified-ads

### IHRSA, International Health, Racquet and Sportsclub Association

263 Summer St.
Boston, MA 02210
(800) 228-4772
http://www.ihrsa.org

### National Alliance for Youth Sports

2050 Vista Parkway
West Palm Beach, FL 33411
(561) 684-1141
(800) 688-KIDS
http://nays.org

### National Association of Sports Commissions

9916 Carver Rd., Suite 100
Cincinnati, OH 45242
(513) 281-3888
http://www.sportscommissions.org

### National Association of Student Personnel Administration

1875 Connecticut Ave., NW, Suite 418
Washington, DC 20009
(202) 265-7500
http://www.naspa.org
Career Link: http://www.naspa.org
/career/default.cfm

## National Intramural-Recreational Sports Association

4185 SW Research Way
Corvallis, OR 97333-1067
(541) 766-8211
http://www.nirsa.org
Career Link: http://www.nirsa.org
/AM/Template.cfm?Section=Jobs

## National Sporting Goods Association

1601 Feehanville Dr.
Suite 300
Mt. Prospect, IL 60056
(847) 296-6742
http://www.nsga.org
Career Link: http://www.nsga.org
/i4a/pages/index.cfm?pageid=4161

## North American Society for Sport Management

NASSM Business Office
West Gym 014
Slippery Rock University
Slippery Rock, PA 16057
(724) 738-4812
http://www.nassm.org

## Sporting Goods Manufacturers Association

1150 17th St., NW
Suite 850
Washington, DC 20036
(202) 775-1762
http://www.sgma.com

## Sports Information Resource Center (SIRC)

180 Elgin St., Suite 1400
Ottawa, ON, K2P 2K3
Canada
http://www.sirc.ca

## Wellness Council of America

9802 Nicholas St., Suite 315
Omaha, NE 68114
(402) 827-3590
http://www.welcoa.org

# Employee Services

## Employee Services Management Association

568 Spring Rd., Suite D
Elmhurst, IL 60126
(630) 559-0020
http://www.esmassn.org

# Therapeutic Recreation

## American Therapeutic Recreation Association

207 3rd Ave.
Hattiesburg, MS 39401
(601) 450-2872
http://atra-online.com/cms
Career Link: http://atra-online
.com/displaycommon.cfm?an=6

## Canadian Paraplegic Association Ontario

1101 Prince of Wales Dr., 230
Ottawa, ON K2C 3W7
Canada
(613) 723-1033
http://www.canparaplegic.org/on

## Canadian Therapeutic Recreation Association

7140C Fairmount Dr. SE
Calgary, Alberta, T2H 0X4
Canada
http://www.canadian-tr.org
Career Link: http://www.canadian-tr
.org/

## The National Clearinghouse of Rehabilitation Training

6524 Old Main Hill
Utah State University
Logan, UT 84322-6524
http://ncrtm.org

## National Council for Therapeutic Recreation Certification

7 Elmwood Dr.
New City, NY 10956
(845) 639-1439
http://www.nctrc.org

### National Therapeutic Recreation Society

22377 Belmont Ridge Rd.
Ashburn, VA 20148-4501
(703) 858-2151
http://www.recreationtherapy
.com/rt.htm
Career Link: http://www
.recreationtherapy.com/jobs

### Therapeutic Recreation Directory

Career Link: http://www
.recreationtherapy.com/jobs

### Therapeutic Recreation Ontario

428 Niagara St.
St. Catharines, ON L2M 4W3
Canada
(905) 646-7473
http://www.trontario.org
Career Link: http://www.trontario
.org/employment.asp

# Appendix B

**Recreation and Leisure Services Journals
and Publications**

Visit the Web site for this book to learn more about the organizations and topics covered in this appendix. http://health .jbpub.com/recreationjobs/2e

Academy of Leisure Sciences

Annals of Tourism Research

Aquatics International

Athletic Business

Athletics Administration

Australian Journal of Hospitality
    Management

Australian Parks and Recreation

Backpacker

Camping Magazine

Canadian Association for Health, PE,
    Recreation and Dance Journal

Climbing

Cornell Hotel and Restaurant Administration
    Quarterly

Cyber Journal of Applied Leisure and
    Recreation Research (LARNet)

Employee Services Management

Event Management: An International Journal

Golf Magazine

International Journal of Contemporary
    Hospitality Management

International Journal of Hospitality
    Management

International Journal of Tourism Research

International Journal of Wilderness

International Review for the Sociology of
    Sport

Interscholastic Athletic Administration

Journal of Ecotourism

Journal of Environmental Education

Journal of Environmental Psychology

Journal of Experiential Education

Journal of Hospitality and Tourism
    Management

Journal of Hospitality, Leisure, Sport and
    Tourism Education

Journal of International Council for Health,
    Physical Education and Recreation

Journal of Interpretation

Journal of Leisurability

Journal of Leisure Research

Journal of Park and Recreation
    Administration

Journal of Physical Education, Recreation
    and Dance

Journal of Sport Management

Journal of Sustainable Tourism

Journal of the Canadian Association for
    Leisure Studies

Journal of the National Association for
    Interpretation

Journal of Travel and Tourism Marketing

Journal of Travel Research

Leisure and Hospitality Business

Leisure / Loisir: Journal of the Canadian
    Association for Leisure Studies

Leisure Sciences

Leisure Studies

Leisure Week

Loisir et societe / Society & Leisure

Managing Leisure: An International Journal

National Parks

Nature Conservancy

Outside Magazine

Park Science

Parks and Leisure (Australia)

Parks and Recreation Canada

Parks and Recreation Magazine

Progress in Tourism and Hospitality Research

Recreation and Parks Law Reporter

Recreational Sports Journal

Research Quarterly for Exercise and Sport

Schole: A Journal of Leisure Studies and
    Recreation Education

Society and Natural Resources

Special Events Magazine

*Sport Marketing Quarterly*

*Therapeutic Recreation Journal*

*Tourism: An International Interdisciplinary Journal*

*Tourism Analysis: An Interdisciplinary Journal*

*Tourism and Hospitality Planning and Development*

*Tourism and Hospitality Research*

*Tourism Geographies*

*Tourism Management*

*Tourism Recreation Research*

*Tourism Review*

*Tourist Studies*

*Travel Holiday*

*World Leisure & Recreation*

# Appendix C

## Top Questions Asked by Interviewers

Appendix C

Visit the Web site for this book to learn more about the organizations and topics covered in this appendix. http://health .jbpub.com/recreationjobs/2e

1. What three people have had the most influence on your life and why? If you could appoint a new team of world leaders, who would they be and what would you ask them? If we were to ask your immediate supervisor to describe you in one word, what word would that be and why?

2. Why are you the best person for the job? What don't you like about your present job? What do you expect from a boss?

3. Describe your areas of weakness or areas that you need to improve. How do you handle personal conflicts with coworkers? Who would give you your best recommendation and why? Who would give you your worst and why?

4. List your three greatest weaknesses.

5. If hired, do you intend to stay at our agency for a long time?

6. Capsulate your total life (birth to present) in 5 minutes, including major personal and professional experiences.

7. What's your strongest trait? The thing you need to work on? Weakness? Leadership style?

8. What do you consider your greatest weakness? Why should we hire you? Now that you know about our programs and facilities, what changes would you make?

9. What is the most difficult situation you have faced in your job and how did you respond to it?

10. How would your friends describe you?

11. When is the last time you failed at something? What makes you angry? Why should I select you over someone else?

12. Describe your most stressful situation and how you dealt with it.

13. What are your professional goals 3 years, 5 years, and 10 years from now. What would you contribute to our program and how? What attracted you to apply for the position?

14. How would a supervisor and then someone you supervise describe your work ethic?

15. Name the one thing your supervisor should know about you to avoid future hard feelings. Name the one person you admire the most and why.

16. What did you do the day before yesterday—in detail? Why do you think we should hire you? Could I trust you with my last dime? Why?

17. Give three adjectives to describe yourself. What are your best qualities in regard to working here? What can you bring to us?

18. What would your present employer say about you as a worker?

19. I'm judging you and your interest in this position by the quality of questions you have for me, so…what would you like to know? Tell me about your biggest mistake in recreation, what you did to correct it, and what you learned as a result.

20. What are you most excited about?

21. Give an example of a poor decision you made and how you learned from it. How do you deal with a coworker who is making your work more difficult? Your

immediate supervisor is involved with some unethical behavior. How would you deal with this?

22. What is the worst mistake you have made at work? How do you manage anger? What is your personal code or philosophy of behavior?

23. How would you accommodate an individual with a disability who wants to play intramurals, participate in club sports, or be in fitness classes? What actions would you take to discipline an employee who was involved in an altercation in your sports program? What specific skills do you bring to this job that are relevant?

24. Briefly describe the most difficult situation you encountered as related to this position. How was the situation resolved and what did you learn from the experience? What is your recreation philosophy and what aspects of this position will allow you to practice your philosophy? What related work experiences have prepared you to assume the responsibilities associated with this position?

25. Tell me a creative idea you would bring to our program.

26. Why did you leave your previous employment?

27. Program X has been losing money for years. Tell how you would make it a money maker. The building has been hit by lots of vandalism over the past years; what would you do to stop this from happening? Participation in our program is down—what would you do to improve participation rates and especially participation by women?

28. Where do you see yourself in five years? Spend the next five minutes talking about yourself.

29. Tell me something I do not know about you. Why are you uniquely qualified?

30. Exchange places with someone in history. What's special about you?

31. How would you change our program or improve this program? Define honesty and ethics. How do you work within those definitions?

32. If you were the president of a negative corporation, sell me on your faults. You've got the job, now what do you do to get started?

33. How do you evaluate your recreation program? How do you justify your programs to the administration? What do you see as the most important component of a recreation program?

34. If you were hiring for this position, what qualifications would you look for? Describe the relationship that should exist between a supervisor and his or her staff. How would you describe the ideal job for you?

35. What recreational activity reflects your personality? Why? As a professional, what do you expect your personal priorities to be?

36. A man comes into the gym with a gun—what do you do?

37. Why does recreation belong in a university setting? Respond to a highly stressful, emotional conflict—what are your actions? Why would you not want this position?

38. What is your vision for success and happiness and how will you accomplish this goal? Please take three minutes to write about your dream vacation.

39. What are your thoughts on affirmative action? What are your thoughts on making decisions by consensus?

40. What separates you from other candidates? What special talents are you offering?

41. What management event or experience have you had that you would have done differently and why? Describe the management style of your current program. What would your references say is the area you need to improve most?

42. Describe your supervisory style. Describe a difficult situation and how you handled it. What three words best describe you?

43. What makes you most uniquely qualified for this job? In what areas of your professional skills do you have the most challenge? How do you anticipate interacting with your colleagues?

44. Who would you take to a dinner and why? (Anyone in the world, dead or alive.) Why should I hire you to work at our institution?

45. What would a previous supervisor say are your strengths and weaknesses? Please tell me of a problem with a coworker and how you resolved it.

46. What is the worst mistake you made? How did you correct your mistake? What did you learn? How do you plan to minimize or eliminate weaknesses? What do you value in an organization?

47. What specific skills will you bring to the position?

48. What would your current staff miss about you; what wouldn't they miss? What haven't we asked you that you want to tell us? How do you handle having an idea not being accepted? What do you do?

49. How does your prior experience lend itself to this position? What have you learned from your mistakes?

50. Since learning more about this job, what areas of concern do you have? What things about the job still seem exciting or attractive?

51. What are your career goals? Tell me what you can contribute to my institution. How long do you plan to stay?

52. Describe your most difficult management scenario. How would you handle it differently the next time?

53. Why are you interested in our position and institution? Can you demonstrate how you can be a team player with our organization? What skills do you possess that would assist you being successful at our institution and within our program?

54. Why should we hire you over all other candidates? How would this position fit your goals? What is the most difficult work-related problem you've had and how did you resolve it?

55. What skills can you bring to the position?

56. Identify your personal and professional goals on a five-year plan.

57. What is the biggest mistake you have ever made? Describe your management philosophy and management style. What do you really want to do in life?

58. How would you define success? Why? Are your weaknesses significant enough for you to do something about them? What could you do? What will you do? If you won't try to correct them, why not? Explain your attitude about loyalty in the workplace (to profession, institution, superior, department, participants, and your values).

59. Describe a difficult situation and your response. How would you handle it differently?

60. Describe to us your perfect job. Part-time employees tend to be motivated by money; on a limited budget, how will you motivate your staff to go beyond the call of duty?

61. What are the positive points about our program? What areas need improvement and how might you help?

62. What is the difference between a good leader and a good manager? How would you dismiss a member of your staff who is a mainstay of the university?

63. Why should I hire you? What would your worst enemy say about your job performance? What areas do you need improvement in?

64. What would your mission statement be?

65. If a group of your supervisors, employees, and colleagues were together in a room and I asked them to describe their concerns about you, what would they say? Tell us about a goal you set for yourself and how you went about accomplishing it. Give us an example of when your personal interest was in conflict with your organization's goals. What did you do about it?

66. Why do you want to work with us? How can you improve our programs?

67. Who do you try to learn as much as possible from? Why? Details? What is your single greatest accomplishment? Why? Details?

68. In one word, what is the most important thing in your life? In the future, when you are reflecting on your career and life, how would you like people to describe you?

69. Why did you choose this profession?

70. What do you look for in a job? What two things do you look for when applying for a job? What did you like least about your last job?

71. What is the biggest challenge you have faced in your previous position? How did you deal with that challenge?

72. If you had $10,000 given to you by your superior to spend in a week (for your program area), on what would you spend it? How do you view the differences between administration and support staff?

73. Define success (or how do you define success?). When told your department will receive a reduction in funding, what options will you consider in order to operate? (You are the director in this particular situation.)

74. Why should we hire you? Based on your experiences and recreational philosophy, describe your ideal recreational facility, and explain why.

75. Act as if you were looking in a mirror. Please describe the person you see. We are interested in a personality sketch.

76. Share three words your previous employer would use to describe you.

77. How did you manage lazy or apathetic group member in school or fellow workers in your previous experiences?

78. Is a poor decision more destructive to an organization's culture than a poor reaction to someone else's poor decision?

# Appendix D

## Top Questions Asked by Candidates

Visit the Web site for this book to learn more about the organizations and topics covered in this appendix. **http://health .jbpub.com/recreationjobs/2e**

1. How can I improve your organization? How do you motivate staff?

2. Who will I work most closely with and what have the previous people in my position gone on to do? Who has worked for that individual? How would you rate your level of job satisfaction within your department?

3. What is your management philosophy?

4. How does the department function within the scope of the organization?

5. What opportunities for advancement exist?

6. What can I do to become better qualified for this position?

7. What would your current employees say about you if I asked them?

8. What are you like to work for? What is your vision for your department?

9. Where do you see this position within your organization now and in the future? What distinguishes this position or agency in your mind?

10. What are your professional goals? Where do you expect to be 10 years from now?

11. What are the job expectations? How does your program compare to others?

12. What are the objectives and long-term goals of your programs?

13. Is there long-term growth and potential with this position?

14. How would you assist me in my job responsibilities?

15. What is the financial outlook for the agency?

16. How valued is your program within the institution?

17. What type of management do you prefer?

18. Where do you see this position five years from now?

19. What is your philosophy about internal development and promotion?

20. What is the work ethic in this department?

21. What evaluation procedures are used with professional staff?

22. What type of relationship does the department have with other departments?

23. What is my potential for growth in this job? What resources will be available?

24. What is your department doing to assist the agency in achieving its objectives?

25. Describe your philosophy of professional staff development.

26. How do you see me fitting into the organization?

27. What do other professionals think or say about your program? What would you want them to say?

28. Do you help your staff advance professionally? How?

29. How do you help student employees balance commitments?

30. How do you lead others?

31. How does your staff coexist, work together, get along, and so on?

32. What type of support do you get from the administration?

33. What are your expectations of someone taking this position?

34. What are your administrative priorities?

35. In addition to the listed job requirements, what other professional opportunities are available to me?

36. Where do you see a person accepting this position being in 3–5 years?

37. What is your philosophy of recreation, fitness, and wellness? If you were able to build the perfect community in which to live, describe that community.

38. What are the program philosophy and future projections for the program? Where does the funding come from? What is the percent breakdown from various sources? What, if any, are the responsibilities of the department to generate money?

39. What do you expect from a person in this position?

40. What vision do you have for the recreation sports program?

41. What are three qualities you look for in employees as a director?

42. What is your philosophy? Where do you see this program going when you leave?

43. What is the most important aspect of this position?

44. What do you and your organization value?

45. What is it like to work here?

46. What are you looking for in an employee?

47. How can I develop professionally in this position?

48. What is your relationship with other university agencies?

49. What is your vision for the program? How do I fit into your vision?

50. How much work will I have to do?

51. Describe work you have done that has promoted cultural diversity. What are some trends in this area?

52. What opportunities do I have for professional development?

53. What is the perceived image of this program relative to being a major impact player in the agency's missions and goals?

54. What is the mission of this department at your agency?

55. What type of person are you looking for in this position?

56. What is the best aspect one experiences while working for your department? What is the worst aspect?

57. If I take the job, what will you do to help me develop as a person and as a professional?

58. What is your vision for this position 5 years and 10 years from now?

59. How do you market your programs?

60. Describe your perfect employee. What steps are you willing to take to ensure my success?

61. Where will my office be located? What does the future bear for me?

62. What is the current political climate and can it affect this position?

63. What kind of a supervisor are you?

64. Describe your departmental philosophy and vision for the future.

65. How can I best serve your department?

66. What is the growth potential of the company?

67. Is there growth potential for new employees to move up within the company?

68. Could I add this (specific meaningful responsibility) to my job description?

69. What current issues on campus affect the position applied for?

70. What is your philosophy on student development?

71. What is the most difficult challenge that you face in your position?

72. What have you done in your department to increase and enhance minority retention?

73. What characteristics are you looking for in this position?

74. What weaknesses do you feel this program currently has?

75. How do you solve problems with difficult employees?

# Index

Index

Visit the Web site for this book to learn more about the organizations and topics covered in this chapter. http://health .jbpub.com/recreationjobs/2e

Rec
June 2012

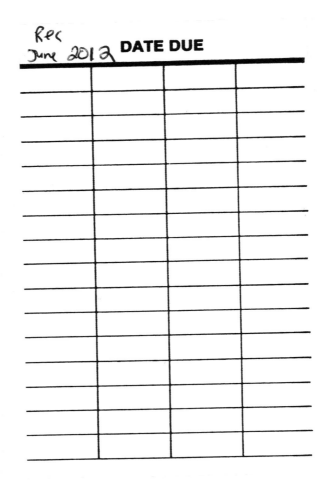

**DATE DUE**